Changin' Times

November 22, 1963 – March 1, 1964

101 Days That Shaped A Generation

D1127822

Copyright © 2013 Al Sussman

All Rights Reserved

ISBN-10: 0989255514

ISBN-13: 978-0-9892555-1-6

Parading Press – an imprint of the Bemis Publishing Group

All images inside from the author's collection, except for public domain images from government sources described within.

Cover design by Richard Buskin

Page Layout by Troy Sanders

Every reasonable effort has been made to contact copyright holders and secure permissions. Omissions can be remedied in future editions.

All rights reserved. No part of this publication may be reproduced, distributed or transmitted in any form or by any means, including photocopying, recording, or other electronic or mechanical methods, without the prior written permission of the publisher, except in the case of brief quotations embodied in critical reviews and certain other noncommercial uses permitted by copyright law.

For permission requests, write to the publisher, addressed "Attention: Permissions Coordinator," at the email address below:

info@paradingpress.com

Changin' Times
November 22, 1963 – March 1, 1964
101 Days That Shaped A Generation

Al Sussman

Parading Press
Chicago, Illinois

Also on Parading Press

Solo in the 70s

by Robert Rodriguez

Beatles 101: The Need-To-Know Guide

by Richard Buskin

(available January 2014)

CONTENTS

FOREWORD

By Bill King

There was something different about the sketch my buddy Chip passed to me in class one day in early February 1964.

Chip was always drawing, but usually it was outrageous hot rods and grotesque drivers inspired by "Big Daddy" Ed Roth's Rat Fink models — the rage among the sixth-grade boys at Barrow Elementary in Athens, Ga.

This time, however, instead of a hot rod it was a drawing of four musicians with pudding-bowl haircuts—like Moe of the Three Stooges—standing behind individual bandstands a la T*he Lawrence Welk Show*.

"Great," I said noncommittally. "What is it?"

"It's The Beatles," he said excitedly.

"What's that?"

"It's a great new singing group from England that's gonna be on Ed Sullivan Sunday night. And they've got LONG hair! You've GOT to see them." (Chip himself hadn't seen The Beatles at that point and was using his imagination when it came to the nonexistent bandstands.)

Now, a singing group appearing on *The Ed Sullivan Show* wasn't something I was likely to get too excited about. My family's one radio was kept tuned to the local middle-of-the-road station, the most-played LPs on my Mom's suitcase portable stereo were the *My Fair Lady* and *Camelot* soundtracks, and my only regular exposure to rock 'n' roll had been watching *American Bandstand* to laugh at the dopey teenagers and their stupid dances.

And long hair on guys? You've got to be kidding, I thought. I had about the longest hair in my class and that simply meant my summer crewcut had grown out enough so that I could comb it. Sounded weird.

But, being half-British, I was intrigued by the fact that they came from England. Besides, Chip seemed excited about this, and he was the guy who'd initiated the class into the facts of life the previous spring, so you didn't dismiss lightly anything Chip was excited about.

There was just one problem. The first part of *The Scarecrow of Romney Marsh* was airing on *Walt Disney's Wonderful World of Color* that Sunday night, and the last half-hour of Disney on NBC clashed with the first half-hour of Sullivan on CBS.

Still, as the week progressed and I read about The Beatles being greeted by a mob of 5,000 screaming fans at New York's newly-renamed Kennedy International Airport, and noticed that even my mother was talking about them, I found myself getting excited—and I still hadn't heard a Beatles record!

Interest in a rock 'n' roll group was completely out of character for me, but so much about the arrival of The Beatles on these shores was out of character for that time and place.

At school, our only previous British fascination had been with notorious party girl Christine Keeler, although we weren't sure exactly what she'd done other than pose nude, as Chip had dutifully informed us. British rock 'n' rollers never had made it here before.

Besides, rock 'n' roll in general was only a peripheral thing for me and my friends. At age 11, we were more interested in playing Swamp Fox in the local woods or reading comic books in my pal David's treehouse. I did like some of the folk music on *Hootenanny*, but up to that point the biggest pop culture event in my circle had been the birth of Pebbles Flintstone the previous spring. (Chip won additional esteem by becoming the first to be able to draw her.)

Looking back at 1964—and it boggles the mind to realize that's looking back half a century—we obviously were ripe for some sort of cultural upheaval. "Camelot" had come to a jarring end the previous November, and the headlines the day The Beatles landed in America told of LBJ pushing the Civil Rights Bill, Castro cutting off the water to the U.S. naval base at Guantanamo Bay, and Jimmy Hoffa, who hadn't yet found his way to the end zone of Giants Stadium, standing trial for jury-tampering. Still, for us, it was a pretty white-bread world, not much different from the Eisenhower '50s. (Mattel also introduced G.I. Joe that same day.)

Our frame of reference was limited: The days of the multiplex were years away and there were only three cinemas in our college town. (Of course, besides the Saturday morning PTA-approved Westerns and adventure flicks, kids my age mostly were allowed to see the new Disney releases, such as the previous fall's animal adventure tale, *The Incredible Journey*, and that Christmas' big animated release, *The Sword in the Stone*.)

On TV, CBS and NBC only recently had expanded their newscasts from 15 minutes to a half-hour and cable TV hadn't yet arrived. We had only three TV channels (plus the educational station), so prime-time network fare was watched by just about everyone. TV Westerns like *Wagon Train* and *The Virginian* were still big, along with doctor shows (the girls in my class loved Richard Chamberlain as *Doctor Kildare*) and variety hours hosted by the genial likes of Garry Moore, Danny Kaye, Andy Williams and Jimmy Dean (before he became a sausage brand). Although primarily aimed at kids, shows like *The Flintstones* and *Walt Disney's Wonderful World of Color* usually drew the parents in as well. And in our household a pair of sitcoms, *The Andy Griffith Show* and *The Dick Van Dyke Show*, were cross-generational favorites—my parents loved them, as did my brothers and me (who looked forward to weekdays off from school when we could watch mid-morning reruns of the earlier seasons). Likewise, the whole family tuned in every week to watch Sgt. Saunders' patrol slog through WWII in *Combat!*

Vestiges of the early days of TV were still in place, with prime-time game shows like *To Tell the Truth* and *I've Got a Secret*. Folks still were singing along with Mitch and Jack Benny remained a Tuesday night fixture. Dr. Richard Kimble had just begun his run from the law on *The Fugitive* and other new programs that season included *The Patty Duke Show*, *My Favorite Martian*, *Burke's Law*, *The Farmer's Daughter* and, in what passed for avant-garde TV at the time, the Orwellian "takeover" of our sets each week by *The Outer Limits* (a favorite of sixth grade boys!). On the cover of *TV Guide* the week The Beatles arrived in the U.S. were the wholesome lovelies of Petticoat Junction, a spinoff of the show that continued to top the Nielsen ratings, *The Beverly Hillbillies.*

Most prime-time programs were shown in black and white, which was just as well as color sets were still somewhat rare—my family didn't have one and neither did any of my friends' families, though my grandmother who lived in a nearby small town was an early adapter. (My brothers and I tried to extend those Sunday visits with her so we could see the Disney show and *Bonanza* in color. The technology was still a bit shaky, though, and if, for instance, one of my brothers jumped off the sofa, the reverberations were likely to turn everyone's face purple on the screen!)

Basically, though, we were still living in times not greatly changed from the 1950s—which is why The Beatles' arrival has been compared to the moment in *The Wizard of Oz* when the film switches from black-and-white Kansas to colorful Oz. We hadn't really been exposed to much that was exotic, and The Beatles were certainly that.

So, at 8 p.m. on February 9, 1964, 73.9 million of us, including many parents, tuned in to Sullivan's show, making it the most-watched program in history at that time. At our house, we nearly wore out the channel selector going back and forth between the Scarecrow on Disney and the Fab Four on Sullivan. It was as if I were caught in a cultural tug of war between my Beaver Cleaver/Opie Taylor childhood and the wide-open new world that The Beatles were ushering in.

I don't need to tell you which side won.

Fifty years on, memories of that era, aside from landmark moments like the JFK assassination and The Beatles' TV debut, have naturally gotten fuzzier. However, now, thanks to Al Sussman, we can relive those days in vivid detail—and my 28-year-old son and 19-year-old daughter can get a new appreciation for the world that shaped their pop culture-obsessed father.

Thanks, Al.

Bill King is a veteran journalist, critic and observer of all things pop culture. He has been the publisher of Beatlefan *magazine since late 1978, covers British pop culture (with his wife Leslie) via the online newsletter* Anglofile, *and is still an editor for the* Atlanta Journal-Constitution, *where he regularly blogs about his other obsession, University of Georgia Bulldogs football.*

Copyright 2013 William Parry King

INTRODUCTION

In Sister Josephine Palmeri's eighth-grade classroom at Our Lady Queen of Peace elementary school in Maywood, New Jersey, it was around 2 o'clock on Friday afternoon, November 22, 1963. It was nearly time for our afternoon break, a perk of being in a ground-floor classroom that was directly adjacent to the playground and having a younger, more liberal nun as our teacher. Before we headed outside, though, there was a knock at the classroom door. A student from a class near the school office was going from classroom to classroom with word that President Kennedy had been shot, news apparently called in by a parent. Sister Jo, as she was known to most of her students, quickly decided that we should take that break immediately.

Outside, many of us were skeptical about this report, thinking it was just a rumor. I was even laughing about it, saying, "Yeah, Barry Goldwater must've shot him." (Goldwater was the front-runner for the 1964 Republican presidential nomination and thus assumed to be Kennedy's opponent in his re-election bid.) After all, the Secret Service appeared to have a pretty impenetrable ring of protection around the president and, even if someone had been able to get off a shot at Kennedy, there was no way that the athletic young president could be wounded seriously. Of course, this was in an era when we had pretty much universal faith in government agencies, especially one with as important a job as guarding the President of the United States.

After about 10-15 minutes, we headed back to our classroom for the homestretch of the school day, but there was a message waiting for us. One by one, classes were being ushered into OLQP's church, where a rosary was being said for President Kennedy. On hearing that news, I realized that apparently this wasn't just a rumor and I could almost literally feel my stomach flip over. We headed upstairs to the other eighth-grade classroom. These were the early days of educational television and some of the classrooms had TVs, which also enabled many of us to see the Mercury manned space flights and, if the teacher cooperated, World Series games (in that era of daytime World Series games). This was one such classroom and, as soon as we walked in, I was greeted with the unusual televised sight of a shirt-sleeved Walter Cronkite at his otherwise-familiar spot in the CBS-TV newsroom. I had barely sat down when Cronkite was handed a bulletin, "The flash, apparently official, President Kennedy died at 1 p.m, Central Standard Time ..."

Now, fast-forward about six and a half weeks. It was Tuesday evening, January 7, 1964. I was supposed to be doing homework for that very same eighth-grade class, but I was concentrating more on the nearby portable radio and what was becoming the biggest Top 40 radio station in America, WABC in New York. It was new survey night and, at 8 p.m., Scott Muni would play the new top seven songs on 77WABC. Muni, the station's prime-time evening deejay then and later one of the founding fathers of FM rock radio in New York, had made a reference during the oldies block in the previous hour to a "beetles fan club." For reasons lost in the mists of time, I apparently hadn't been listening to the radio for a couple of days so I had no idea what Scottso (his self-applied nickname) was talking about. But, hey, fan clubs with weird names were pretty common on Top 40 radio so I didn't give it a second thought and continued with my homework.

Eight o'clock came and my attention to homework was severely compromised as Muni counted down the ballad-heavy Top 7, most of which seemed to be holding their slots from the previous week, though "Popsicles and Icicles" by The Murmaids and the Singing Nun's "Dominique" had both dropped a couple of slots. Bobby Rydell's "Forget Him" … Bobby Vinton's "There! I've Said It Again" … The Kingsmen's "Louie Louie," the No. 1 song the past three weeks and the one piece of real rock 'n' roll in the lot, had dropped to No. 2. I had no idea what could have replaced it. On came the familiar jingle, "It's now number one / On 77WABC" and on came a song that I had never heard before, and to which I had an immediate negative reaction because it was unlike anything I'd ever heard. After the record ended, I found out from Scottso that this song had leaped from No. 35 on the previous week's All American Survey to No. 1. The song was called "I Want to Hold Your Hand" and it was by a group called The Beatles.

* * *

For much of the "baby boom" generation, the assassination of President Kennedy is a generational demarcation line, much as the Japanese attack on Pearl Harbor on December 7, 1941, was for our parents and September 11, 2001, would be for the children of boomers, because of the out-of-nowhere shock and long-range effects of all three events. It's hard to actually put into words, but for my generation nothing was ever quite the same after November 22, 1963. I've always felt, though, that the demarcation line needs to be widened to take in the historic breakthrough of The Beatles in America, since many of those same boomers

2

can vividly recall every detail of either their first listen to "I Want to Hold Your Hand" or seeing the live American TV debut of The Beatles on the February 9, 1964, *Ed Sullivan Show.*

* * *

Relying on my own memories of that time and some preliminary research, I quickly realized that there was a story to tell that went beyond JFK and The Beatles. Change was in the air. A pope traveled by air out of Italy—and to the Holy Land, at that. The first U.S. government-mandated report on smoking was released. The most sweeping civil rights legislation since Reconstruction was passed by the House of Representatives, and was hand-delivered to the Senate at the end of February.

And on Sunday night, March 8, 1964, The Dave Clark 5 made their live American debut on the Sullivan show, the event that really kicked off the musical "British Invasion" because it showed that there was more coming to America from England besides the overwhelming phenomenon of The Beatles.

Due to 1964 being a leap year, the distance between November 22, 1963, and March 1, 1964 (the Sunday before that U.S. debut of the DC5) was 101 days, and the more I dug into all that happened during this time and all that would happen as a result of what was bubbling under the surface during those 101 days, it became evident to me that this was a textbook example of a period of change. Thus *Changin' Times: 101 Days That Shaped a Generation.*

My other impetus for examining this period is that December 1963 is something of a boomers' black hole, a time from which most people remember very little, if anything. Before I began my research, all I remembered from that month was the kidnapping of Frank Sinatra Jr. and the Chicago Bears' 14-10 victory over the New York Giants in the pre-Super Bowl era NFL championship game, a source of irritation for me for half a century. But the fact that so little from December '63 was memorable, save for one's own personal memory bank, contributed to the myth that grew over the years of a nation paralyzed with grief over the murder of its young president. I found that, in reality, life went on rather quickly, despite the enormous psychic body blow of the JFK assassination, something that *Time* magazine took note of in a lead article called "The Mood of the Nation," published in mid-December.

My inspiration for taking on this "moment in time" concept goes back to a short-lived ABC News series from the 1986-87 season called *Our World.* Anchored and principally co-written by Linda Ellerbee, better known today as the host of Nickelodeon's *Nick News*, and Ray Gandolf, then the weekend sports anchor for ABC's evening network newscasts, the series took a look each week at a different slice of 20th century American history. It might be an entire summer (1969), 13 days (the Cuban missile crisis), or one night (Halloween 1938). Unfortunately, the first half-hour of *Our World* was up against *The Cosby Show* at just about the peak of that show's massive popularity so, not surprisingly, ABC canceled *Our World* after that one season due to low ratings. But many, including Ellerbee and Gandolf, look back on *Our World* as a noble experiment. I'm proud to say that this book is a part of the legacy of *Our World*.

My primary sources for the period material in this book were the *New York Times* and *Time* magazine. Most major libraries have the *Times* on microfiche, going back to the paper's birth, and the periodicals staff at the Johnson Public Library in Hackensack, NJ, allowed me to spend an abnormal amount of time going through each day's paper for the period and taking notes. Individual articles are available free online to physical or digital subscribers to the *Times* and for a fee to nonsubscribers at http:// www.nytimes.com/ref/membercenter/nytarchive.html.

Time magazine's entire archive is available online—again, to subscribers—at http://www.time.com/time/archive.

For the chapters dealing with pop culture, my primary sources were the indispensible IMDB (Internet Movie Database —http://www.imdb. com), the lesser-known but very useful IBDB (Internet Broadway Database — http://www.ibdb.com/index.php), and the increasingly-clunky but still useful TV.com at http://www.tv.com . For pop music, B*illboard* is the industry standard and does have a website, but for research purposes one has to go with Joel Whitburn's *Record Research* books and the *Billboard* data in those books is courtesy of Billboard Publications Inc. and Joel Whitburn's *Record Research* Publications. The other major record industry publication in that era was *Cash Box*. The magazine itself has not existed since 1996, but the *Cash Box* singles and album charts live on at http://www.tropicalglen.com/Archives and the current online incarnation of *Cash Box* is at http://cashboxmagazine.com/wp-content.

Additionally, Allan Sniffen, the creator of the New York Radio Message Board, also created wonderful websites chronicling WMCA and WABC, the most popular Top 40 radio stations of that era in New York, including a complete set of each station's weekly surveys. The WABC Musicradio77 website is at http://www.musicradio77.com/index.html while the associated WMCA site is at http://www.musicradio77.com/wmca/home.shtml.

Wikipedia is a good resource for follow-up research, but the need does exist to confirm information found in Wikipedia via other sources. For instance, much of the information relating to *Funny Girl*'s bumpy ride to Broadway came from a Barbra Streisand fan site's detailed section on the show at http://barbra-archives.com/live/60s/funny_girl_broadway_1.html.

By its very nature, this has been almost entirely a solo project. But my editor and professional guide through the project has been Bill King, a veteran professional journalist/editor for the *Atlanta Journal-Constitution* who has been editing my work for some 34 years through his role as publisher of *Beatlefan* magazine. Bill knows my written work better than anyone in the world, so it was a no-brainer for me to ask for his assistance. But he had to edit my work for this project while also working a full-time job, publishing *Beatlefan* every two months, being a parent and husband and having to deal with other serious family issues. I very much appreciate his patience with my often-obtuse questions about form and mechanics and my oft-times not-very-subtle nudging regarding the status of a particular chapter. I hope that the results here are worthy of Bill's editing and counsel. As well, I should give a shout-out to other friends, primarily from the Beatleworld, who have given me advice and helped me over the often-bumpy road through this project. They would include fellow writer/editor Susan Ryan, Beatleworld jack-of-all-trades Tom Frangione, *Fest For Beatles Fans* promoter and longtime friend Mark Lapidos, and authors Wally Podrazik, Bruce Spizer and Jude Southerland Kessler.

This book, then, is dedicated to them and to others who kept the faith through the long and winding road that this project has taken, despite "often overwhelming oddities."

And so, let's return to a very different time, a Friday morning in November 1963, as Americans departed for work and school, unaware that history was just hours away from an irrevocable turning point …

President Kennedy and First Lady Jackie arriving in Texas on
Thursday, November 21.

CHAPTER 1

A FRIDAY IN NOVEMBER

As it dawned, November 22, 1963 looked to be a very ordinary day. It was the Friday before Thanksgiving so schoolchildren were looking ahead to a few days off, while students away at college were looking forward to coming home as grownups were busy planning the traditional holiday festivities. For many families in 1963, those festivities included the relatively new traditions of parades and football. Detroit was all set for its nationally televised double feature of J.L. Hudson's Thanksgiving Day Parade and the annual pro football clash at Tiger Stadium between the Detroit Lions and the Green Bay Packers (the latter being defending National Football League champions).

In New York, a six-page advertising supplement pegged to Macy's Thanksgiving Day Parade was scheduled to run two days before the parade, while a college football game between Syracuse and Notre Dame was set for Thanksgiving afternoon at Yankee Stadium. The holiday's marquee college football matchup, though, was the annual meeting between the No. 1-rated University of Texas Longhorns and Texas A&M, to be followed that Saturday by Army's traditional battle with No. 2-ranked Navy, including the Midshipmen's Heisman Trophy-bound junior quarterback, Roger Staubach. And on this Friday morning a Navy man who had attended the last two Army-Navy games, the president of the United States, was in the middle of a two-day swing through Texas.

There was general consensus that John F. Kennedy's trip was little more than a pre-1964 campaign trek through a state he badly needed in his re-election effort. Indeed, that morning's *New York Times* had a report on the president's trip on the front page above the fold—but in the far-left-hand column, indicating that a number of stories were deemed to be more important. For instance, Prince Norodom Sihanouk of Cambodia was rejecting military and financial aid from the United States as he pursued a stance of seeming neutrality for his country in the ongoing Cold War between the superpowers. Meanwhile, the new chancellor of West Germany, Ludwig Erhard, was emphasizing the need for cooperation among his portion of the divided Germany, the US, and the always-difficult Charles de Gaulle's France. And the Second Ecumenical Council at the Vatican had authorized the use of native languages for the sacraments of the Roman Catholic Church rather than the traditionally universal Latin. All told, that Friday looked to be, as they say, a slow news day.

In his 2004 book *The Beatles Are Coming!*, author Bruce Spizer reveals that *The CBS Morning News With Mike Wallace* for that Friday morning was light enough on hard news that there was room for a report filed that week by the bureau chief of CBS's London news bureau, Alexander Kendrick, about a British rock and roll band called The Beatles. This new British pop sensation's second LP was being released that day in England with unprecedented advance orders, and scenes of massive fan hysteria in London earlier that fall had attracted the American broadcast and print media. *Time* and *Newsweek*, the two leading US newsmagazines, had recently run short pieces on the group and a report for NBC News had run on *The Huntley-Brinkley Report* the previous Monday evening. Kendrick's piece, like the others, dealt mostly with the fan mania (or "Beatlemania," as it had been dubbed by the British press) and the group's floppy hairdos; also included was a brief interview with the members of the band that touched hardly at all on their music. But the piece was offbeat enough that, according to Spizer's research, it was scheduled to run again on that evening's *CBS Evening News with Walter Cronkite*.

As Americans of all ages began their day, they had ample reason to feel good about the way things stood at that moment in time. It had been just over a year since the US and the Soviet Union went to the brink of nuclear war over Cuba, but with the signing of a nuclear test ban treaty and the installations of "hot lines" between the White House and the Kremlin late in the summer of '63, there appeared to be a slight thaw in

8

the icy relations between the world's two great superpowers. The economy was, for the most part, robust.

The civil rights movement had been gaining momentum for much of the year, with a major positive turning point being the August 28 March on Washington. Many government officials (including some at the White House), fearing that the gathering would turn into a race riot, made sure that the march's leaders weren't granted a meeting with the president until after the event's peaceful conclusion. The march turned out to be an unqualified triumph and gave needed credibility to the Kennedy administration's belated drive for the passage of a comprehensive civil rights bill. But in September, four little black girls were killed in the bombing of a church in Birmingham, Alabama. As fall set in, the civil rights bill languished in a congressional committee. Nonetheless, the drive for black equality was in a far better place than it had been just a year earlier.

There was an increasingly annoying little civil war in Vietnam in which the US was becoming more and more involved, extending to covert American approval of a military coup that ousted the regime of President Ngo Dinh Diem at the beginning of November. But this guerrilla war in the jungles of Southeast Asia seemed very far away to most Americans that morning. Besides, nearly complete faith in the government and its agencies, headed by a president who was extremely popular in much of the country, was held by *most* in the country.

President Kennedy was not universally beloved, especially in the South, where he was perceived to be an appeaser in his dealings with the Communist bloc and a meddler intent on pushing an unwanted civil rights agenda. In fact, in the *New York Times*' best-selling non-fiction book list, already printed and ready to run that Sunday, the number one book was a right-wing examination of the Kennedy presidency by noted conservative writer Victor Lasky, *JFK: the Man and the Myth*.

Texas, especially Dallas, was a hotbed of right-wing extremism. Senator Barry Goldwater of Arizona, the leading contender for the Republican presidential nomination in 1964, figured to reap the benefits. JFK had barely won Texas in the 1960 election, amid whispers of chicanery possibly tied to vice-presidential candidate Lyndon Johnson: he badly needed the state in '64 as an insurance policy against the defection of other Southern states over civil rights. As well, there was a battle going on within the Democratic Party in Texas between Senator Ralph Yarborough and the state's freshman governor, John Connally. Connally was a longtime political ally of Vice President Johnson and a former secretary of the Navy under Kennedy. Johnson in particular felt that a presidential trip to Texas could do nothing but help heal the party rift and enhance the chances of a Democratic victory the following year.

But Ambassador to the United Nations Adlai Stevenson had been roughed up and hit over the head with a placard following a speaking engagement in Dallas late in October. The incident made Stevenson very apprehensive about the president's well-being during a possible visit to the city, but the former two-time Democratic presidential nominee's reservations were overruled. A two-day trip was set up for a presidential party that would include JFK, LBJ, Governor Connally, Senator Yarborough, Lady Bird Johnson, and—in a rare political appearance—First Lady Jacqueline Kennedy. Jackie had been keeping a very low profile since the death of the Kennedys' second son, Patrick, two days after his birth in early August, so this was a renewed coming-out of sorts for the woman who was deemed to be one of JFK's primary political assets.

The presidential party had made ceremonial stops in San Antonio and Houston on Thursday, November 21 before spending the night in Fort Worth. Friday was set to be virtually all politics, with the president speaking before the Fort Worth Chamber of Commerce, a short flight to Dallas's Love Field, followed by a motorcade through Dallas, a speech at the city's Trade Mart, back to Love Field for a flight to Austin for a fund-raising dinner, then on to the LBJ Ranch for the night and a flight back to Washington on Saturday. Pretty routine political stuff and little wonder why the rest of the country wasn't paying much attention to this presidential trip.

*****

From the vantage point of the early 21st century, the technology of 1963 must seem rather quaint. Consider, for instance, that there is no professional film record of what happened at 12:30 p.m., Dallas time, in that city's Dealey Plaza, All that exists is home movie footage, including, of course, the short piece of film taken by Abraham Zapruder that is the only close-by film document of the shooting of President Kennedy. But two pieces of long-since-outdated technology played a crucial role in getting word to the nation of the shooting.

One was the radio-telephone, one of the very few means of mobile communications in the pre-portable/cell phone era. AT&T, then the all-encompassing phone company, generally provided a "pool" car for reporters that was equipped with a radio-telephone near the front passenger seat. Merriman Smith, the veteran White House correspondent for United Press International, generally situated himself as close to the radio-telephone as possible and he was in that spot as the motorcade neared an overpass that would lead it to the Trade Mart. When Smith heard what many thought were firecrackers or a police motorcycle back-fire, he immediately recognized the noises as gunfire. He waited for a moment but when he saw spectators diving to the ground, a commotion in the area of the presidential limousine and Secret Service agent Clint Hill suddenly sprint to the car, Smith knew something abnormal had happened.

He grabbed the radio-telephone and dialed UPI's Dallas bureau. It was 12:34, Dallas time, when Smith dictated the first bulletin, "Three shots were fired at President Kennedy's motorcade in downtown Dallas." From the back seat, Associated Press correspondent Jack Bell demanded the radio-telephone but Smith, with perhaps the scoop of the century, wasn't letting go of the line and curled himself over the phone while the pool car took off after the presidential limousine. Bell began flailing away at Smith's back to no avail until the car reached the emergency entrance of Parkland Hospital. Only then did Smith flip the receiver to Bell. Smith and Bob Clark of ABC News made a beeline for the limousine. The president was lying in a blood-covered back seat, with his head being cradled and covered by Jackie. The reporters asked Hill how badly Kennedy had been hurt and the agent quickly said, "He's dead." Smith ran into the emergency entrance and was able to commandeer a phone from which he called UPI with an updated bulletin that Kennedy had been "seriously, perhaps fatally" wounded. That bulletin went out at 12:38 p.m., Dallas time.

In that pre-computerized era, an omnipresent part of most newsrooms was at least one teletype machine, with big-time news operations having separate machines for each of the major wire services. News copy would clatter out of the machines like an automated typewriter and the machine's long, continuous rolls of paper would be torn off at regular intervals. If a major bulletin had come in, a series of bells would go off on the machines to signal big news. The sound of teletype machines and the periodic bells became synonymous with news and, years after teletype machines had been retired in favor of computer terminals, the sound of teletype machines/news tickers would provide the organic soundtrack for some all-news radio stations.

In 1963, the sounds of the CBS newsroom in New York was the nightly background for *The CBS Evening News with Walter Cronkite* and, at 1:38 p.m., Eastern Time, Cronkite was standing near the UPI teletype

CBS NEWS WITH WALTER CRONKITE 7 PM TONIGHT & EVERY MONDAY THROUGH FRIDAY WHDH-TV CH-5

Arguably America's most famous newsman by the early sixties, Walter Cronkite delivered to much of the country the news of the assassination of President Kennedy.

machine, eating his lunch, when the bells signaling a major bulletin went off. Cronkite, a print reporter for United Press in the '40s, knew those bells very well. He looked at the machine, saw Smith's bulletin, ripped the copy from the machine, headed for a sound booth, and had the CBS News "BULLETIN" slide put onscreen. At 1:40 p.m., Eastern Time, the bulletin interrupted the soap opera, *As the World Turns*. Meanwhile, the tube-powered cameras of that era had to be warmed up in the newsroom before the shirt-sleeved Cronkite could go on camera and similar preparations had to be made at the other networks and at local TV stations all over the country.

Indeed, radios and TVs were being switched on throughout the nation as news of the shooting began to spread. As would be the case on September 11, 2001, wild rumors began to circulate, including one that was broadcast that a Secret Service agent had been killed and a not-aired rumor that Vice-President Johnson had suffered a heart attack. There was virtually no official information on the conditions of Kennedy or the also-wounded Governor Connally for roughly an hour after the shooting. Scraps of information came from doctors at Parkland, Senator Yarborough, Texas congressman Albert Thomas, police, and two priests who had been summoned to give the president the last rites of the Catholic Church. CBS Radio in New York even ran with information gathered from sources by reporter Dan Rather at CBS's Dallas affiliate and made a quite premature announcement of the president's death, complete with the playing of the national anthem, without Rather's go-ahead.

Of course, we would later learn that Kennedy was, for all intents and purposes, clinically dead by the time the limousine reached Parkland, confirming agent Hill's snap judgment. In that Cold War era, though, no one could be sure that this wasn't the first part of an attack on the country so official sources were being very circumspect. About an hour after the shooting, though, the bits of information began to take on an ominous tone. The crowd that had been growing outside of the hospital was moved back as Johnson left Parkland for an undisclosed destination that turned out to be Love Field and Air Force One. The two priests left the hospital and told some reporters that Kennedy was dead. Finally, the media was ushered into a small classroom within the hospital complex.

At 1:33 p.m., Dallas time, Malcolm Kilduff, acting press secretary in the absence of Pierre Salinger, who was en route with a number of Cabinet officers to a trade conference in Japan, announced that President Kennedy had died at 1 p.m. Within about five minutes, the impact of that bulletin was symbolized for all time by the unforgettable image of Cronkite delivering the news and then battling to keep his on-camera composure.

*****

"It was the least likely thing to happen in the whole world. If anyone else had died—Sir Winston Churchill, de Gaulle, Khrushchev—it would have been something that somehow we could have understood and even perhaps accepted. But that Kennedy should go. Well, we just didn't believe in assassination anymore. Not in the civilized world, anyway." Those words from 24-year-old David Frost, co-creator and anchor of the popular British satirical TV show, *That Was the Week That Was*, opened a hastily-assembled special edition of the show some 24 hours after the news of the JFK shooting reached London. In America, "stunned disbelief" quickly became the go-to phrase to describe the general reaction. Like Pearl Harbor, just short of 22 years before, and September 11, 2001, the assassination of President Kennedy was too huge and too out-of-nowhere to take in right away, but certainly this ordinary November Friday had suddenly become quite extraordinary.

It wasn't just that a young, charismatic president had been gunned down. It was also the first time in a little over 62 years that shots had been fired at an incumbent US president, and the fact that those shots found their target destroyed the Secret Service's image of near-invincibility in protecting the president. Most Americans had assumed that the Secret Service had created a wall of protection for the president that would easily prevent the kind of handgun attacks that resulted in three presidential assassinations in 36-plus years between 1865 and 1901. But that assumption didn't take into account the more modern possibility of at least a lone assassin with a high-powered rifle in the upper floors of a building. Clearly, the Secret Service hadn't secured the entire motorcade route in Dallas. In later years, there would even be claims that Secret Service men were out on the town in Fort Worth the night before a trip to a city rife with extremism.

That day marked the beginning of the erosion of the American people's total faith in governmental agencies. Indeed, later that afternoon, a sudden rush of information, presumably from the FBI, on the background of a young man arrested in Dallas's Oak Cliff section in connection with the murder of a Dallas policeman, J.D. Tippit, not long after the assassination suddenly appeared on the wire services. A cottage industry in conspiracy theories surrounding the JFK assassination would eventually include people who believed that various government agencies, including the FBI, were in on Kennedy's murder.

Oliver Stone's 1991 film, *JFK*, would be merely the most famous example of that particular conspiracy scenario. Prior to November 22, 1963, the thought of US government complicity in the assassination of an American president was simply the stuff of espionage novels and/or movies like 1954's *Suddenly* or 1962's *The Manchurian Candidate* (incidentally, both starring Frank Sinatra). That latter film, in fact, disappeared from circulation for many years following the Kennedy murder. As well, the pending release of *Seven Days in May*, a film about an attempted military coup against the US government, was in doubt for a short time after the assassination, despite the fact that the Kennedy White House had given the film the go-ahead.

The numerous conspiracy theories that would sprout up in the coming years would contribute to making the murder of the young president arguably the most written-about event of the 20th century, a century that included two world wars and a massive economic depression. But for Americans living through it, that afternoon took on a surreal quality, especially with details on the whereabouts of the new president and even

The new First Family, with big-haired teenager (and soon-to-be Beatles fan) Luci Baines at the upper left, older sister Lynda Bird, LBJ, and wife Lady Bird.

the body of the murdered chief executive being kept secret after the announcement of Kennedy's death. It wasn't until Air Force One was in the air and headed toward Washington that official word was released that Lyndon Johnson had taken the oath of office on the plane and that Mrs. Kennedy and the coffin with her husband's body were also on the plane.

From Dallas came word that that young man arrested in the Tippit killing, one Lee Harvey Oswald, was also being questioned regarding the assassination, once it became known that he worked in the Texas School Book Depository: the building believed to be the source of the shots that killed Kennedy. Shortly after that, the spate of information on Oswald's background suddenly became a torrent of information about his years in the Soviet Union as an American expatriate and his eventual return to the US Meanwhile, the only visual evidence Americans had of the orderly transfer of power was a still photograph taken on Air Force One of LBJ taking the oath of office from a Texas district judge named Sarah T. Hughes. In the photo, the new president was flanked by Lady Bird Johnson and a visibly-shell-shocked Jacqueline Kennedy, still dressed in the now-bloodstained pink outfit she had worn at the breakfast in Fort Worth and the presidential party's arrival at Love Field that morning.

Shortly before 6 p.m. (Washington time), what had happened that afternoon became stark reality for a shocked nation now returning home and gathering around TV screens. Air Force One landed at Andrews Air Force Base amid the illumination of hastily-rigged floodlights and TV cameras. A van was wheeled up to the plane and JFK's inner circle had to drag the coffin onto the van's platform before it could be loaded into a hearse that had pulled up behind. Then, Attorney General Robert Kennedy appeared on the platform with Jackie, sporting dried blood-stains on her skirt and stockings. She had to be helped down to ground level from the platform before she walked to the hearse for the trip to Bethesda Naval Hospital for an autopsy. The sight of the coffin and the bloodstained first lady provided the first real visual confirmation of what so many Americans found so hard to believe. Meanwhile, the new president and Lady Bird waited for the hearse to drive off before they walked off the plane and to a bank of microphones set up for the new president to make a brief first public statement before helicoptering to the White House grounds. In effect, the arrival back in Washington of the new president and the body of the murdered chief executive put a punctuation mark on the story of the day's events, even though it was only early evening.

Later that night on NBC, David Brinkley spoke of how quickly what he called "one of the more horrible days in American history" played out, terming it all "too much, too ugly, and too fast." Brinkley referred to the aftermath of the death in April 1945 of Franklin Roosevelt, whose body was returned to Washington on a train following his death from a stroke in Warm Springs, Ga. As Brinkley recalled, this gave Americans a chance to absorb the shock of FDR's death after 12 years in the presidency. In contrast, in a span of some five hours on this day, President Kennedy had gone from being very alive in the motorcade in Dallas to his body having been returned to Washington on the same plane with his widow and a new president. As Brinkley put it, "the sheer speed of it was just too fast for the senses ... there is seldom time to think anymore and today there was none."

*****

November 22, 1963 and the story of how they first heard the news of the shooting of President Kennedy is burned indelibly into the memory of virtually every person old enough to remember that day. That night, American families came together in front of their TV sets and, to a great extent, remained there for the next three days. In that era, most homes with a television had only one. Most children and teenagers did not have their own TV, let alone the video games and personal computers of later decades. The kids might have their own record player in their room but TV viewing was generally a family affair, and so it was that weekend. All regular television programming and commercials had been canceled and, while much of the coverage of the tragedy had amounted to radio with pictures, the three TV networks put their best journalistic and technological foot forward in covering the biggest story in the relatively short history of network television news. Indeed, TV historians have referred to that weekend as the time when television news grew up and truly began to realize its potential. So aside from the estimated quarter of a million people or more who journeyed to Washington to view President Kennedy's flag-draped coffin in the Capitol's rotunda, the memories of that weekend for the majority of Americans are black-and-white images from the TV coverage.

Saturday, November 23:

It was a gray, rainy day in Washington; very appropriate as the shock of the day before gave way to sorrow. In a tradition that goes back to the assassination of Abraham Lincoln, crowds gathered in a quiet vigil in Lafayette Park, across from the White House. The flag had been lowered to half-staff on Friday afternoon and mourning bunting was in view. The coffin, which had arrived from Bethesda in the early hours of Saturday morning, was on display in the East Room, resting on a catafalque similar to the one that had borne Lincoln's coffin nearly a century before. A steady stream of dignitaries arrived at the White House to pay their respects, including former Presidents Harry Truman and Dwight Eisenhower. (Herbert Hoover, the only other living ex-president, was quite elderly and frail by that time and was less than a year from his own passing.) In a jolting illustration of the sudden change of power, JFK's personal effects, including his famous rocking chair, were being moved out of the Oval Office. Late in the afternoon, the new president solemnly announced that Monday, the day of President Kennedy's funeral and burial, would be a national day of mourning. Kennedy, a Navy veteran who served heroically in World War II, would be buried Monday afternoon at Arlington National Ceremony.

In Dallas, a very different scene was playing out at the city's police headquarters. Police Chief Jesse Curry and Homicide Capt. Will Fritz didn't really seem to mind the sudden influx of media attention from all over the world. Oswald had been formally charged with the Kennedy murder late on Friday night and throughout Saturday he was moved from room to room, providing several photo ops for the growing throng of media. As well, the rifle recovered from the sixth floor of the Texas School Book Depository was given its own media spotlight. There had been so many reporters and photographers there on Friday night that lost in the crowd was a familiar face to the Dallas police, a strip club owner and erstwhile small-time Chicago hood professionally known as Jack Ruby. The circus-like atmosphere contrasted with the growing melancholy in much of the country, but that contrast would become even starker on Sunday.

Sunday, November 24:

Two years, 10 months, and four days after television had covered John F. Kennedy's inaugural parade, the networks were preparing to cover a procession over a similar return route that would bring his body from the White House to the Capitol for public viewing of the closed coffin in the Great Rotunda. First, though, even as final preparations were being made for the solemn parade, there was the seeming formality of transferring the accused assassin from Dallas's city jail to the county jail. It should have been done very quickly and quietly but the move was made into a media event and NBC was even covering it live at about 11:20 a.m., Dallas time. After nearly two days of interrogation, Oswald had given the Dallas police precious little in the way of cooperation while repeatedly, in that pre-Miranda era, requesting legal representation.

Now, the handcuffed Oswald was led down a ramp toward an armored police van for the move to the county jail. Suddenly, a man in a fedora entered the picture, rushed toward Oswald, and fired a shot into his midsection. A wild scene ensued, with the assailant knocked down by Oswald's police escort. At least two of them recognized him and one called out, "Jack, you son of a bitch!" It turned out that the shooter was the same Jack Ruby who had been hanging around the station on Friday night. Oswald was carried back inside, put on a stretcher, and carried back down the ramp to an ambulance that seemed to get to the station instantaneously. On the stretcher, he was already unconscious and pale. The ambulance then rushed, ironically, to Parkland Hospital and Oswald was moved into an emergency cubicle not far from the one where one of the two men he was accused of killing on Friday had died. After being worked on by a team of doctors, though, Oswald expired at 1:07

p.m., Dallas time, virtually assuring that we would never definitively know exactly what happened in Dealey Plaza at 12:30 on Friday afternoon, November 22, 1963.

Approximately a half-hour after what became television's first live handgun murder, the nation's attention returned to Washington. The widowed first lady and her two young children waited as the coffin departed the White House and was placed on the same horse-drawn caisson that had transported the coffin of Franklin Roosevelt over 17 years before. Saturday's rain had given way to cold temperatures and a brilliant blue sky, the setting for a series of images and sounds that would become a permanent and prominent part of the collective memory of Americans of a certain age: the caisson—the riderless horse—the cadence of the muffled drums—the eerie silence of the huge crowds lining the procession route—the dirge-tempo playing of "Hail to the Chief" at the Capitol plaza before the coffin was taken off the caisson—the Navy hymn "Eternal Father Strong To Save" played as the coffin was carried by the military honor guard up the steps and into the rotunda.

That catafalque had borne the coffins of many great Americans in that same spot in the center of the rotunda and would again numerous times in decades to come. An emotional eulogy from Senate Majority Leader Mike Mansfield followed: the kind of larger-than-life, straight-out-of-central-casting political figure we just don't have any more. Further indelible vignettes followed: the young widow and daughter Caroline kneeling at the coffin; Jackie gently kissing the flag and Caroline patting the coffin. Lastly: beginning at mid-afternoon, the procession of hundreds of thousands of people in a line stretching for miles into the streets of Washington, filing past the honor-guard-flanked coffin.

That night, the images of the people paying their respects to their fallen president, with solemn classical music as a soundtrack, alternated on the TV networks with memorial concerts and scenes of the unprecedented assemblage of dignitaries arriving in Washington for the following day's state funeral. NBC, which had already scheduled an American version of *That Was the Week That Was* to debut in January, had a videotape of the previous night's special edition of the British series flown over for showing on Sunday night. That broadcast gave most Americans their introduction to young David Frost, who would become a familiar face on American TV in the late '60s and the '70s.

There was also news film of the crowds at the seven National Football League games played that afternoon. A smattering of college football games had been played on Saturday but most high schools, colleges, and the professional American Football League had either canceled or postponed their games for that weekend. NFL commissioner Pete Rozelle, after consulting with press secretary Salinger, felt that since President Kennedy was a football fan he would want the games to go on. Rozelle announced that Sunday's NFL schedule would go on but with no bands or halftime shows or any of the normal festivities of a football Sunday in the early sixties.

While the crowds at the games were close to normal NFL attendance, many fans were there only because they had season tickets and felt obligated to go. Many of the players expressed misgivings about having to play and the games themselves were lackluster and unmemorable. For the remainder of his life, Rozelle said that playing the games that day was the biggest mistake he made as commissioner.

Monday, November 25:

The people kept coming past the coffin all through the night and into Monday morning until the line was stopped at around 8:30 a.m., with an official estimate at 250,000 people paying their respects. Hundreds of thousands more lined the route of the funeral procession, while millions more nationwide and around the world went to their places of worship that morning before returning to what some had dubbed America's electronic chapel for that weekend. Upwards of 200 foreign dignitaries representing 92 countries arrived in Washington to attend President Kennedy's funeral and burial.

Once again, brilliant sunshine and the late-autumn chill set the scene as the funeral procession moved from the Capitol back to the White House. Mrs. Kennedy had specifically requested the participation of the Royal Highland Regiment Pipers of The Black Watch, who had played for the first family on the White House grounds only a couple of weeks before. From the White House, with the tolling of bells nearly the only sounds, the procession moved on foot to St. Matthew's Cathedral. Mrs. Kennedy, walking hand-in-hand with JFK's surviving brothers, Robert and Ted, was a poignant, black-veiled picture of dignity. Behind walked the massive collection of dignitaries, with the tall, uniformed French President de Gaulle and Ethiopia's medal-bedecked Haile Selassie at the front of the group.

The gravel-voiced Richard Cardinal Cushing, an old Kennedy family friend, officiated at the funeral Mass. The archbishop of Washington, the Reverend Philip Hannan, read excerpts from Kennedy's speeches, including the entire inaugural address, and passages from the Bible. One of those passages was the excerpt from Ecclesiastes 3.1 that Pete Seeger had adapted for his song "Turn Turn Turn (To Everything There Is a Season)". Interestingly, The Byrds would record Seeger's tune two years later and, on the same album, would include an adaptation of the old folk tune "He Was a Friend of Mine" with new lyrics by the group's Jim McGuinn in tribute to President Kennedy.

The coffin was taken from the church and returned to the caisson for the final trip to Arlington to the strains of the hymn "Holy God We Praise Thy Name". On his third birthday, John F. Kennedy, Jr. fidgeted outside of the church. He had learned how to salute the American flag so his mother bent down and suggested that he salute the flag that was covering his father's casket. Young John stepped forward and did indeed salute: perhaps the most poignant moment of the entire sad weekend.

From the church, the funeral procession resumed, passing the Lincoln Memorial as it traveled over Arlington Memorial Bridge and on to the burial site. Once again, individual sights and sounds are the memories that endure from that late afternoon: the sadness in the voice of Cardinal Cushing. The dazed, vacant look in the eyes of Robert Kennedy, who would be buried not far from that spot some four years later. The fly-over with the missing lead aircraft. The 21-gun salute followed by the playing of "Taps", with one appropriately flattened note. The Navy hymn playing as the flag that covered the coffin was folded and given to the young widow. Mrs. Kennedy lighting the eternal flame that she had requested be installed. And perhaps the last unforgettable image of an unforgettable weekend, the eternal flame glowing in the late-autumn dusk following the burial ceremony.

*****

Change, in the most shocking way imaginable, had come to America. And nothing would ever again be quite what it had been on that ordinary Friday morning in November.

21

A JOYOUS THANKSGIVING NIGHT SPECIAL!

"THE ARTHUR GODFREY SHOW"

STARRING **TONY BENNETT ★ CAROL LAWRENCE**
SHARI LEWIS ★ ORSON BEAN ★ LIZA MINNELLI

PRESENTED BY

MOHAWK CARPET MILLS

See and hear about the Fall Spectacular of Mohawk Carpet Values...on sale at all Mohawk dealers!

NBC-TV·CH④·10 PM-11 PM
IN COLOR!

Longtime CBS radio & TV host Arthur Godfrey starred in this NBC Thanksgiving night special as the nation struggled to move on from the murder of its young president.

CHAPTER 2

DON'T LET IT BE FORGOT

"LIFE GOES ON"

T hat was the headline on the front page of the *New York Daily News* on Tuesday morning, November 26, above the photo of John F. Kennedy, Jr. saluting his father's flag-draped coffin outside St. Matthew's Cathedral the previous afternoon. Despite the psychic body blow of the assassination of President Kennedy, life did go on for Americans following the long, history-altering weekend. For instance, the New York Stock Exchange had gone into a half-hour free-fall before trading could be closed off on Friday afternoon in the wake of the shooting in Dallas. When the exchange reopened on Tuesday morning, the market staged the largest one-day rally in its history to that point in time, a rally interpreted as an expression of confidence in President Johnson.

The scheduled six-page newspaper supplement to promote Macy's famous Thanksgiving Day Parade ran that morning and, later in the day, Macy's announced that the parade would go on as scheduled on Thursday. Officially, Macy's didn't want to "disappoint the millions of children" who would either be along the parade route or watching on TV. Of course, even children too young to understand what was going on must have realized something very bad had happened when they weren't able to watch their normal kiddie shows and cartoons over the weekend and saw the demeanor of their parents and older siblings.

There may also have been monetary considerations in going on with the parade, particularly the telecast of the parade. While the NBC telecast of the Macy's parade wasn't the three-hour nonstop commercial for Christmas shopping and Broadway shows of later decades, the 90-minute show of that era had a heavy emphasis on commercials for toys. Given the huge losses in commercial revenue suffered by all three networks that weekend, not to mention the production costs of the non-stop coverage, NBC may very well have been reluctant to give up more ad revenue had the parade been canceled. In any case, once Macy's announced that the New York parade would go on, J.L. Hudson's decided that the Detroit parade would go on as well. But the Army-Navy game, scheduled for that Saturday, was postponed a week to December 7, with the game's festive traditions sidelined.

Life went on in Washington as well that Tuesday. The new president moved into the Oval Office and it was announced that LBJ would address a joint session of Congress at midday on Wednesday. Meanwhile, the Senate Judiciary Committee rather prematurely announced that it would begin a probe of the assassination. Ironically, Senator James Eastland of Mississippi, the committee's chairman, was a noted opponent of any civil rights legislation and figured to be a particular Senate obstacle in the way of the bill that the Kennedy administration had sent to Congress. Not surprisingly, the expressions of support for President Johnson by members of Congress from the South did not include support for the civil rights bill, but Johnson would lobby in that address to Congress for passage of the bill as a tribute to Kennedy.

Ted Sorensen, JFK's chief speechwriter, took on the same job for the new president's first full-length address, despite his deep depression over the loss of a close personal friend. Delivered before a somber Capitol Hill audience, the speech would perhaps be best-remembered for its opening line, "All I have I would have given gladly not to be standing here today" and the exhortation, in the spirit of the "let us begin" line in Kennedy's inaugural address, "Let us continue." That phrase would become a theme for the following summer's Democratic convention that would nominate Johnson for a term in his own right.

Obviously, the assassination had brought the first Republican maneuverings toward the '64 campaign to a halt. Maine Senator Margaret Chase Smith, who had placed a rose on JFK's old desk in the Senate chamber during a brief Monday morning Senate session prior to the funeral, postponed until January her entrance into the race as the first female candidate for a major party presidential nomination. Indeed, a moratorium on overt political activity would be observed until after the official 30-day period of mourning and then the Christmas/New Year's holidays. New York Governor Nelson Rockefeller would resume his already launched campaign just after the New Year and the GOP frontrunner, Barry Goldwater, would announce his candidacy the same week.

Thanksgiving Day 1963 was a somber affair across most of the country. Restaurants in New York City saw an upward bump in their business because some families felt that it wouldn't be appropriate to have the usual Thanksgiving celebration six days after the murder of the nation's young president, and even the level of dinner conversation in those restaurants was muted. JFK's Thanksgiving proclamation was widely read at public functions and religious services. Tens of thousands, including Mrs. Kennedy, visited the late president's grave at Arlington, now surrounded by a white picket fence. Late in the day, the new president made an appearance on national TV and, continuing the theme of renewal from his address to Congress the day before, called for the nation to aspire to "a new American greatness."

He also announced that, at Mrs. Kennedy's suggestion, NASA's Florida-based Launch Operations Center would be known as the John F. Kennedy Space Center as a tribute to Kennedy's enthusiastic support of the space program. As well, Cape Canaveral, site of the actual launches, was renamed Cape Kennedy, a name change that would be reversed some 10 years later, though the space center would still carry Kennedy's name. A number of efforts would soon take shape to name places and things, some not even built yet, after the slain president. For instance, momentum was building to have the long-proposed National Cultural Center named for JFK, who had been one of the center's chief proponents. By December 3, President Johnson had announced his support. Formal legislation to name the cultural center for Kennedy was introduced that day in the Senate by Arkansas's J.W. Fullbright and in the House by future House Speaker, Carl Albert of Oklahoma.

As promised, Macy's Thanksgiving Day Parade did indeed go on. The only overt reminders of the nation's loss were the flags at half-mast and the black streamers on flags and banners in the parade. Otherwise, the parade went on as intended, with the upcoming New York World's Fair the lead theme. The fair's symbolic Unisphere was saluted in the lead float. The main Broadway float was for the new Meredith Wilson musical, *Here's Love*. TV/movie teen heartthrob Troy Donahue and comedian/musical parodist Alan Sherman were two of the celebrities who appeared in the parade, along with NBC personalities James Drury, Michael Landon, Mitch Miller, and Leslie Uggams. The two marquee football games scheduled for that day went on as well: in Detroit, after the Hudson's parade, the NFL's Lions and Packers battled to a tie while Texas preserved its number one college football ranking by beating traditional rival Texas A&M.

*****

Following her Thanksgiving visit to Arlington, Jacqueline Kennedy flew with Caroline and John Jr. to the Kennedy compound at Hyannis Port, Mass., to spend some private time before preparing to move out of the White House. On Friday, Theodore H. White—the author of *The Making of the President 1960* and a Kennedy family friend—came by the Cape Cod house for an interview with Jackie, one of a scant few she would give in the three-decade remainder of her life. One week after the assassination, she suggested that White do an essay on President Kennedy for *Life* magazine, one of a number of publications for which White wrote. They talked for some four hours and White, with Jackie acting as a de facto editor, wrote the piece in just 45 minutes. The piece, "For President Kennedy: An Epilogue," ran in the following week's issue of *Life* after the presses had been held on Friday night for White's essay.

Despite her breathy public voice and the fairly traditional role she played as political wife and, then, First Lady, the former Jacqueline Bouvier was a very savvy woman who knew how to cultivate an image. (It's not surprising that she spent much of the last two decades of her life as a book editor for a major publishing house.) On that very same Friday, Michigan Congresswoman Martha Griffiths suggested that Jackie be appointed ambassador to France: such was the high esteem with which she was held.

Just one week after his death, the young widow had decided that didn't want Jack Kennedy's legacy left to historians or to what she considered "bitter" writers and columnists of that era. She was also aware that his image would be tarnished by stories of her husband's philandering, once they became public knowledge. So with that one interview, she deftly co-opted the revisionists by creating a mythology for the Kennedy presidency.

Jackie related a story about how JFK loved the cast album from the Broadway show *Camelot*, how the couple used to play it at night before they went to bed, and how Jack especially loved the finale and the last few bars of the title song's reprise, with the lyrics "Don't let it be forgot/ That once there was a spot//For one brief shining moment/That was known as Camelot."

White's notes from the full interview, which were not made public until after both he and Jackie had passed on, are very interesting. They include her detailed, graphic account of the assassination and the hours after and—given how the coming years would play out—ironic comments about whether she would ever live in Europe and her son's interest in planes. She also declared that she was against "changing the name of something," that her only direct tribute requests were the eternal flame on JFK's grave and the change to Cape Kennedy so that name might be "on just that one booster-the one that would put us ahead of the Russians." Otherwise, she was against going "out on a Kennedy driveway to a Kennedy airport to visit a Kennedy school." White's *Life* essay included hardly any of this material.

Instead, White emphasized the *Camelot* angle and gave the Kennedy years their historic identity, at least in the public mind. The original, self-applied slogan for JFK's presidency, "The New Frontier," was largely forgotten. The myth that the Kennedy years were a magic, idyllic moment in time cut short by tragedy began to grow and would never really die, despite the revisionist history and tawdry revelations of later years.

*****

On that same Friday, the new president announced the formation of a formal investigative body to probe the assassination of President Kennedy. The Warren Commission, as it became known, would be headed by Supreme Court Chief Justice Earl Warren. The commission would include both a Democratic and Republican US senator and a Democratic and Republican congressman. As it happened, the GOP representative from the House, Gerald R. Ford, would himself become president under historic circumstances less than 11 years later. The commission also included former Central Intelligence Agency director Allen Dulles and former World Bank president John McCloy.

It was Ford who recommended that the commission bring aboard as an assistant counsel a not-quite-34-year-old Philadelphia lawyer named Arlen Specter, a future moderate Republican senator from Pennsylvania who would turn Democratic in the last years of a lengthy career. While serving on the commission staff, Specter helped come up with the "single-bullet theory," which claimed that the first shot that hit Kennedy passed through his neck and also hit Governor Connally. Warren Commission critics would seize on the single-bullet theory and even the announcement, just a week after the JFK murder, of the commission's formation as indications that from the start the commission was mandated to conclude that Lee Harvey Oswald was the lone assassin so that any suspicion of an international conspiracy would be squelched.

That day also saw the release of a heavily-detailed report on the efforts by the doctors at Parkland Hospital to save President Kennedy and *Life* magazine released still images from Abraham Zapruder's film of the shooting. Both the testimony of the doctors at Parkland and, of course, the Zapruder film would be major components in the Warren Commission probe. The saga of the Zapruder film is quite a story in itself, one that has been the subject of a number of books, but the bottom line is that *Life* purchased all still and moving-picture rights to the film and Zapruder would end up with a lot of money, $25,000 of which he would almost immediately donate to a fund for the widow of J.D. Tippit.

Life soon published color slides from the film, but minus the shot to the head that killed Kennedy. It would be over 11 years before a complete copy of the film would be shown on US network television by Geraldo Rivera on ABC's late-night *Good Night America*.

Three days after the Warren Commission was announced, a previously announced Texas Board of Inquiry investigation of the assassination and the murders of Tippit and Oswald was "postponed indefinitely." That investigation was to be headed by a prominent Houston attorney named Leon Jaworski. Almost exactly 10 years later, Jaworski would be named to succeed Archibald Cox as the Watergate special prosecutor in the wake of the infamous "Saturday night massacre."

Bearing a reputation as a "Southern moderate," Jaworski would engineer a grand jury's naming of Richard Nixon as an "unindicted co-conspirator" in the Watergate cover-up and then take his pursuit of 64 White House tapes to the Supreme Court. The high court would rule that Nixon had to hand over the tapes in late July 1974 and within three weeks Nixon would resign the presidency. So, while his old friend and client LBJ deprived Jaworski of heading up a state investigation of the murders in Dallas with the formation of the Warren Commission, Jaworski would become an American hero a decade later.

*****

By the early 21st century, the Friday after Thanksgiving had long since become known as Black Friday, the biggest shopping day of the year and the symbolic kickoff to the Christmas shopping season. In the early '60s, that Friday was a big shopping day but not to the ridiculous lengths of later decades. In 1963, terming a day of rampant consumerism "Black Friday" would have been very inappropriate. Indeed, retail figures for the period from November 22 through November. 29 showed a 30 percent drop in volume from the same period in 1962. In that era, most stores were closed on Sundays and certainly on Thanksgiving Day, but many had also closed for that Monday's national day of mourning (as well as some hours on November 22 once word of the president's death became official). As well, though, the somber atmosphere that permeated so much of the country that week certainly had an effect on the normal Thanksgiving week shopping habits.

*****

Extremists of all stripes were beginning to share their particular spins on the JFK assassination. After the Soviet Union had blamed the killing on a right-wing conspiracy, right-wing extremist Gen. Edwin Walker claimed it was the work of a Communist plot organized by Fidel Castro. Walker added that Southern integration was also the result of a Communist plot and he continued to fly his US, Texas, and Confederate flags at full-mast during the official 30-day mourning period. It also came to light at this time that Oswald was believed to have taken a shot at Walker earlier that year, apparently with the same rifle he was accused of using to kill Kennedy. The John Birch Society would use the assassination as the focal point of anti-Communist ads in mid-December but would hold the publication of the December issue of the society's magazine because it contained two articles critical of the Kennedy administration.

At the other end of the extremist spectrum, Malcolm X, the apostle of black separatism, likened Kennedy's murder to "chickens coming home to roost" due to Kennedy's "twiddling his thumbs" during high-profile murders of blacks and the coup in South Vietnam. Those remarks would earn Malcolm a suspension from public appearances representing the Black Muslims and may have marked the beginning of the break between Malcolm and the Nation of Islam hierarchy. Some 15 months later, Malcolm X would himself be assassinated.

*****

Collateral damage from the JFK assassination was symbolized by a now-legendary line by controversial comedy icon Lenny Bruce. There are various accounts of when and where Bruce delivered the line but a consensus indicates that it was probably at the Village Theater in New York and it was at the beginning of Bruce's first gig after the assassination. Most accounts say that Bruce came on stage, took the hand mi-

A 1963 cash-in paperback featuring Vaughn Meader and the cast of the *First Family* albums.

crophone, looked at the audience in silence and then whistled and said, "Vaughn Meader is screwed!"

Vaughn Meader was a young comedian who had rocketed to sudden stardom a year earlier as a result of his facial resemblance to and spot-on vocal impersonation of President Kennedy. An ensemble comedy album, *The First Family*, with Meader in the lead role as JFK, was a runaway hit during the 1962 Christmas shopping season; one of the fastest-selling LPs to that point in time. In fact, the president was reported to have bought a number of copies to give as gifts that Christmas. *The First Family* was the No. 1 album in the country for 12 weeks at the end of '62/early '63 and won the Grammy award as album of the year. Although Meader was anxious to move on from the Kennedy image, he was roped into doing a follow-up *First Family* LP, which wasn't as successful as the original but was still a Top 5 album in the summer of '63.

In early November, Meader recorded a new album, called *Have Some Nuts*, which was completely devoid of any Kennedy material and would be the first release of his new record deal with MGM/Verve. On November 15, he taped an appearance on a TV special starring Joey Bishop that was slated to air in February, right around the time *Have Some Nuts* was scheduled for release, supported by Meader with a series of club gigs. A filmed special called *The Best on Record*, saluting the Grammy award winners in that era before the actual Grammy awards show was carried live, would have a segment featuring Meader and was scheduled to air on November 24. He was in a cab on Friday afternoon, November 22 when he heard the news that would permanently alter his career.

The Best on Record, preempted along with all regular programming that weekend, aired on December 8 with Meader's segment excised. His segment on the Bishop special was erased, according to the *New York Times* in early December. In January, Meader played an engagement at the famous Blue Angel in Manhattan, got rather good reviews, and was held over for an extra week. But the *Have Some Nuts* album would gather dust in record store bins. His career went into free-fall, marked by that era's all-too-familiar pattern of bouts with drugs and alcohol. He would later begin playing bluegrass in bars and dives. At one point, Meader would even talk bravely about doing a one-man show as JFK but nothing would ever come of it. He would make an appearance in the very forgettable 1975 film *Linda Lovelace For President* and made one last vinyl appearance on a Reagan-era Rich Little comedy album.

Meader's health would worsen as the new century began. He would pass away just a few days before the 2004 presidential election, a few weeks short of 41 years after Lenny Bruce uttered his prophetic line.

*****

As a still-mourning Robert Kennedy returned to work at the Justice Department on December 4, New York City Mayor Robert F. Wagner announced that he would urge the City Council to rename what was officially called New York International Airport but was popularly known as Idelwild. The new name would be John F. Kennedy International Airport. Two days later, the late president and Pope John XXIII, who had passed away in early June of that year, were each awarded a posthumous Presidential Medal of Freedom by LBJ. Meanwhile, Mrs. Kennedy and the children moved out of the White House and into the home of Under Secretary of State W. Averell Harriman in nearby Georgetown. Mrs. Kennedy would soon purchase a home in the same tony neighborhood. The Johnson family moved into the White House the next day, 15 days after the assassination.

As that first full work/school week since November 22 ended, there were already indications that people were moving on with their lives and weren't as paralyzed with grief as later portrayals of this period would imply. Retail sales made a big upward jump that week as Christmas shopping began in earnest and even Christmas light displays could be seen dotting many neighborhoods. Newspaper articles that led with the premise of a somber holiday season ended up portraying a near-normal atmosphere. But *Time* magazine, in mid-December, ran a more upfront assessment of a nation having a relatively normal Christmas season in a leadoff piece in the magazine's main news section called "The Mood of the Nation." The piece concluded with a description of the scene outside of a Detroit office building, with people entering and leaving amid the usual holiday hustle and bustle and hardly noticing that the wreath over the building's entrance was not a Christmas decoration but a black mourning wreath.

There was a reduction in the number of corporate Christmas parties that year but a majority of such cancellations had been made earlier that fall, due to budgetary considerations and/or the reputation for "inappropriate behavior" those parties had earned. That said, some companies did cancel their parties in the aftermath of the assassination. But, on the evening of December 12, the annual Rockefeller Center Christmas tree lighting festivities were held in New York. The tree lighting was held later in the season than it would be in later decades and the television coverage was a local 15-minute program beginning at 6:15, not the bloated two-hour network plugathon into which it would eventually morph.

Meanwhile, the New York City Council voted unanimously on December 10 for the renaming of Idelwild Airport for JFK and President Johnson asked Congress to authorize a Kennedy 50-cent piece, which was quickly approved. On December 12, veteran New York Times columnist James Reston commented on the growing "Kennedy legend": "It is clear now that he captured the imagination of a whole generation of young people in many parts of this world, particularly in university communities." And the Sunday papers for December 15 included ads for a growing number of pieces of JFK memorabilia--bronze busts, framed portraits, record albums of his best-known speeches, and a Decca LP of the November 23 special tribute edition of *That Was The Week That Was*.

That episode had featured the debut of a new tribute song called "In the Summer of His Years," with lyrics by Herbert Kretzmer, who would later write English lyrics for the score of *Les Miserables*. The following week, Millicent Martin, who had debuted the song live, went into a London studio to do a professional recording of "In the Summer of His Years" in a session produced by George Martin, England's hot record producer of the moment. A smattering of renditions of the song were released in America over the next several weeks, including Martin's and versions by Mahalia Jackson and Kate Smith. The most commercially successful of those was by Connie Francis, one of the most popular female vocalists of the late '50s/early '60s. Her single of "In the Summer of His Years" reached the US Top 50 in the first weeks of 1964. By December 21, seven JFK memorial LP releases were reported to have sold a combined 5 million copies.

On December 17, the Public Works committees in both the House and the Senate approved legislation to name the national cultural center the John F. Kennedy Center for the Performing Arts. Given the snail's pace at which the cultural center project had progressed, going back to the first congressional resolution in 1938, it's not surprising that ground wouldn't be broken by President Johnson until December 1964, and full construction wouldn't begin for another year. The Kennedy Center would have its official opening in September 1971. The annual Kennedy Center Honors for luminaries in all of the performing arts would become a modern December tradition, with Caroline Kennedy taking over hosting duties for the Honors Gala from Walter Cronkite in 2003.

The name switch from Idelwild to John F. Kennedy International Airport was completed very quickly. Mayor Wagner signed the bill on December 18 and the rededication ceremony was set for 11 a.m. on Christmas Eve morning at the International Arrivals Building. Robert Kennedy was expected to represent the Kennedy family, but in that age before it was deemed proper for men to show emotions in public, RFK didn't feel up to making that appearance so the youngest of the Kennedy brothers, Ted, and his sister Jean accepted the honor for their family. Being in New York, the ceremony became a major media event, of course. The next big media event at the airport's International Arrivals Building would be on February 7, with the arrival in America of The Beatles.

*****

On December 18, a former New York State assemblyman and frequent defense lawyer named Mark Lane submitted a 10,000-word brief to the Warren Commission and also released it to a "progressive newsweekly" called the *National Guardian*. The brief urged the commission to appoint defense counsel on behalf of Lee Harvey Oswald and Lane indicated that he would be available to fill such a position. The commission's response was that it wasn't conducting a trial so there was no need for defense counsel. By mid-January, though, Marguerite Oswald, mother of the accused assassin, had retained Lane to represent her before the commission.

Unlike Lee Oswald's wife Marina, who had come to the US from Russia and could barely speak English, his mother took to the limelight quite nicely, posing for photographers at her son's grave and weeping seemingly on cue. Given that neither she nor Lane was at all a shrinking violet, they made an interesting team. Lane had already suggested that Mrs. Oswald file a wrongful-death suit against the city of Dallas and his primary position was that there was insufficient evidence to charge Oswald with Kennedy's murder. Marina Oswald testified before the Warren Commission early in February and Lane's reaction was to imply that she had been brainwashed by the Secret Service and the FBI.

Relations between Lane and the commission, particularly special counsel J. Lee Rankin, had quickly become so adversarial that when Marguerite Oswald testified before the commission on February 10 Lane remained outside the hearing room and Mrs. Oswald was represented by Washington lawyer John F. Doyle. She entered the hearing room with a black bag full of documents that she said would exonerate her son. Mrs. Oswald testified for three days and charged that Lee was a US intelligence agent who was set up to take the fall for the assassination but, despite that bagful of documents, Earl Warren said that she supplied no evidence to support her claims.

The following evening, Lane and Mrs. Oswald appeared at a public meeting sponsored by the National Guardian at New York's Town Hall. Earlier that day, Dallas police officials announced that tests indicated that the rifle Lee Oswald used to shoot at Gen. Edwin Walker was the same one used in the assassination of President Kennedy. However, Lane played a tape recording of an interview he said he had conducted earlier that day with a schoolteacher who was one of the closest witnesses to the shooting of the president and Governor Connally. She said she heard 4 to 6 shots coming from the grassy knoll and saw a man running from that area, 1,500 people attended the meeting and cheered Mrs. Oswald. Less than three months after the assassination, conspiracy theories were already gaining momentum. Meanwhile, the trial of Jack Ruby for Oswald's murder began in Dallas the day before the Town Hall event, despite defense efforts to have the trial moved out of Dallas and a motion for acquittal for Ruby on the grounds of temporary insanity.

The adversarial relationship between Lane and the Warren Commission would culminate in the 1966 publication of *Rush to Judgment*, one of the first books to take on the commission's September 1964 report;

particularly the conclusion that Oswald had acted alone and was not part of any conspiracy. Spurred along by the growing number of protests against the escalation of the war in Vietnam and the increasing distrust in government, the various Kennedy assassination conspiracy theories would become another element in the tumult of the mid-to-late '60s but would live on well beyond that time. Indeed, with each passing decade the likelihood of ever finding out what really happened that day in Dallas would become ever more remote.

*****

On a cold late Sunday afternoon in Washington, about 14,000 people turned out for a candlelight ceremony at the Lincoln Memorial on December 22 to officially conclude the 30-day mourning period for President Kennedy. Three members of the new first family, seven Cabinet members, and two Supreme Court justices were among the dignitaries at the ceremony. LBJ symbolically turned the page after delivering his remarks. He returned to the White House, where the mourning bunting had been taken down and Christmas decorations put up, and turned on the White House Christmas tree. The next morning, the Johnson's flew to Texas to spend the holidays at the LBJ Ranch.

While Americans did move on and enjoyed a relatively normal Christmas season with record retail sales figures for a Christmas buying season six days shorter than that of 1962, the memory of President Kennedy and his death was never far from the minds of most people. The thousands who paid their respects at his grave or left wreaths in Dealey Plaza during the holiday season were proof of that. So were some 800,000 letters, cards, and telegrams sent to Mrs. Kennedy since November 22, which required a staff of volunteers to acknowledge. Another indicator was the nonfiction best-selling book list on the final weekend of the year. Topping the list was *Profiles in Courage,* the 1955 book written by JFK (and, reportedly, Ted Sorensen). As well, though, after 14 weeks on the list, hanging in at No. 4 was Victor Lasky's conservative take on the Kennedy presidency, *JFK: The Man & the Myth.*

As the year ended, JFK's personal secretary, Mrs. Evelyn Lincoln, who had been part of the presidential entourage in Dallas on November 22, was going through all of Kennedy's personal papers and organizing them for storage and an eventual move to the JFK Library, then in the very first planning stages of what would become a long, bumpy process before its dedication in 1979. Mrs. Lincoln was also part of a rather bizarre fact sheet that began circulating during this time, a list of similarities and/or coincidences linking Kennedy with Abraham Lincoln. Among those was the fact that Lincoln's personal secretary was named Kennedy and JFK's was named Lincoln, along with the more well-known item that both were succeeded by vice presidents named Johnson and the bizarre coincidence that the full names John Wilkes Booth and Lee Harvey Oswald each had 15 letters.

On the first business day of the new year, Philadelphia Mayor James Tate signed a bill to rename Philadelphia Stadium, the home of the Army-Navy game in that era, John F. Kennedy Stadium. Production of the new Kennedy 50-cent piece was scheduled to begin in February, with the coins available to the public in late March or early April. And a 5-cent stamp honoring the late president would be issued on JFK's 47th birthday, May 29. This continued a tradition of stamps honoring presidents who died in office going back to Lincoln.

The following week, the completion of a piece of unfinished business from November 22 was announced for late January. As the shots were fired in Dallas, a delegation of Cabinet members led by Secretary of State Dean Rusk was in a plane over the Pacific en route to a trade and economics conference in Tokyo. Upon the news of the president's death, the plane returned to Washington, arriving late that Friday evening. On January 6, it was announced that virtually the same delegation would attend the rescheduled conference toward the end of that month.

With the standard edition of *Profiles in Courage* at the top of the best-seller lists, a new memorial edition of the book with a forward by Robert Kennedy would be hitting bookstores within the first couple of weeks of February. Writing that very personal forward in December was part of the process through which RFK came to grips with the sudden loss of his brother and confidant. By early January, Bobby was coming out of the deep depression that had gripped him in the weeks immediately after the assassination. He had decided to stay on as attorney general, despite his, at best, frosty relationship with the new president.

LBJ, for his part, had asked Kennedy to continue to sit in on National Security Council meetings and sent him on a diplomatic mission to Southeast Asia soon afterward. Given RFK's experience as an advisor to his brother during the Cuban missile crisis, Johnson was intending to use Bobby as an advisor on Cuba and other Latin American matters. For the future, RFK was considering options that included leaving politics and going into either practicing law or teaching, entering state politics in Massachusetts, or even the vice-presidency, though that seemed a very remote possibility. As 1964 began, ending that year as a US senator-elect from New York would have seemed to be an even more remote possibility for Robert Kennedy.

On January 13, RFK announced an ambitious "oral history" of the Kennedy presidency that would be put together through an extensive series of interviews with associates of the late president and eventually placed in the JFK Library. The next day, with her brothers-in-law sitting nearby, the widowed first lady made her first on-air public statement since the assassination of her husband from RFK's Washington office. It was primarily a chance for Jackie to thank the public for the messages of sympathy that had been received. She added that all of those messages would be included with her husband's papers at the JFK Library.

The next day, Ted Sorensen became the first member of the late president's inner circle to leave the White House, departing so he could write a book about the Kennedy years. Less than two weeks later, special assistant Arthur M. Schlesinger Jr. resigned with the same intent. And in March press secretary Pierre Salinger departed the White House to run for the US Senate from California. But LBJ was able to limit the departure of JFK's closest aides. He convinced Kenny O'Donnell, Dave Powers, and Larry O'Brien to stay beyond the '64 election. O'Brien, in fact, was one of the highest-ranking officials in Johnson's election campaign, a prelude to his later work as chairman of the Democratic National Committee. And, of course, Kennedy's national security and foreign relations team, headed by Secretary of State Rusk, Secretary of Defense Robert McNamara, and national security advisor McGeorge Bundy, remained and was largely responsible for the escalation of US involvement in the war in Vietnam.

Sorensen and Schlesinger did indeed write books about the Kennedy years. Sorensen's *Kennedy* was an international best-seller and Schlesinger's *A Thousand Days: John F. Kennedy in the White House* won Schlesinger his second Pulitzer Prize. Neither book could be described as a "warts and all" account of the Kennedy presidency but that's not what the public wanted at that juncture. The revisionists would have their say in later years and there would be a flood of tawdry revelatory books but in the first months and, indeed, the first years following John F. Kennedy's murder, most of the public was willing to take its cue from the nation's widowed First Lady. For the moment, America accepted the image of the Kennedy years as an exciting, hopeful, idyllic "one, brief shining moment known as Camelot."

The day before President Kennedy's assassination, Vietnam was still an increasingly-annoying civil war in Southeast Asia that produced scenes like this one from November 21, 1963.

CHAPTER 3

THE WHOLE WORLD IS FESTERING

Prior to his days as a Songwriters Hall of Fame-bound lyricist for Broadway shows, Sheldon Harnick wrote comic and social commentary songs for Broadway revues in the '50s. One of those was a humorous vision of a world in turmoil in the nuclear age, "The Merry Minuet." A fledgling folk music group called The Kingston Trio recorded the song in August of 1958 at the Hungry I in San Francisco for the live album that would be their big-time breakthrough. By the fall of 1963, Sheldon Harnick had become one-half of a very successful songwriting duo with Jerry Bock. They'd written the score for one of the most popular shows then on Broadway, *She Loves Me*, and would have an even bigger success the following year with *Fiddler on the Roof*. But the world still hadn't changed a whole lot from the days of "The Merry Minuet."

Not only were we just a year removed from the US's near-apocalyptic face-off with the Soviet Union over the presence of Soviet missiles in Cuba, there seemed to be hot spots all over, some of which flew under the radar of most Americans. For instance, on November 18, three days before President Kennedy flew to Texas, there was a military coup in Iraq, a country a goodly number of Americans of that time probably couldn't find on a globe. The coup ousted the Baathist Socialist government, which had just recently secured an approximately $84 million loan from Kuwait in exchange for recognition of Kuwaiti sovereign-

Better than a year after the missile crisis over Cuba, the island's premier, Fidel Castro, was accepting support from both the Soviet Union and Red China.

ty by the Baghdad government. With outside agitation from Egypt and Syria, the situation in Iraq seemed to be eternally chaotic. Indeed, when the news of the murder of the American president reached Baghdad, one Iraqi said, "We are used to this kind of thing in Arab countries. But in America?" But the instability of the Iraqi government was of scant interest to most Americans and totally unknown to them was a young Baath with an already-growing rap sheet of contributing to that instability named Saddam Hussein.

Of much more immediate concern to Americans, especially in the days following the assassination of JFK, was the ongoing "merry minuet" with the Soviets and increasing worry about Cuba's attempts to increase its influence throughout Latin America. In his first days in office, President Johnson took pains to affirm US support for the North Atlantic Treaty Organization (NATO) while putting out diplomatic feelers regarding a possible get-acquainted meeting with Soviet premier Nikita Khrushchev. Khrushchev, who had taken the unusual step of expressing his condolences in person at the US embassy in Moscow on November 23, was reportedly satisfied that Johnson would continue to pursue better relations with the Soviets.

Given its proximity to the US mainland, though, Cuba was of utmost concern. Only a week after LBJ took office, charges were being aimed at Fidel Castro's regime that it had sent leftist terrorists into Venezuela to sabotage that country's December 1 elections. The leftist agenda was rejected as the Democratic Action Party won the Venezuelan elections. Nonetheless, two days after the elections, the Organization of American States (OAS) voted to investigate possible Cuban efforts to influence the vote.

Another source of concern was the deepening ideological split between the Soviet Union and Communist China, which had been brewing since 1960 but had been exacerbated by the Soviet back-down in the Cuban missile crisis and, some 10 months later, the nuclear test ban treaty. By the last weeks of '63, the two Communist superpowers were still throwing ideological brickbats at each other, despite US encouragement for talks to soften the split. Indeed, the Peking government was accusing the Soviets of collaborating with the US in pursuit of "world domination." The US responded by saying that the door was still open to possible US/China talks but only if the Red Chinese would cease their "venomous attacks" on America. If anyone had suggested that, a half century later, the US and China would be doing frequent commercial business with each other and that China would be a voice of reason in responding to bellicose threats from the leadership of North Korea, that person would have been accused of having, at the very least, flights of fancy.

By early February, Peking was making noises about formally splitting with the Soviets and forming its own branch of the Communist movement, rather than play second-fiddle to Moscow and its allies. Not helping matters was ongoing communication between the Cuban hierarchy and the Red Chinese government. Reports in early December had Castro's minister of industry, Ernesto "Che" Guevara (yes, *that* Che, the future counterculture t-shirt face of rebellion), meeting with Chinese Premier Chou En-lai. At the same time, Cuba was pressing for economic help, especially in the area of agriculture, from the Soviet bloc, even though the Russians were having their own economic problems and were in the process of buying wheat from the Americans.

Contributing to Cuba's economic difficulties was the fact that the Cuban sugar harvest for 1963 was the country's lowest in 20 years, so Fidel and Che were looking for whatever help they could get and from whichever party they could get it, such as the 450 buses Cuba was able to buy from Britain in early January (much to the displeasure of the US). Two weeks later, Castro suddenly turned up in Moscow, ostensibly for a wintertime vacation, but also to wangle a deal with the Soviets for a goodly amount of that Cuban sugar over the next several years.

It wouldn't become public knowledge until mid-February, but

91-year-old British philosopher/pacifist/left-wing intellectual Bertrand Russell sent a letter to the Soviet leadership on December 2, appealing to Khrushchev for better treatment of Soviet Jews. The letter was signed by a number of luminaries in science, literature, philosophy, and Socialist politics, including six Nobel laureates, and by Great Britain's Queen Elizabeth II.

Other than expert followers of the machinations of the Soviet hierarchy, not many people noticed on December 19 when Leonid Brezhnev was retained by the Supreme Soviet as president of the Soviet Union. The 57-year-old Brezhnev was looked on as a protégé of and possible successor to Premier Khrushchev. In February, *Time* magazine ran a lengthy article on Russia's agricultural and industrial difficulties and placed much of the blame on Khrushchev, who had been spouting overly positive propaganda about the Soviet economy virtually since he took power. Brezhnev was on the cover of that issue of *Time*, even though he was not the focus of the article, with the implication that the ruling Politburo might well have plans for him. Sure enough, less than eight months later, Khrushchev would be deposed by the Politburo and a troika of Brezhnev, Alexey Kosygin, and Communist Party elder Anastas Mikoyan installed to replace him. It wouldn't be long until Brezhnev would become the undisputed Soviet leader and would remain so until his death in 1982.

Holiday cheer must have been flowing on Christmas Day at *Pravda*, the primary Soviet news organ. That day, *Pravda* had news that Khrushchev had sent 70th birthday greetings to Red China's leader, Mao Tsetung, and a report from America painted a more favorable, more conciliatory picture of the US attitude toward relations with the Soviets. On December 30, Khrushchev and Brezhnev sent New Year's greetings to President Johnson, with hope for continued improved relations between America and the Soviets. A goodwill note to all nations proposed a reduction of force in territorial or border disputes and a European East-West non-aggression pact.

The Russians were also about to begin talks with the US toward a two-year extension of the cultural exchange agreement between the two superpowers. And among 69 nominees for the '63 Lenin Prize for literature was Aleksandr Solzhenitsyn, whose critical work on the Soviet forced-labor camps system, *One Day in the Life of Ivan Denisovich,* had been approved by Khrushchev and had become a best-seller in the West. Solzhenitsyn didn't win that prize, but following the deposing of Khrushchev, he would become a symbol of KGB-enforced repression and would be awarded in absentia the Nobel Prize for literature in 1970.

By late January, the normal ideological tensions had resurfaced and were only exacerbated when France moved to establish diplomatic relations with Red China, a first for any of the powers of the non-Communist world, while also attempting to continue official relations with Nationalist China. By February 10, though, France had virtually forced Nationalist China into cutting off diplomatic relations with the French by opening the Chinese mission in Paris to the Red Chinese. Next, President de Gaulle proposed a neutralization plan for all of the former French possessions in Southeast Asia, a plan that would be implemented by France in conjunction with Red China. According to the proposal, Cambodia, Laos, and North and South Vietnam would have no ideological ties and "no foreign interventions" would be allowed in any of those nations.

Without giving immediate official reaction, the feeling in Washington was that de Gaulle's remarks were "naive and misguided." And, at a February 1 news conference, President Johnson said that there was no chance that the de Gaulle plan could be implemented. Mao, though, felt so comfortable with the new relationship with France that he opened up to a French parliamentary delegation visiting Peking in February, telling the visitors that he considered Khrushchev a "traitor" because of the test ban treaty and wished him dead.

Meanwhile, Secretary of Defense Robert McNamara outlined for the Senate Armed Services Committee a theoretical "damage-limiting strategy" in which the US would have available forces powerful enough to destroy munitions and war-making capabilities of the Soviet Union, Red China, and their allies. As well, Midas satellites were being developed for the Air Force by Lockheed Aircraft. They would be capable of detecting the launching of Soviet missiles and clandestine nuclear tests in space. And astronauts in NASA's upcoming Gemini program were expected to experiment with electronic and optical instruments designed to detect missile launchings.

On February 10, a scenario right out of spy novels suddenly emerged during the resumed 17-nation disarmament conference in Geneva. A member of the Soviet delegation, 36-year-old KGB officer Yuri Nosenko, defected and was given diplomatic asylum by the US Almost immediately, speculation developed that Nosenko might have been operating as a double agent for some time and, in fact, he had off-and-on contact with the CIA for some months before claiming that he had been found out by the KGB and needed to defect. Nosenko also would claim to have had contact with Lee Harvey Oswald when Oswald defected to the Soviet Union in 1959 and that the KGB had briefly considered Oswald for intelligence work but found him to be "unstable." But lie detector tests would find Nosenko to be lying about Oswald and he would spend much of the next few years in solitary confinement at a CIA "safe house" undergoing daily interrogation. At the same time, Nosenko would be subjected to sensory deprivation and various means of psychological torture, including, according to Nosenko, being fed LSD by CIA operatives. It would take just over five years from his defection for Nosenko to be cleared of suspicions by the CIA, declared a genuine defector, and released from CIA custody.

Berlin, one of the chief Allied spoils of victory at the end of World War II, had been one of the primary fronts in the Cold War since the late '40s, but particularly since August 1961, when the Soviet-controlled government of East Germany decided to close its borders and build a wall to cut off the steady flow of young professionals to the West. With the construction of the Berlin Wall, residents of either part of the city could not cross to the other side, literally dividing many families and sealing off East Berliners from lucrative jobs on the Western side of the wall. While the US had backed away from a direct confrontation with the Soviets over the construction of the wall, President Kennedy's visit to the wall in June '63 and his "Ich bin ein Berliner" speech gave the West an ideological victory. It was shortly after Kennedy's assassination that talks between the two German governments began regarding the possibility of visits by West Berliners to East Berlin over the Christmas holidays, which had not been permitted the previous two years. By December 17, an agreement had been hammered out. East Berliners still could not visit the Western side of the wall but West Berliners would be issued passes to visit relatives in East Berlin. The next day, 25,000 West Berliners lined up for the first permits. By the time the visitation period began on the morning of December 20, 170,000 passes had been given out and, by the first few days of January, West Berlin Mayor Willy Brandt could claim that at least 1,300,000 had passed through to the east side of the wall before the visitation period ended on January 5. The holiday seasons of 1964, '65, and '66 would see similar visitation periods.

On the eve of the fifth anniversary of the overthrow of the Batista regime, Castro gave an interview to ABC's Lisa Howard and said he hoped for restoration of good relations with the United States and that President Kennedy had been leaning in that direction before he was killed. However, in a two-hours-plus anniversary speech the next day,

Castro repeatedly attacked LBJ and the US, including an accusation that US agents had sunk a Cuban torpedo boat on Christmas Eve, despite the fact that an anti-Castro Cuban exile group had claimed responsibility for the attack. At the same time, Secretary of State Dean Rusk said that Cuba could return to good standing in the Western Hemisphere only by abandoning its interference in the affairs of other Latin American countries.

Just over a month later, though, tensions suddenly flared anew. On February 3, the US Coast Guard seized four Cuban fishing boats that had strayed into US territorial waters some 65 miles from Key West, Florida. Radio contact with Havana had continued until the Coast Guard "escorted" the boats to Key West. Havana called it "kidnapping." Three days later, the Cuban government cut off the normal water supply for all but one hour a day to the US naval base at Guantanamo Bay in reprisal for the seizure of the four fishing boats. That precipitated a high-level meeting at the White House the next morning to determine the official US response. An unofficial and not very helpful response came from Barry Goldwater, who said that the Marines should be sent in to turn the water back on, and a few days later suggested a missile-crisis-style naval blockade to cut Cuba off from receiving military supplies.

Instead, the US government's response was to cut off money flowing to the Cuban government by discharging 2,500 Cubans who worked but did not live at Gitmo and to grant a $4 million contract to Westinghouse Electric for a self-sufficient salt water conversion system for the base. Then, the base's commanding officer, Adm. John D. Bulkeley, had the Cuban pipes leading into the base cut off, shutting off any water coming from Castro's system. As for the fishing boat personnel that started all this, a judge in Key West freed the 25 crewmen but found the captains of the four boats guilty of poaching, fined each $500, and gave them suspended six-month sentences. They were all then put back on their boats and told to go back home to Cuba and not return to US territory.

In South Vietnam, things had reportedly stabilized enough following the November coup that 1,000 of the estimated 16,500 US "advisors" there were set to be sent home by Christmas, but that stability was short-lived. Meanwhile, Cambodia's Prince Norodom Sihanouk was lobbying for a "neutral confederation" between his country and South Vietnam. On December 12, though, a diplomatic brushfire broke out between Cambodia and the US The American delegation to Cambodia had expressed unhappiness with what it felt were disrespectful comments Sihanouk had made in the wake of the assassination of President

Kennedy. Sihanouk responded by recalling the entire staff of the Cambodian embassy in Washington and putting relations with Britain "on hiatus." Some observers looked on this as being a consequence of Sihanouk cozying up to the Red Chinese. Indeed, by mid-February, Sihanouk's pronouncements were becoming nearly as bellicose as those of Mao's government. Sihanouk made continual demands for a multi-national conference on Cambodian neutrality, held the US responsible for the bombings of Cambodian villages by South Vietnamese planes, and demanded that the US finance truce points along the Cambodia/South Vietnam border, as per the International Control Commission.

Cambodia had cut off diplomatic relations with South Vietnam while the Diem regime was still in power the previous August, but since it was suspected that Cambodia was being used as a supply route for the Communist guerrillas infiltrating South Vietnam, the new South Vietnamese military junta sent a goodwill mission to Cambodia in mid-December. The purpose of the ultimately unsuccessful mission was to explore the restoration of diplomatic relations between those two governments. Meanwhile, a civil war was continuing in nearby Laos and that country's leadership contended only North Vietnam or the Soviet Union could bring the war to an end and that the pro-Communist Pothet Lao forces were controlled and supplied by North Vietnam.

By late December, an increase in the frequency and ferocity of attacks by the Viet Cong convinced US officials that the war in Vietnam would last longer than they had projected. The plan for total withdrawal of American troops by 1965 was no longer considered viable and the priority now was cutting off the possibility of Communist domination of Southeast Asia, preventing what later would be known as "the domino theory." With Defense Secretary McNamara making a pre-Christmas fact-finding visit to Saigon, the new South Vietnamese government was looking for assurances that the US would see South Vietnam on to victory over the Communist guerrillas. As part of that effort, the military junta arranged for several thousand South Vietnamese students to stage an anti-de Gaulle demonstration outside the French Embassy in Saigon to protest the French president's proposals for South Vietnamese neutrality.

That same week, after 15 months covering the war, David Halberstam reported in the *New York Times* that the war had reached a critical stage. The Viet Cong had taken the military initiative, but with the Vietnamese "dry season" coming between January and April South Vietnamese military operations against the guerrillas could be somewhat easier, according to Halberstam. He would win a 1964 Pulitzer Prize for his coverage of the war for the Times, a prelude to 1965's aptly-titled *The Making of a Quagmire*, the first of his classic books on the war.

In a scene that would become much more familiar once America's role in the war escalated, a peacenik affiliated with the Committee for Non-Violent Action burned his draft card and used the burning card to light a candle "for peace on earth" in front of a draft board in New York City on Christmas Eve. The day after Christmas he received his draft notice, which he said he would refuse to honor. In mid-January, Lt. Gen. William Westmoreland was appointed deputy commander of the US forces in South Vietnam at the suggestion of McNamara and amid speculation that he would replace Gen. Paul Harkins as overall commander by July, at which point Harkins would reach the retirement age of 60. Harkins had been criticized in the fall of '63 for making overly optimistic comments about the progress of the war, but in one of his last press conferences President Kennedy had expressed confidence in Harkins. The ruling military junta associated Harkins with the Diem regime and wanted him out but defense department sources were denying reports of discord in January. Westmoreland would assume command in June and, as the war dragged on, would become notorious for making assessments that were even more unreasonably optimistic.

On January 29, though, the military junta was suddenly ousted. Unlike the violent end to the Diem regime, a quick, bloodless coup brought to power Gen. Nguyen Khanh, 36-year-old leader of the South Vietnamese army's 1-Corps. The coup's leaders claimed that at least two members of the junta had been conspiring with French agents to force South Vietnam into Laos-type "neutralism," and they were placed under house arrest. But Gen. Duong Van "Big" Minh, the leader of the junta, quickly accepted a role as an advisor (nominal chief of state) to Gen. Khanh. The timing of the coup, hot on the heels of France's official recognition of Red China, was seen as no coincidence. The official US reaction was to deny any involvement in this coup but to praise the fighting spirit of Gen. Khanh, who installed himself as premier in yet another new South Vietnamese government, this one an unwieldy and fractious 53-man junta.

The Viet Cong guerrillas responded by stepping up the ferocity of their attacks on American personnel. On February 9, two Americans were killed and 23 wounded when two bombs exploded in the bleachers during a game at Pershing Field, a military softball field just outside of Saigon. Less than a week later, a bomb exploded in the lobby of a Saigon movie theater, killing three Americans and injuring at least 50. And, in a battle waged in a peasant village 45 miles northwest of Saigon, a 500-man Viet Cong attack left a government-stated toll of 94 dead and 32 wounded. By the beginning of March, McNamara was back in Saigon for yet another fact-finding visit, his third in six months.

*****

There are some conflicts that have seemingly been going on for centuries, perhaps will never be truly resolved, and flare up anew with little provocation. For instance, the ages-old feud between Turks and Greeks over the island of Cyprus suddenly erupted again in late December, interrupting the holiday vacations of diplomats representing the two antagonists and Great Britain, which had retained a pair of bases since Cyprus attained independence in August 1960. As would be the case with other international brushfires that winter, this one began with teenage terrorists and rooftop snipers but also involved the very sensitive issue of the tiny country's constitution, which tried to serve both the Greek Cypriot majority and some 100,000 Turkish Cypriots. In and around the capital city of Nicosia, violence flared anew just before Christmas. Turkish and Greek troops and police faced off against each other on the streets of Nicosia. Turkey's government sent units of the Turkish fleet to patrol the Cypriot coast and jet fighters to make low "warning" passes over Nicosia. NATO's council met in special session in Paris and Britain sent several hundred combat troops to Cyprus to help restore order.

In the middle of the Christmas/New Year's holiday week, the UN Security Council met in a special night session in New York to discuss a solution. In the first week of January, Archbishop Makarios, the Cypriot president who was in favor of Security Council involvement, announced that the British, Turkish, and Greek governments had signed on with the Cypriot government for a conference in London later that month. A 10,000-man UN expeditionary force was proposed to police Cyprus over the next three months, an idea that got a cool reception from the US and Britain because of the possible involvement of personnel from Communist countries. Predictably, two homemade bombs exploded outside the US embassy in Nicosia early in February, causing about 600 American dependents to be flown out of Cyprus to the then-relative safety (in that era) of Lebanon. Even with ongoing Security Council talks helmed by UN Secretary-General U Thant pointing toward a British-led multi-national peacekeeping force, the proliferation of weapons on both sides simply made the atmosphere on the island so tense that one high-ranking Cypriot official said, "I don't think there can ever be any hope of coexistence between Greek and Turk here." Or, as a British major put it, "Bloody mess, this is."

As the crisis in Cyprus was just beginning to heat up, the Greek Line cruise ship *Lakonia*, four days into a holiday cruise to Madeira and the Canary Islands, suddenly erupted in an uncontrollable fire on December 22. More than a thousand passengers, crew, and crew relatives were aboard. The ship was on its maiden voyage for Greece after 33 years as a Dutch liner and service during World War II as a British troop ship. With a majority of the passengers elderly Britons and a crew apparently unprepared for a calamity at sea, the raging fire began in the hair salon and caused the ship to be abandoned less than an hour after the first distress signal went out. Five ships and rescue planes from America and Britain headed toward the ship. With the *Lakonia* some 180 miles northwest of Madeira, though, it would take time to reach the scene and a *Titanic*-like scene played out onboard.

A number of lifeboats were unusable or were lowered improperly and many passengers were forced to dive into the water. Despite a water temperature of 64 degrees, a number of passengers, mostly elderly or children, perished from exposure. By the time the rescue fleet reached the area before dawn, they encountered a scene of broken lifeboats and dead bodies bobbing in the sea. After the survivors had been lifted to the rescue ships, many told horror stories of crew incompetence, lack of communication, and opportunism. The death toll in the *Lakonia* disaster was 128: 95 passengers and 33 crew members, with 53 people killed as a direct result of the onboard fire. On December 29, while the burned-out hulk of the ship was being towed to Gibraltar, the *Lakonia*, which had been increasingly listing, suddenly rolled over and sank. The following week, *Life* magazine ran a spread of color photos of the smoking hulk with a blaring cover headline, "FIRE AT SEA."

A two-year Greek Merchant Marine Ministry investigation would find that the *Lakonia* never should have passed safety inspections before sailing from Southampton on December 15 and that the fire started as a result of faulty wiring that caused a short circuit. The ship's captain, first officer, and security officer were charged with gross negligence.

*****

Another Western Hemisphere diplomatic brushfire suddenly broke out on January 9 when Panama abruptly cut off its often-tense relations with the United States over a disturbance involving Panamanian and American teenagers and the flags of the two nations that escalated to the point where US Canal Zone forces were accused of killing six people. Within a day, Panamanian President Roberto Chiari demanded "complete revision" of the treaties under which the US operated the Panama Canal. By January 11, the anti-American rioting, spurred on by Castro followers and other agitators, had claimed 20 lives, including three American soldiers, and the US Embassy in Panama City had been evacuated. US troops stationed on the border of the Canal Zone were removed because of sniper fire. Complicating matters was the fact that there had been no US ambassador to Panama since October, much to the displeasure of the Senate Foreign Relations Committee, so LBJ, his newly appointed assistant secretary of state for Latin American affairs, Thomas Mann, and the new deputy secretary of defense, Cyrus Vance, had to try to defuse the crisis. As well, the Organization of American States and the UN Security Council took up the dispute while violent demonstrations continued in the streets of Panama City.

Attempting to cool the tensions, the US promised to make sure that the flags of the two nations would fly side by side in the Canal Zone. But students in Nicaragua burned American flags to show solidarity with their brethren in Panama, newspapers in London and Paris denounced America's "colonial-like" control of the Canal Zone, Red China's official press hailed Panama's "patriotic struggle against imperialist aggression," and Moscow radio and newspapers assailed the "crime in Panama" and accused US soldiers of "staging a massacre of Panamanians." By January 14, the US and Panama had agreed to restore diplomatic relations and within about a month to begin negotiations regarding all issues of dispute between the two nations.

But, apropos of the long-term-tense relations between the two countries, grandstanding on both sides threatened to capsize those negotiations. President Chiari recalled the staff of Panama's embassy in Washington, remaining US Embassy personnel were ordered out of Panama, and the OAS mediators returned to Washington and waited for cooler heads to prevail on both sides. It would take over thirteen more years for the US and Panama to hammer out a new treaty that would see the end of the Canal Zone as an entity as of October 1, 1979, and the end of American control of the region as of December 31, 1999.

*****

India and Israel had become independent entities within a nine-month period between August 1947 and May of '48 and each had endured, to say the least, tumultuous times in the 16 years between then and the winter of 1963-64. Both had been led by long-serving original prime ministers. David Ben-Gurion had declared the independence of the state of Israel in May 1948 and except for a self-imposed sabbatical in 1954-55 served as prime minister from then until June '63. Jawaharlal Nehru had served as India's first and only prime minister since India declared its independence from Britain in August of '47 but the 74-year-old Nehru's health had begun to decline following the 1962 Sino-Indian War. In the midst of a violent revival of tensions between Hindus and Moslems in January that went back at least to India's first days as a nation, Nehru suffered a serious stroke. The Indian government tried to downplay the debilitating effects of the stroke and stage-managed public appearances by Pandit Nehru but those appearances would quickly lessen in frequency. A reported heart attack would follow the stroke and, in the early morning hours of May 27, the man who many still consider India's greatest leader would pass from his earthly life.

As for the state of Israel in the early months that followed Ben-Gurion's tenure as prime minister, the eternal 800-pound gorilla in the desert was the relationship between the Jewish state and the Arab countries surrounding it, a saga that goes back to the days of the Bible. As 1964 began, Israel outraged the Arab nations again by announcing that it intended to divert the waters of the River Jordan to irrigate the Negev desert. Egypt's Gamal Abdel Nasser called for a united effort by the Arab countries, and to that end arranged for a summit of Arab leaders, several of whom were enemies of each other. For instance, King Saud of Saudi Arabia, who had once tried to have Nasser killed, embraced and kissed the United Arab Republic leader when they met at the summit's outset at Cairo's Nile Hilton Hotel. The Saudis and King Hussein's Jordan reopened diplomatic relations with Egypt. And vague reports leaked out of a secret plan by the Arab nations for the destruction of Israel. That turned out to be just so much posturing and it would be better than three years until the Six-Day War, which would end up solidifying Israel's role as the dominant force in the Middle East.

A friendly summit meeting of black America's two, philosophically-opposed leaders, Rev. Dr. Martin Luther King and Malcolm X, with Rev. Ralph Abernathy to Dr. King's left.

CHAPTER 4

TRANSITIONS

In the aftermath of the JFK assassination, the leaders of the civil rights movement served notice that there would be no moratorium on the movement's activities. Indeed, a leadership conference organized by the Student Non-Violent Coordinating Committee (SNCC) opened as scheduled on November 29 with a keynote speech by author James Baldwin and an opening address by SNCC national Chairman John Lewis. The 23-year-old Lewis was already a hardened veteran of the civil rights struggle, with the visible scars to prove it, having been directly involved with the student sit-ins and Freedom Rides of the early '60s,

Lewis had become very impatient with the deliberate pace at which the Kennedy administration had addressed the civil rights situation. He was the youngest speaker at the March on Washington and his original speech included a passage that questioned the administration's commitment to civil rights. The March elders had Lewis strike that portion of his speech but, clearly, he was something of an irritant, however well-intentioned, to the more moderate leaders of the movement. So it wasn't surprising that Lewis saw no need to halt SNCC activities following the assassination. But, on December 7, Bertrand Russell warned that outbreaks of violence tied to the civil rights movement could set the movement back for "many decades."

Meanwhile, despite the new president's exhortation for swift passage of the civil rights bill, it was still sitting in the House Rules Committee at the end of November and House Majority Leader Carl Albert indicated that he saw no hope of getting the bill to the House floor for debate before the Christmas recess. Nonetheless, the administration was very happy with late-year figures showing gains in equal employment opportunities and black families integrating white neighborhoods. Conversely, many Northern cities, notably Boston, had been found to be heavily-segregated, with blacks relegated to two or three neighborhoods.

One hundred blacks were arrested on December 16 for demonstrating in downtown Columbia, South Carolina, even as the Justice Department was filing voter discrimination suits against two counties in Mississippi and two in Alabama. A day earlier, Dr. Martin Luther King, Jr. led 2,500 blacks in an Atlanta demonstration to protest that city's lack of desegregation in schools, housing, public accommodations, and hospitals. On Christmas Eve, two male SNCC members and the wife of comedian-activist Dick Gregory were arrested for trying to sit at a segregated Atlanta lunch counter and spent Christmas Day in an Atlanta jail cell. With Dr. King having moved back to Atlanta and SNCC already based there, Atlanta would be the center of civil rights demonstrations that winter. Indeed, on January 7 Lewis led a march of 150 high school students in Atlanta, urging the students to "play hooky for freedom" and "learn civics in the streets." Hoping to short-circuit further demonstrations, Mayor Ivan Allen, Jr. announced on January 11 that 14 major Atlanta hotels were dropping racial restrictions, but the Negro Leadership Conference voted to continue demonstrations and mass gatherings in the city.

An uneasy peace was broken on January 25, when a violent confrontation broke out near an Atlanta hotel at which a UN human rights committee was staying. On one side of the conflict were black demonstrators, largely from SNCC and the SCLC, but also including Gregory. They were confronted by members of a local Ku Klux Klan chapter, but one of the prime instigators was a leader of the Atlanta Citizens' Council, a restaurant owner and staunch segregationist named Lester Maddox, who had run for mayor against Allen in 1961 and for lieutenant governor in '62 and would be elected governor of Georgia in 1967.

A committee on voter registration and participation released its report on December 20 and recommended that states eliminate literacy tests. It also suggested that states consider lowering the voting age to 18. No recommendations were made in the report for federal action, though, so the drive to lower the national voting age wouldn't gain momentum until the turbulent late '60s. But voter registration efforts in the South between April 1, 1962, and December 23, 1963, had garnered some 327,600 black voters. The largest numbers came from Texas and the smallest, not surprisingly, came from Mississippi, site of the most virulent resistance against voter registration of blacks.

As 1963 came to an end, *Time* magazine voted Dr. King its "Man of the Year," partly for his role as the leader of the social revolution that had the most impact on the nation that year but also as the symbol of the positive strides black Americans were making. Despite the fact that blacks, or "Negroes" as they were still popularly known, comprised anywhere from 1 to 3 per cent of the nation's college professors, physicians, lawyers, salaried managers, and journalists, there were 35 known black millionaires in the US and 16% of non-whites held white-collar jobs, according to Time. The lead article ended with a comment from Carl T. Rowan, then the US ambassador to Finland and about to be appointed Edward R. Murrow's successor as director of the United States Information Agency. Rowan was also a veteran journalist and his comments would resonate almost exactly 45 years later, when what seemed inconceivable in the last days of 1963 became reality, the election of the first black President of the United States. Rowan's comments: "Every Negro American in a position of responsibility who discharges his duty faithfully and well, whose conduct is laudable, is making a real contribution to the struggle by bringing along a segment of the white population. However, he is also obliged to speak out where speaking is called for."

On the subject of speaking out, while the NAACP had been promised greater integration of Pasadena's New Year's Day Tournament of Roses parade to avert picketing of that parade, the Congress of Racial Equality (CORE) and the Committee for Freedom Now were threatening to disrupt Philadelphia's Mummers parade that same day with "human blockades" if any of the Mummers appeared in blackface, a long-standing tradition. Snow and freezing rain forced the parade to be postponed until January 4 and in the interim a Philadelphia court injunction banned blackface from the parade but also prohibited picketing of the parade, which went on with no blackface and no incidents but a much-smaller-than-normal turnout. That same week, CORE decided to test Washington D.C.'s new fair-housing regulations, which barred discrimination in the sale or rent of public housing, by sending both whites and blacks into predominantly white neighborhoods.

With Congress returning to work in earnest the first week in January, the civil rights bill would become top priority for both the White

House and the leaders of the movement. For instance, on January 6, the NAACP's Roy Wilkins warned Washington Democrats not to expect automatic black support if they allowed undue delays in moving the bill through the legislative process and added there would be stepped-up voter registration efforts in the coming months, particularly in the North. Nearly two weeks later, Wilkins, CORE's James Farmer, the Urban League's Whitney Young, and Dr. King dropped in on LBJ at the White House for an update on the bill's progress. At the same time, a survey showed that blacks were registered in every parish and/or county in Louisiana for the first time since Reconstruction and a Louisiana statute requiring a political candidate's race to be listed on the ballot was unanimously struck down by the Supreme Court.

On January 27, a federal court in Americus, Ga., ordered Terrell County officials to halt intimidation, threats, and coercion against a black voter-registration campaign. That same day, in a development seemingly unrelated to the American civil rights movement, the International Olympic Committee withdrew its invitation to South Africa for that nation to participate in the 1964 Summer Olympics in Tokyo due to South Africa's ongoing policy of racial apartheid. On January 18, 16-year-old Larry Joe Sims was convicted by an all-white jury in the murder of a 13-year-old black in Birmingham, just a few hours after the September 15 church bombing. The jury deliberated for four hours and Sims would spend seven months in jail. Justice in the case of the church bombing itself would take a lot longer to be served.

A constitutional amendment that would eliminate poll taxes, long used to discourage black voter registration, had been moving through the state-by-state ratification process since Congress passed the 24th amendment late in August of 1962. Only five Southern states still used poll taxes and the amendment would only apply to federal elections but on January 23, South Dakota became the 38th state to ratify, just beating out the Georgia legislature, and the 24th Amendment officially became law. The Supreme Court would rule all poll taxes, including those in state elections, unconstitutional in 1966.

January ended with the civil rights bill being voted, by an 11-4 margin, out of the House Rules Committee and onto the House floor. As this was happening, the Norwegian Nobel Committee received a letter from eight members of the Swedish Parliament, nominating Dr. King for the Nobel Peace Prize. And LBJ was asked at a meeting of the executive board of the National Newspaper Publishers Association about the possibility of a black being seated on the Supreme Court. Johnson replied that he hoped the time would come soon. "Soon" would come a lot sooner than many people expected; just three and a half years later Johnson would nominate Thurgood Marshall to be the first black Supreme Court justice. But, as the president was making those comments, an all-male, all-white jury was being seated in Jackson, Mississippi, for the trial of Byron de la Beckwith in the murder of Medgar Evers. It was the first trial with racial overtones in that hotbed of hatred since the infamous trial in the murder of Emmett Till in 1955, which also had an all-male, all-white jury. Like that trial, this one was expected to end with an acquittal or a hung jury and, indeed, the judge did declare a mistrial, with the jury deadlocked at 7-5 for acquittal. A second trial later that year also would end in a mistrial and de la Beckwith would remain a free man for the next 30 years. He finally would be convicted of first-degree murder in February of 1994 but would serve less than seven years before dying in January, 2001. Mississippi's reputation as the South's leading outpost for racial hatred and violence was rapidly growing and, in a foreshadowing of events later that year, Attorney General Robert Kennedy received a telegram from CORE at the beginning of February, requesting that federal troops be sent to protect voter-registration workers in Mississippi. The request came in the wake of the murder of Lewis Allen, a civil rights activist in the state. RFK's Justice Department said that it had requested that the FBI begin a preliminary investigation.

Even as debate on the civil rights bill began on the House floor, Southern forces were trying to defang it. Attempts at weakening the voting rights and public accommodations sections of the bill were defeated during the first week in February, even as 45% of the New York City school system's enrolled student population stayed home in an organized one-day boycott to spur integration in the city's schools. This was just one of a number of school boycotts in Northern cities being organized that month. Old-line members of the Chicago branches of the NAACP and the Urban League opposed the proposed February 25 boycott in that city, but Dr. King gave the boycott "my moral support and deepest sympathy." In Massachusetts, state attorney general Edward Brooke ruled that the scheduled February 26 Boston boycott was illegal but the boycott leaders said that they would go ahead with their plans. Nearly three years later, Brooke would become the first black in the 20th century to be elected to the US Senate by popular vote. Both the Chicago and Boston boycotts were termed complete successes and the leader of the New York boycott, the Rev. Milton Galamison, announced plans for a mid-March boycott and a demonstration on the opening day of the New York World's Fair in April. The day after the NYC boycott, nationally known civil rights lawyer Constance Baker Motley became the first black woman elected to the New York State senate. That weekend a series of demonstrations in support of a public accommodations ordinance for Chapel Hill, North Carolina similar to the hotly debated section in the civil rights bill, resulted in more than 90 arrests on and around the campus of the University of North Carolina.

A little-known congressman from New York City's "silk stocking" district came to prominence during the House debate. John V. Lindsay was officially a Republican but was really a young, good-looking, Kennedy-esque liberal, and his work on the House floor in support of the civil rights bill led to speculation about a possible Lindsay run for mayor of New York in 1965 or even governor in '66, in the event that Governor Nelson Rockefeller was elected president. That fall, Lindsay would buck a national Democratic landslide by being re-elected to his House seat and a year later he would indeed be elected New York mayor. Then, after leading the city through perhaps the most tumultuous period in its history, he would finally move to the Democratic party and make an unsuccessful primary run for the party's 1972 presidential nomination.

Thanks in part to Lindsay's efforts, the civil rights bill was passed by the House of Representatives on February 10 by a 290-130 vote after just nine days of debate. The bill was then slated to be hand-delivered to the Senate and "met at the door" of the Senate a week later and placed before the Senate clerk, who gave the bill a first reading by titles. After a second reading was waived, Senate Majority Leader Mike Mansfield gave the bill the second reading himself on February 26 and proposed that the bill be sent immediately to the Senate floor for debate. Under Senate Rule 14, that would place the bill on the Senate calendar, rather than have the bill sent to the Judiciary Committee, chaired by Senator James Eastland of, yes, Mississippi. Eastland was prepared to prevent the bill from ever being passed by burying it in committee. Senate Rule 25, passed in 1946, required that the bill be sent to committee, which none of the bill's proponents wanted. So a motion was made to call the bill off the calendar and onto the floor for debate. Given all of the parliamentary maneuvering, formal Senate debate on the civil rights bill wouldn't begin until March, with the Southern filibuster quickly commencing and lasting 57 days. It would take the support of Senate Minority Leader Everett Dirksen to cut off the filibuster through a rarely used vote of cloture on June 10, which would lead to the passage of the strongest civil rights bill since Reconstruction nine days later and the formal signing by President Johnson on July 2.

*****

Another signpost toward change of a more general variety, but which has faded into the mists of history was the Supreme Court decision on February 17 in the case of Wesberry v. Sanders. The case was brought by residents of Georgia's 5th Congressional District, which included the city of Atlanta and had an official population of almost 825,000, the second most populous such district in the country. Despite the fact that that figure was more than double the average population of Georgia's 10 congressional districts, the much larger district's votes in congressional elections didn't represent as much as those in the more sparsely populated districts. The high court, with Justice Hugo Black writing the majority opinion, found that the disparity in representation was a violation of Article 1, Section 2 of the Constitution, that each citizen's vote should be equal to another's: one person, one vote. Thus, congressional districts all over the country had to be reapportioned according to population. So the Atlanta area was split into two separate districts, the average population of Georgia's districts rose from nearly 330,000 to more than 455,000, and the concept of overrepresentation of rural areas in the House of Representatives would come to a gradual end through the decade.

*****

In the 1960s, major airplane crashes happened much more frequently than in later decades. For that reason, it was not a huge story when a Trans-Canadian jetliner crashed in Montreal just a week after the president's assassination, killing 118 in the worst air disaster in Canadian history to that point in time. Just over a week later, on December 8, a Pan American World Airways 707 caught fire in the air during a thunderstorm and exploded while en route from San Juan to Philadelphia, killing all 81 aboard. Predictably, the House Health and Safety Subcommittee held hearings on airline safety in January and officials of the major airlines and the Federal Aviation Administration agreed that air traffic controllers should not have say over possible cancellations of flights because of bad weather on the flight route.

In the latter part of '63, there was much talk about a possible American supersonic transport aircraft to compete with the proposed British Airways/Air France Concorde. On December 20, Federal Aviation Administration Deputy Chairman Gordon Bair said that a US supersonic

59

plane could be used for high-speed travel to large American cities, flights of "perhaps 1,200 miles," rather than just transcontinental flights. By mid-January, Boeing, Lockheed, and North American Aviation had all submitted proposed SST designs to the FAA. Each of the three proposed American SSTs was to be bigger than the Concorde and attain a speed of Mach 3 (three times the speed of sound). Proposals for the plane's engines were submitted by General Electric, United Aircraft, and Curtiss-Wright. All of these proposals were to be evaluated by a team of 210 aeronautical experts from the government, as well as the nation's airlines, with contracts to be awarded in May and a target date of 1972 for commercial service for the American SST. Environmental concerns over sonic booms and the effect of engine exhaust on the ozone layer, though, would cause Congress to drag its heels regarding support for the project and, ultimately, drop funding in 1971, some two years after the first flights of the French and British Concorde prototypes.

*****

A distraction of sorts from the grim post-assassination atmosphere in Washington was the Capitol Hill soap opera surrounding Bobby Baker. A Senate page as a teenager, Baker had quickly moved up to chief page, and had cultivated friendships with a number of Democratic bigwigs of the era, most notably the Eisenhower-era Democratic leader in the Senate, fellow Southerner Lyndon Baines Johnson. Baker rose in the ranks to secretary to the majority party after Johnson became Senate majority leader, established himself as a Capitol Hill insider and power broker, and became a very wealthy man despite his modest official salary of around $20,000. When LBJ became vice president, it enhanced Baker's Washington power base, since he was already known as "Lyndon's boy." In just one example of Baker's various investments and more, he and another associate founded a company in 1962 that provided vending machines for companies that dealt with federally granted programs; as of July of that year, Baker claimed a net worth of $826,000 and assets worth about $1.5 million. It was after a disgruntled one-time government contractor sued Baker and his partners in civil court in September '63 that Baker's power base began to topple. With Republicans having forced an investigation into Baker's business dealings by the Senate Rules Committee, he resigned his Senate position in October.

By the time the committee began devoting real time to the case in early December, Baker's Capitol Hill mentor had become president and the Johnson White House pledged full cooperation, even while putting out conflicting signals regarding how well LBJ really knew Baker. When word leaked out that the committee was also likely to look into the role of "party girls" in Baker's business dealings, *that* got the attention of the TV networks. After all, the British Fleet Street press had gotten months of mileage out of the John Profumo/Christine Keeler call girls/espionage scandal. The prospect of even a hint of Capitol Hill hanky-panky was enough for NBC to schedule coverage of the first day of public hearings, especially when the first scheduled witness was the bee-hived blonde widow of one of Baker's business associates. When Trudy Novak's testimony at the hearing turned out to be a lot less spicy than expected and a lot more mundane stocks and mortgages-oriented, the network bailed on its coverage and went back to the more dependable quiz shows and dramatized soap operas. Then again, no one on the committee or in Congress seemed wild about the prospect of the hearings becoming a media event, lest certain revelations cause embarrassment for many on Capitol Hill.

For instance, Novak was a Senate clerk who had been collecting cash payments from Baker for the operation of a million-dollar Ocean City, Maryland, motel owned by Baker and Novak's family that was subsequently sold to the aforementioned vending machine company, Serve-U-Corp, in which Baker was a major stockholder. There was Baker's personal Senate secretary (and, in some accounts, mistress), Nancy Carole Tyler, a one-time Tennessee beauty queen who *Time* magazine described as a "sultry, shapely brunette" and who Baker identified as his cousin when he set her up as the occupant of a Washington townhouse he had bought. And then there was Ellen Rometsch.

Rometsch's name came up in the hearings regarding her deportation that August and her connection with Baker. She had been a sometime "hostess" (some have alleged that she was a flat-out prostitute/call girl) at Baker's Quorum Club, a "watering spot" for Washington insiders in the Carroll Arms Hotel, and had quickly developed quite a reputation for her sexual abilities. Baker, in his 1978 book *Wheeling and Dealing: Confessions of a Capitol Hill Operator*, revealed that he introduced Rometsch to Jack Kennedy and that after their first time together Kennedy called Baker to tell him that, to paraphrase, it had been one of the best sexual experiences of his life. Rometsch gave JFK very high marks, too, and they saw each other several more times.

Rometsch was married at the time to a member of the West German military but whispers of KGB connections involving the East German-bred Rometsch began circulating and reached the FBI in the summer of '63. Now, the affair between Kennedy and Rometsch was going on at roughly the same time as the president was also getting his jollies with Chicago Mafia goumada Judith Campbell Exner, among others. FBI Director J. Edgar Hoover was keeping close watch on all of this. He took his dossier on the president's philandering to Attorney General RFK that July, and according to some accounts, threatened to take it public unless Rometsch was deported. Indeed, some of the more exotic conspiracy theories surrounding the JFK assassination have sprung from Kennedy's affair with Rometsch, including stories linking Rometsch with the Profumo/Keeler scandal. Others contended that Hoover blackmailed RFK into authorizing FBI wiretaps of Dr. King. There have also been accounts of Hoover and RFK making separate visits to Capitol Hill and indicating to Senate Majority Leader Mansfield and Minority Leader Dirksen that the FBI had plenty of dirt on plenty of members of Congress so no one should even consider going public with any kind of White House expose. Rometsch was soon deported and alleged to have been paid large sums of hush money to stay silent about her dalliance with JFK. How much of this the Senate Rules Committee knew is debatable, if only because of the committee's questioning of Baker about whether he had anything to do with her deportation.

The hearings continued once Congress returned from the holiday recess. A closed-door hearing in January produced testimony from a longtime Baker business associate, insurance man Don B. Reynolds. Over a span of 10 years, Reynolds had paid Baker $15,000 for referring him to the right contacts in Washington, including Majority Leader LBJ, in need of life insurance after his 1955 heart attack. Reynolds was able to procure $100,000 in life insurance for Johnson and, at the suggestion of Johnson aide Walter Jenkins, also bought more than $1,000 in advertising on Lady Bird's radio/TV station in Austin.

Reynolds also testified that in 1959 Baker suggested that Reynolds give the Johnson's one of the new stereo phonographs, which he purchased and had installed at their home for $588. Subsequently, LBJ purchased another $100,000 in life insurance through Reynolds. As well, Reynolds testified that Baker had arranged for him to meet a Philadelphia contractor, Matthew McCloskey, who put in the winning bid for the construction of the stadium in Washington originally called D.C. Stadium. McCloskey met Reynolds in Baker's Senate office and then wrote a performance bond on McCloskey. Reynolds received a $10,000 commission from which he paid Baker $4,000.

Jenkins, who would be arrested on a morals charge late in the '64 election campaign, denied that there had been any arrangement for Reynolds to buy TV time on Lady Bird's station. As well, press secretary Pierre Salinger and LBJ himself implied that the stereo had come from Baker as a family present. Despite Republican attempts to frame the Reynolds/Baker/LBJ relationship in an improper light, nothing unlawful had taken place. And the hearings droned on until Baker himself took the witness table in late February and on the advice of famed attorney Edward Bennett Williams denounced the hearings as unconstitutional and invoked the First, Fourth, Fifth, and Sixth Amendments. Nancy Carole Tyler took a similar tack the day after Baker's turn at the witness table, albeit after scolding the committee for fostering insinuations about her character.

Ultimately, the committee would take no action against Baker, a "hometown" decision in the opinion of many, and Barry Goldwater would try to make the Baker case a campaign issue that fall to no avail. But the Justice Department would indict Baker on fraud and tax evasion charges in 1966. Baker would be convicted in '67 and, after several appeals, serve 17 months in jail in the early '70s. There is one link between the Baker hearings and the 21st century. One of the members of the Senate Rules Committee at that time was the by-then senior senator from West Virginia, Robert Byrd, who would soon participate in the Southern filibuster against the civil rights bill. Byrd eventually would become the first senator to serve for 50 uninterrupted years, a mark he reached just a few months before his death in 2010 at the ripe old age of 91.

*****

Despite the Republican moratorium on active campaigning during the official mourning period for President Kennedy, behind-the-scenes maneuvering was very much ongoing. It was hardly a secret that the titular head of the GOP, former President Dwight D. Eisenhower, felt that Goldwater was too conservative to be the party's standard-bearer and was looking for more moderate alternatives. His former vice president and the 1960 Republican nominee, Richard Nixon, passed the New York bar exam in early December and was making plans to practice law as a partner in a prestigious Manhattan firm while privately keeping his options for '64 open. Nixon's running mate on the '60 GOP ticket, Henry Cabot Lodge, was now the US ambassador to South Vietnam and Ike was reportedly urging Lodge to leave the ambassadorship, return home, and be either an active candidate or make himself available for a possible draft for the nomination.

Some saw this as a backhanded slap by Eisenhower at both Nixon and New York Governor Nelson Rockefeller, though Rocky, in particular, was perceived as being more liberal than moderate. That might come as a surprise to those who remember the very reactionary Rockefeller of the early '70s, the New York State official held most responsible for the bloody reaction to the 1971 Attica State prison revolt and a series of tough state drug laws still in effect but judged by many to be archaic in the first decade of the 21st century. But Jackie Robinson, the man who broke the color barrier in major league baseball in 1947 and an outspoken proponent of the drive for civil rights, had been a Rockefeller supporter going back to Rocky's first run for New York governor in 1958 and, at the end of January, Robinson resigned from his position as a director of the Chock Full O' Nuts company to join the Rockefeller presidential campaign.

When asked about Lodge as a potential GOP candidate, National Urban League President Whitney Young replied that Lodge would have a "more advanced point of view" than Goldwater. Lodge's comment on all this was that he would consider Ike's suggestion but intended to stay in South Vietnam until late spring or early summer, pretty much ruling out any active campaigning in the primaries. In the likely event of a non-run by Lodge, two more moderate alternatives who didn't have the political baggage of either Nixon or Rockefeller were Pennsylvania Governor William Scranton and George Romney, the first-year governor of Michigan who had achieved fame in the business world as the president of American Motors. Senator Margaret Chase Smith of Maine was also preparing to enter the Republican race, the first woman to enter major party primaries but also 66 years old. On Christmas Eve, former President Harry Truman, asked by a reporter about whether a woman should be nominated for president or vice president, said, "Why not? They're in control of everything else, so I don't see why not politics, too." And an opposition figure from the Truman era also threw his hat into the ring. Harold Stassen announced that he would make his fourth run (out of an eventual 10 tries) for the GOP presidential nomination.

Nixon, who would spend the winter saying "no, no, no" while keeping a travel schedule that said "maybe, maybe, maybe," had moved with wife Pat and daughters Julie and Tricia into a $100,000 co-op apartment on Fifth Avenue and was telling everyone that he loved being a New Yorker. The Nixon's had come east with their two dogs, the famous 12-year-old Checkers and year-and-a-half-old Vicky, and Nixon's secretary for the previous 10 years, Rose Mary Woods. (A decade later, Woods would take one for her boss when she assumed responsibility for at least part of the 18 1/2-minute gap in one of the Watergate-related White House tapes and would demonstrate how she did it in a photo op with a pose that, as one pundit put it, "looked as if she was sliding into third base.") Continuing his dance of the seven veils in late January, Nixon gallantly told Walter Cronkite that he would accept a draft for either the presidential or vice-presidential nomination in the event of a deadlock at the convention but added that he doubted that scenario would play out.

In the midst of all of this jockeying by the party moderates, Goldwater officially announced his candidacy on January 3 to give Americans a "clear choice." Rockefeller immediately challenged Goldwater to a face-to-face debate, a challenge that Goldwater deflected by saying that he didn't believe in intra-party debates. The following Sunday, Goldwater appeared on *Meet The Press* and showed his hard-line attitude toward the Soviets by saying that he would threaten the Kremlin with the loss of diplomatic relations as a means of extracting concessions. He made his first public appearance as an announced candidate on January 6 at a GOP fund-raising dinner in Grand Rapids, Michigan at which he was introduced by Governor Romney, who was keeping a high political profile while insisting that he had no plans to become a candidate. A week later, an article written by Goldwater appeared in *Life* magazine in which he proposed a policy of "nuclear sharing" with America's NATO allies through which each nation would be equipped with nuclear weapons, not exactly a comforting thought.

Even before that incendiary piece appeared, Goldwater was assailed by liberals from both parties for comments he had made to the elite Economic Club of New York. He had said that the poor and unemployed caused their poverty through their attitude ("low intelligence or low ambition") and that those on welfare needed to have work on community projects imposed on them. He referred to the Johnson White House as "the Santa Claus of the free lunch, the government handout, the something-for-nothing and something-for-everyone." Rockefeller's very-Democratic-esque response to Goldwater's charges about those trapped in the poverty vortex pointed out that "people who don't have an education and who don't have the preparation for jobs -- it is not because they're either stupid or indolent and don't want to know, it's because they haven't had the opportunity."

That same week, New York State Congressman William E. Miller, who doubled as the chairman of the Republican National Committee, announced that he would retire as party chairman after the GOP convention and from his congressional seat at the end of his term. Before that could happen, though, Miller would end up as Goldwater's vice-presidential running mate that fall. Years later, Miller's brief time in the limelight would earn him an American Express credit card commercial and, still later, his daughter Stephanie would become a liberal radio talk show host who would spend much air time in 2011-12 lampooning Governor Romney's son Mitt.

On the night of January 29, the Republican National Committee presented a rather unique 21-city "Go Day" network of fund-raising events, which drew 25,000 GOP supporters at $100 a head, despite a new Gallup poll that showed LBJ trouncing all of the Republican candidates and non-candidates. The centerpiece of "Go Day" was a closed-circuit TV discussion featuring Goldwater, Rockefeller, Nixon, Romney, Scranton, Miller, and Eisenhower. Nixon told the party faithful, "I say with confidence tonight that one of those whom you will hear on this program will be the next President of the United States." It would take almost exactly five years for Nixon's prediction to come fact, but LBJ's successor as president would be ... Richard Nixon.

A couple of weeks later, the increasingly chatty Nixon, who had fared better than any other Republican in that Gallup poll, offered his opinion that LBJ didn't have the "idealism and sense of purpose that the world expects from the President of the United States," characteristics that Nixon felt Eisenhower and Kennedy were able to project. Nixon was also of the opinion that mass demonstrations and boycotts would harm the civil rights movement and create an atmosphere of hate. This was, of course, coming from the same man who in the White House would refer to anti-war demonstrators as "bums." And he told newsmen that he was surprised that LBJ was taking the same attitude with his critics that he was with enemies abroad. That indicated to Nixon "a grave misunderstanding of the two-party system." This was coming from a man who in the White House would cultivate an "enemies list" of his political/sociological opponents.

*****

In December, President Johnson began holding a series of informal, mostly impromptu news conferences rather than formal televised press conferences that would invite immediate stylistic comparisons to JFK. At the first of these on December 7 he announced that he would be addressing the United Nations General Assembly on December 17 and was looking for the Defense Department to cut spending and payroll in the '64 budget. The U.N. visit would be his second trip to New York in a week and a half, his first excursions outside of Washington since November 22. Any trips away from the White House raised concerns, not only because the shooting in Dallas was so recent but because there was no vice president and there wouldn't be one until the next scheduled inauguration on January 20, 1965. Until then, first in the line of succession was the nearly-72-year-old House Speaker, John McCormack, followed by 86-year-old Carl Hayden, president pro tempore of the Senate. So there was immediate talk of changing the line of succession and the usual speculation about possible vice presidential running mates for LBJ in 1964. Among the names being bandied about were Peace Corps director and JFK brother-in-law Sargent Shriver, both of Minnesota's US Senators, Hubert Humphrey and Eugene McCarthy and UN Ambassador Adlai Stevenson. California politicos were beginning to lobby for that state's governor, Edmund "Pat" Brown while New York Democrats were pushing Mayor Robert F. Wagner, who was also being talked about as a possible Democratic US Senate candidate against incumbent Republican Kenneth Keating. Others suggested Johnson tap Attorney General Kennedy as his running mate, despite the well-founded rumors of antipathy between the two. In light of how the next four years would play out, a scenario with either Kennedy or McCarthy as Johnson's vice president is, to say the least, quite intriguing. The only hint of a challenge to Johnson within his own party in '64, though, came, not surprisingly, from Alabama's segregationist Governor George Wallace, who said in January that he was considering entering five Northern state Democratic primaries. As for the presidential disability and succession problem, the road to the 25th Amendment to the Constitution began that same month with Senate debate on the matter that would lead to passage of the amendment in July 1965 and ratification by February 1967.

Not unlike the calls for renewal in his first speeches after assuming the presidency, LBJ used his speech before the UN's General Assembly to call for an end to the Cold War "once and for all" and for a "peaceful revolution" in the world. He also echoed his predecessor's words from that summer by saying that "peace is a journey of a thousand miles and it needs to be taken one step at a time." As for the president's desire for Defense Department budget cuts, along with the proposed closing of 26 military installations and the first tentative thoughts of an all-volunteer army, one of the first casualties was development of the interestingly named Dyna-Soar space glider while a manned orbiting laboratory/ space station was slated for launch in late 1967 or early '68, according to the Pentagon. As well, after nearly a year of indecision, the Defense Department had decided to develop a military telecommunications system, with the first seven satellites to be launched in early 1965 and the system to be fully operational by '66. The manned laboratory would, in effect, be used as a spy space station and a command post for targeting politically hostile satellites, quite a different agenda from NASA's science-driven program. The end of Boeing's Dyna-Soar project, though, would be a blow to Seattle's economy, since it would mean the loss of 5,000 jobs at Boeing.

LBJ also had to make some major decisions regarding NASA's budget for 1964. With the Mercury manned flight phase winding down and the two-man Gemini phase still to come, JFK's goal of a manned moon landing by the end of the decade was still deemed doable but to accomplish it some of NASA's scientific projects might have to be sacrificed in the new budget. In fact, Nobel Prize-winning chemist Harold C. Urey publicly expressed his disappointment that scientific aspects of Project Apollo, the portion of the manned space program that would accomplish the moon landing, would have to be curtailed for budgetary concerns, including sending scientists to the moon. In early January, it was announced that the Johnson White House would ask Congress to grant NASA $5.3 billion in appropriations, $200 million less than the '63 NASA budget and $600 million less than the agency had requested. Officials called this budget "barely adequate" to continue the effort toward a manned moon landing by 1969.

Counting scientific and military projects, the US had launched some 55 payloads into space during 1963, three times as many as the Soviet Union was believed to have launched. Nine orbital launches, including Gordon Cooper's 22-orbit final Mercury flight, were all successful, a substantial increase in overall success. The Soviets had launched about 16 satellites and an unsuccessful unmanned lunar spacecraft but did send the first woman into space. Valentina Tereshkova married a fellow cosmonaut in the fall of '63 and was reported to be pregnant by January, with her first baby due in the summer of '64. A rare collaborative effort between the US and the Soviets, Echo 2 was a balloon satellite designed for communications experiments. It launched from Vandenberg Air Force Base in California in late January.

With the ultimate prize of a manned lunar landing at the top of NASA's list of priorities, a 16-story, 20,000-pound Saturn rocket was launched from Cape Kennedy on January 29 and its liquid hydrogen-fueled upper stage went into orbit. This was the first launch for what was slated to be the family of booster rockets that would take the Apollo spacecrafts into orbit on their way to the moon. It marked the heaviest spacecraft payload launched to that point in the space race. The next day, the sixth Ranger spacecraft began a 66-hour trip to the moon with six TV cameras on board that, if all went well, would send back some 3,000 close-up pictures of the lunar surface in the 10 minutes before Ranger made contact with the moon. Ranger 6's projected target was 150 miles in diameter in the Sea of Tranquility.

Unfortunately, previous Ranger missions had a history of malfunctions and, sure enough, on February 2 the cameras failed to operate at the appointed time, even though the rest of the mission had been problem-free. With a large media presence at the Jet Propulsion Laboratory in Pasadena, Ranger 6 hit its target right on time and within a few miles of a bull's-eye but with no signal from the cameras, the sixth straight failure of one type or another for the Ranger program. Finally, at the end of July a Ranger mission would pay off as Ranger 7 sent back dazzling, detailed pictures of the lunar surface, crucial toward determining a possible landing site for an Apollo lunar mission and deciding if the terrain was level enough for the planned lunar exploration module (LEM) to land safely.

After the failure of Ranger 6, government sources began putting forth spin that a manned moon landing still could happen by the end of 1968 but, on February 6 an associate administrator for manned space flight at NASA appeared before the House Committee on Science and Aeronautics. He told the committee that the agency's more realistic target for the lunar landing remained mid-1969. The first moon landing would take place on July 20, 1969. Not a bad estimate, four-and-a-half years out.

*****

In sharp contrast to the grim atmosphere surrounding his first presidential speech before Congress, the mood on Capitol Hill for President Johnson's first State of the Union address on January 8 was business-like but upbeat. Along with an end to racial discrimination and passage of the civil rights bill, Johnson announced that his nearly $98 billion budget would lower the federal deficit to just under $5 billion. He announced a 25% reduction in the production of nuclear materials by the US, the first such substantial cutback in the nuclear age, and called on "our adversaries" to do the same. And he announced a domestic "war on poverty" that would be fought through "better schools and better health and better houses and better training and better job opportunities to help more Americans, especially young Americans, escape from squalor and misery." Within a month, he had appointed Peace Corps Director Shriver to head the war on poverty and Shriver's brother-in-law RFK had announced a three-year, $12 million program to aid the youth of West Virginia. Called Action for Appalachian Youth, Kennedy said it would serve as a prototype for LBJ's war on poverty programs. Aid for the chronic poverty in Appalachia would later be one of RFK's pet projects as a senator. A week after his address to Congress, Johnson pledged that "we have just begun to fight" for a Social Security-based program for financing medical care for the aged but it would take another year and a half before the program would finally be passed, as Medicare and Medicaid, by Congress as part of LBJ's "Great Society" programs. Nonetheless, Johnson sent a special message to Congress on February 10 in which he lobbied for Congressional approval of a program for hospitalization and home health care for the aged and renovation of obsolete and inefficient hospitals in major cities.

As well, there was the issue of older workers forced to retire at a specific age, depending on individual company policies. So the cabinet-level Council on Aging reported to LBJ that state anti-discrimination laws were needed, along with programs that would allow older workers to "taper off" their hours, rather than be forced to retire.

The literary muse for the war on poverty was a 1962 book called *The Other America: Poverty in the United States* by Democratic Socialist and future Nixon enemies list member Michael Harrington. Harrington's book was a JFK favorite and he even took to using Harrington's phrase "the invisible poor" in discussing poverty in America. Johnson became a convert via White House economic advisor Walter Heller. While Harrington felt that "centralization can lead to an impersonal and bureaucratic program," he was convinced that the only way to attack poverty was through the Federal government. That belief gave birth to the war on poverty.

According to the administration's economists, the reduction in the Federal debt would benefit private businesses seeking to borrow money and buyers of homes looking to finance mortgages. The reduced deficit would "ease pressure on the money markets and help maintain funds available at reasonable interest rates" for private use. Another shot-in-the-arm for business was a $9.1 billion tax cut that LBJ signed into law in late February, which added an average $4.50 to the take-home pay of workers and sent the Dow-Jones industrial average on Wall Street up 3.10 points to an all-time high of 800.14. The tax cut was slated to raise total personal income by $29 billion in '64. Government forecasts were for personal spending to increase by $24 billion, with industrial production to rise by 4.7% and a $36 billion increase in the gross national product, which would result in the creation of some three million new jobs. In an election year, these were all very positive figures.

*****

February 12, 1964, was the 155th anniversary of the birth of Abraham Lincoln. The Great Emancipator had received a good deal of attention in recent months, given that the pivot point of the March on Washington was the Lincoln Memorial and the numerous links between Lincoln and America's most recent assassinated president. But a couple of unexpected sources called attention to Lincoln as his birthday, still a semi-national holiday in that era, approached.

Perhaps it was the beard that Lincoln wore while he was president that gave Fidel Castro and Che Guevara a feeling of simpatico, but the official Havana media saluted Honest Abe, painting him as a revolutionary for his freeing of the slaves. Even more bizarrely, the Jackson, Mississippi-based Citizens' Council of America placed ads in a number of newspapers that were headlined "Lincoln's Hopes for the Negro," featuring out-of-context but fairly typical mid-19th century comments by Lincoln on separation of the races and the superiority of the white man. Council members contended that they had received "a sack-full of mail" in response to the ad but didn't elaborate on whether the response was positive or negative. Iowa congressman and Lincoln expert Fred Schwengel called the ad "ugly, unhistoric, unscholarly misuse of the facts of history" but didn't deny that Lincoln had made the remarks, which were largely conventional wisdom of the day. In that era, even those opposed to slavery and sympathetic to the cause of blacks still felt that the races should be segregated and that whites were just naturally superior to blacks. And Lincoln experts pointed out that his views on these matters didn't remain static but evolved while he was president.

In those states in which Lincoln's birthday was a holiday (it was never a Federal holiday because many Southern states refused to recognize it), schools were closed and so were most stores. In 1964, Washington's Birthday, which was a Federal holiday, fell on a Saturday, February 22. Again, most stores, as was customary, closed for the holiday, which meant that many major stores were closed on both that day and Sunday,

71

President Johnson gives his friend and colleague, Democratic Sen. Russell of Georgia, the up-close-and-personal "LBJ treatment."

February 23. Within just a few years, Congress would designate Washington's Birthday to be celebrated on the Monday nearest February 22, making it a three-day weekend for Federal workers beginning in 1971. That would lead to stores opening and running huge sales on what became known in many states as Presidents' Day (a compromise name widely used to honor both Washington and Lincoln), quickly making the holiday one of the biggest shopping days of the year, quite a change in a very short time. Lincoln's birthday would continue to be observed as a holiday for state workers in a shrinking number of states.

*****

With the end of February, the new president had completed 100 days in office and had already put his own brand on the office. The tax cut that LBJ had just signed into law had originally been submitted to Congress early in '63 by President Kennedy and, like the civil rights bill, was still languishing there on November 22. Johnson's skill at expediting legislative action, dating from his days as Senate majority leader, was very much in evidence during the drive to get the tax bill passed in the last weeks of '63 and early '64. Nonetheless, of the 62 pens he used to sign the bill, LBJ presented four of them to Jacqueline Kennedy at a housewarming for her new home in Georgetown. The civil rights bill, of course, would face a tougher road to passage once Senate deliberations

72

began in early March.

Johnson's personal style, so different from Kennedy's, took some getting used to in the first weeks after the assassination, but by late February he felt comfortable enough to hold a live press conference at the State Department auditorium, where Kennedy had held virtually all of his celebrated press conferences. He was devoting more and more time to active campaigning, including a late February trip to Florida with an eye toward the November elections. He named recently retired St. Louis Cardinals baseball icon Stan Musial to succeed politics-bound former Oklahoma football coach Bud Wilkinson as director of The President's Council on Physical Fitness. LBJ also transformed the formerly staid White House dinners for members of Congress into informal affairs at which he showed off another facet of his style, dancing with virtually every woman in sight. And the Hat Corporation of America announced plans to bring out an "LBJ hat," a 2-to-3-gallon, 2-inch-brimmed version of the Johnson 5-gallon Stetson that was on display whenever Johnson was home at the LBJ Ranch.

CORVAIR—A CAR THAT'S NEVER HAD SO MUCH ENGINE BEFORE! Got a hill nearby? Go climb it in a '64 Corvair, and watch it disappear. Almost 19% more horsepower in the standard engine. 110 horsepower in the extra-cost engine. And 150 hp in the Turbocharged engine of the new Monza Spyder Series. (If you suspect that each year we push the Corvair a bit more into the sports car class, you're right.) Some nice interior refinements, too. Like thicker, more deeply tufted bucket seats in the Monzas and sporty map pockets on each front door. Did we mess with the way it parks? Or handles? Or its unbelievable rear-engine traction? Never. **CORVETTE—A CAR THAT'S NEVER BEEN SO EXCITING BEFORE!** And that wasn't easy. New *one-piece* rear window in the coupe, so you can see who's behind you better. Two new extra-cost V8's up to 375 hp. And the ride is smoother and quieter. On the one hand, you'll be surprised at what a beautiful boulevard car the '64 Corvette is. On the other hand, it's still a superb sports car.

CORVAIR and CORVETTE and

Straight out of Detroit, Chevrolet's '64 models of the classic Corvette and the gone-by-decade's-end Corvair.

CHAPTER 5

THE TIMES THEY ARE A-CHANGIN'

O n the night of December 31, tens of thousands gathered in New York's Times Square for an annual tradition that went back to 1905: the dropping of an illuminated ball at midnight to celebrate the new year. But that was the extent of New Year's Eve Times Square festivities in those days: no appearances by popular rock acts— no light shows or fireworks—no celebrities to push a symbolic button to lower the ball. Just the lowering of the ball on the former Times tower, by then the Allied Chemical building, and the tolling of a pre-recorded bell that rang 12 times as the ball descended its pole before a turnout far smaller than the hundreds of thousands that would become the norm for New Year's Eve in Times Square in later decades. Traffic between 42nd and 47th streets at the confluence of Broadway and Seventh Avenue wasn't closed until 11:10 p.m. and was reopened just 20 minutes after the ball dropped and the area quickly emptied.

The real action was further east on 42nd Street, at Grand Central Terminal, where a Bell Ringer's Ball for Mental Health was held from 7 p.m. to 2 a.m. The very middle-aged, dressed-to-the-nines crowd of about 1,000 sedately danced the evening away. The highlight of the night was the appearance of Mr. New Year's Eve, Guy Lombardo, and his Royal Canadians for the CBS telecast of the festivities from 11:15 to 12:15, with the big moment the playing of "Auld Lang Syne" at midnight. Alternatives to spending the evening at Grand Central could be found at the city's posh supper clubs. Singer Leslie Uggams was headlining at the Persian Room of the Plaza Hotel at a cost of $32.50 per person. $30 per person at the Royal Box of the Americana Hotel gained admission to see veteran singer/comedienne Pearl Bailey. And a bargain-priced $15-$25 could get one into the city's best-known night club, the Copacabana, where Italian crooner Jerry Vale was headlining. And, with the arrival of 1964, the Census Bureau announced that the population of the United States stood at 190,695,000.

*****

Given its longstanding resistance to change, 1963 had been a tumultuous year for the Roman Catholic Church. There was the passing of the beloved and surprisingly progressive Pope John XXIII, the election of Pope Paul VI, and the second session of the Second Vatican Council. The first session, presided over by John XXIII, had set the rusty wheels of change within the church in motion. The second session, which adjourned in early December, had called for changes in the presentation of the Mass and the sacraments that would be implemented over the next couple of years, with the council's third and fourth sessions.

Then, at the close of Vatican II's second session, came the announcement that Pope Paul VI would travel to the Holy Land in early January. It would be the first time that a pope had travelled outside of Italy since 1809. The pope was making this trip despite the fact that the Vatican did not yet officially recognize the existence of Israel and the council had not yet modernized the Catholic Church's attitude toward Jews, long blamed by Catholics for the death of Christ. Despite that, the Israeli government officially welcomed the pope's trip. But while one of the purposes of the pilgrimage was to mend fences with the Eastern Orthodox Church, Paul VI was forced to skirt the issue of Israel and the Jews. A glaring example of the very deliberate pace at which the Catholic hierarchy moved through most of the 20th century is the fact that the Jews would be "forgiven" for the death of Jesus at the conclusion of Vatican II in 1965 but the Vatican wouldn't establish diplomatic recognition of Israel until 1993.

On the Sunday after the early December announcement of the pope's trip, Bishop Fulton J. Sheen, the star religious figure of television's early years, appeared on ABC-TV's "Page One" and hinted that Pope Paul might well visit America some day. "Some day" turned out to be less than two years away. Obviously, the days when the pope was tethered to Vatican City and the world would have to come to him were rapidly

July 2, 1963: The first meeting between a reigning pope and a U.S. President as the newly-installed Pope Paul VI meets JFK. Secretary of State Dean Rusk stands behind the pope.

coming to an end. On January 3, Pope Paul became the first pontiff to travel by plane as he departed Rome for Amman, Jordan, where he was greeted by King Hussein. The papal party then made the 54-mile drive to Jerusalem and the pope stopped by the banks of the River Jordan. Surrounded by a huge crowd and a massive turnout of newsmen, he celebrated Mass at the Church of the Holy Sepulcher and meditated at the Garden of Gethsemane.

The real highlight of the trip, though, was the meeting in Jerusalem of Pope Paul and Patriarch Athenagoras I, the first meeting between the heads of the Roman and Greek Orthodox Catholic churches since the churches split in 1054. It ended with a commitment from the pope for a continued dialogue between the two churches. Next, the pope travelled from Jerusalem to Bethlehem, where he said Mass in Manger Square, the traditional site of the birth of Jesus, and gave an address on the need for Christian unity and world peace. Then, back to Jerusalem for a second meeting with Athenagoras before the pope returned to Amman for the flight back to Rome. The entire trip lasted barely two and a half days.

Pope Paul was greeted like a conquering hero on the ride from the airport in Rome to the Vatican, with more than a million people lining the streets to see the pontiff's open-topped car (the Pope-mobile and the need for one was still some two decades away) and some 35,000 in Vatican Square to hear the pope's first back-home remarks. The pontiff's trip to the Holy Land had very little immediate impact and felt more like a media event than a papal pilgrimage. Israel was quite unhappy with the pope's lack of recognition for the Jewish state and his outspoken praise of Pope Pius XII's World War II efforts on behalf of Jews. Charges that would linger into the 21st century had been leveled that Pius had ignored the Third Reich's rounding-up of Italian Jews, including a new Rolf Hochhuth play, *The Deputy*, that was just weeks away from its Broadway debut. But official channels would indeed open up between the Vatican and Israel before the end of the century, including an official trip to Israel by Pope John Paul II in 2000, and the promised communications with the Eastern Orthodox church would also come to pass, though the two churches would remain separate.

*****

From the vantage point of an era in which prime seats to regular season major league baseball games and big-time music concerts have gone well past the $100 mark, it's quite an eye-opener to see the price of Christmas gift booklets for the 1964 New York World's Fair, which went on sale in December of '63. The base price of admission to the fair was $2 (with additional admission to some of the individual pavilions), with volume discounts for booklets of 50 and 100. For instance, a book of 100 tickets cost $67.50. And just across the road from the fair grounds Shea Stadium, the new home of the baseball Mets and football Jets, was scheduled to open a few days before the fair's opening day. The best seats in the house, field level box seats for baseball, cost $3.50 -- yes, three dollars and fifty cents!

Meanwhile, the Top of the Fair restaurant at the World's Fair site had already opened by early December. Prices at the restaurant were considered to be "moderately expensive." For instance, prices on the lunch menu ranged from $2.75 to $4.00 while dinner prices ranged from $3.00 to $6.75. But a New Year's morning settlement that averted a possible citywide transit strike kept the bus and subway fare, including routes to the World's Fair grounds in Queens, at 15 cents, so a day at the fair or even just lunch there wasn't a budget-buster.

For further perspective on those prices, consider what a fairly typical month's rent cost for an apartment on New York's prestigious Central Park West that winter. A two-bedroom apartment could be had for $200-$225 a month, a one bedroom for $150-$175, and a studio apartment went for $125-$150. A deluxe co-op apartment at the tony address of 812 Fifth Avenue, on the other side of Central Park, could be bought for anywhere from $48,600 to $200,900. Consider also the cost of a college education at that moment in time. At as prestigious a university as Notre Dame, undergraduate tuition was $1,400 a year while graduate tuition was $1,000 a year.

Then again, the Educational Policies Commission of the National Education Association was recommending that students in need of "intellectual growth" be given two years of tuition-free education beyond high school. That wouldn't happen, for the most part, but there would be acceleration in the growth of publicly funded, cost-friendly community colleges. At the beginning of 1964, there were only 425 such schools (then still widely known as junior colleges) in the country.

For those already in the job market, the average hourly wage for a factory worker in the US in 1963 was $2.46 and rose to $2.50 in December. The Labor Department reported that the average weekly wage in '63 was $99.38 and rose to $102 in December. According to figures released in January, Americans were buying appliances at an unprecedented rate. Sales of "machines that cool, clean, cook, and entertain," as *Time* magazine put it, increased 7% in '63 to $9 billion. January sales were up 10% from '63's first month. Millions of families owned more than one air conditioner or refrigerator or automatic washer or, most significantly, TV. In February, RCA brought out a $113 portable TV amid forecasts of a 75% increase in sales of portables that year. Sales of color TVs had leaped 72% in '63, with forecasts of a doubling of sales in '64 and availability of color portables by 1967.

But in a scenario that would play out many times over the coming decades and force many existing appliance dealers out of business, deep discounting of major and private label appliances meant for a very small profit margin for dealers. Average refrigerator prices had dropped 25% in 13 years by the end of '63, washers had dropped 10%. And the technology of the future was beckoning. General Electric had already begun manufacturing self-cleaning ovens, with affordable home microwave ovens expected by the end of the decade or the early '70s.

*****

Despite this rosy economic picture, one of the oldest manufacturers of modes of transportation ended better than a century of operation that December in South Bend, Indiana. The Studebaker Corporation, which began manufacturing wagons in the 1850s and became one of the more innovative and dependable automobile manufacturers of the first half of the 20th century, ended a precipitous decline through the '50s and into the early '60's with the closing of the South Bend plant. Taking into account the costs of shutting down production in South Bend, Studebaker took nearly a $17 million red ink bath in 1963. Production would continue at Studebaker's satellite plant in Hamilton, Ontario, for a little over two years before the company would leave the auto business completely in March of 1966, the third US auto manufacturer to cease production since World War II. Only four major American auto concerns remained: General Motors, Ford, Chrysler, and American Motors. By the start of the 21st century, only the "Big Three" would remain, following Chrysler's buyout/absorption of AMC in 1987.

Despite the demise of Studebaker's US production, overall US auto production in 1963 was the second-best in history, nearly 7,637,000, the greatest production since the record high of more than 8 million in 1955. Registered auto sales, including foreign imports, topped 7 million for the second straight year, with '64 expected to be as good or better. More cars were sold in December of '63 than any previous December. And as the year ended GM was looking to break its own record for corporate earnings in one year, thanks to big sales years for Buick, Pontiac, and Oldsmobile. To put that in perspective, by the end of the first decade of the 21st century, GM had gone through the process of bankruptcy (with Oldsmobile history since 2004 and Pontiac destined for the same fate) and the US had become the third-leading auto-maker in the world, trailing both Japan and China. In the winter of 1963-64, such a development was pretty much inconceivable.

But even in that era GM wasn't immune from coming up with the odd clunker. Early in February, Buick and Oldsmobile introduced "domed" station wagons, featuring a 4-inch curved, partially glass roof over the rear two-thirds of the wagon and long, narrow windows in the front and on the sides. The new "vista domes" were scheduled to reach showrooms on February 20, with list prices ranging from $2,900 to $3,200. Then again, the next day Ford confirmed the scheduled April debut of a new sports car that would be considerably more successful and memorable. The new vehicle, a four-seat sports car available in hardtop or convertible, would carry a list price of about $3,000 and so would be dubbed "the poor man's Thunderbird." Ford named its new sports car the Mustang.

*****

A typical wintertime snowstorm in mid-January caused the closing of schools in 14 states and heavy telephone activity, including large-scale use of pay phones on the snow-covered streets of New York. Thus, New York Telephone's 8,000 operators were asked to work overtime to handle the heavy volume of operator and information calls, all of which routinely went through live personnel. Some 32 million phone calls were placed at the height of the storm on January 13, with more than 433,000 calls placed to the WE-6-1212 weather hotline in the era when area codes were gradually replacing letter prefixes in phone numbers and all-news radio was just beginning. Indeed, on February 8 the White House went the all-numeric route, changing its phone number to 456-1414, the sixth different phone number since the first White House telephone was installed in 1878.

With the success of the first generation of communications satellites, new technology was being developed. For instance, AT&T had racked up in excess of $1.5 billion in net income on operating revenue of $9.5 billion between November '62 and November '63. Nonetheless, Ma Bell had decided that as the decade progressed it would increase its reliance on satellites for trans-Atlantic phone service, rather than via cables. A privately owned but government-created company called Communications Satellite Corporation had hopes of a network of communications satellites that would be capable of relaying TV, telephone, telegraph, and facsimile signals anywhere in the world. Comsat, as it came to be known, would be the parent of the first commercial orbiting communications satellite, Early Bird (officially Intelsat I), which would be launched and activated in the spring of 1965. And an experiment in "subscription TV" was being planned to begin in the fall of 1964 in England.

In mid-December, *Time* magazine reported on a new company called Law Research Service Inc., which offered automated research for New York lawyers through the use of Sperry Rand's Univac III computer. Founded by New York attorney Ellias Hoppenfeld so that lawyers had an alternative to manually researching cases through voluminous archives, Law Research lawyers would boil an inquiry down to a few words or phrases, put that information onto a punch card, and feed the card into the computer. Univac would then scan reels of magnetic tape at the rate of 120,000 cases a minute and type out the applicable rulings. That data was then put into a high-speed printing machine that would call up the full texts of the decisions. Within 24 hours after Law Research received a question, the inquiry would be answered for a mere $20 per inquiry. Of course, in the 21st century this sounds like horse-and-buggy technology, since the same information can very likely be accessed for free via a few mouse clicks or keystrokes on a desktop or laptop computer or even a portable device with many times the computing power of the huge Univac machines. Nonetheless, even this primitive form of data processing was a major time and work saver, two decades before the debut of the desktop PC.

Another example of the new technology was unveiled on January 23 when RCA Communications introduced what the *New York Times* trumpeted as "the world's first computerized international public telegraph system: the fastest, most accurate, and versatile commercial message system ever developed." It was capable of handling 900,000 words per second. Scheduled to go into 24-hour operation in the spring of '64, fewer than 20 people were required to run the system, as opposed to more than 150 people required to run the then-standard punched-tape system. Less than two weeks later, RCA introduced a new kind of computer memory, RACE (Random Access Computer Equipment). RACE had a maximum storage capacity of 651 million characters, which would approximate about 8 megabytes in 21st century computing. The data was put on large magazines of magnetic cards, which were then stored in the huge computers of the era. The *Times* story on this was accompanied by a photo of an RCA executive gleefully holding one of the magazines, little realizing that what he was holding would be totally obsolete 25 years later.

Another tiny signpost toward the technological highway of the future was just beginning to attract attention: the microcircuit. According to *Time* magazine, this "simple, solid piece of silicon" reduced the size of an entire electronic circuit board of transistors and other components. Engineers at Texas Instruments had developed a complete circuit a thousandth the size of a corresponding vacuum-tube circuit and a hundredth the size of a transistorized circuit. According to *Time*, Sperry Rand was thus able to compress the computing power of one of those huge Univac computers into a 6-inch box using 1,243 microcircuits that could be expected to run continuously for two years. Thus began the journey that would lead to the gradual miniaturization of computers, hearing aids, pacemakers for heart patients, making reality out of science-fiction-type gadgets such as TVs that could hang on a wall or wireless two-way mobile communication.

The Internal Revenue Service took its first step toward full computerization with a "national identity file" that would be able to check any income tax return. The file would be in partial use for the '63/'64 tax filing season and was slated to be completely in operation by January 1965.

Ford Motor Company Chairman Henry Ford III said in mid-January that those who were blaming automation for unemployment were wrong, and he called for more spending by the company so that workers could learn new technology that would enable them to move on to other skilled positions, rather than to become unemployed.

The Cinerama Corporation, the wide-screen pioneer, provided a literal peek at the future at its New York theatre in mid-December with a demonstration of the first affordable home videotape recorder. Earlier in the year, Ampex and Sony had each introduced home VTRs but both were far too expensive for the average person. Late in June, though, a fixed-head longitudinal VTR called the Telcan was demonstrated on the BBC in London and shortly thereafter on NBC's *Today* show. It used standard 1/4-inch reel-to-reel tape and was developed by the Nottingham Electric Valve Company With the fixed-head format, the machine could only record about 20 minutes of low-resolution black-and-white programming on each side of a tape, but the basic Telcan kit cost less than $300. The Telcan had to be wired into and mounted onto an existing TV but a more expensive "Combi" unit was also available. And for about $150, the company offered a tiny TV camera for recording video at home. Instantaneous playback of recorded material was possible, and with the reel-to-reel format commercials could be edited out. With a timing device, a primitive version of what would become known as "time-shifting" could be used.

Cinerama acquired worldwide rights to the Telcan shortly after the *Today* segment was shown and the company talked bravely of professional companies recording Broadway shows and music concerts and releasing them on commercial videotapes, a la long-playing audio records. But media reaction to the quality of recordings shown at the New York demonstration of the Telcan was not very enthusiastic and the kits were too complex for the average consumer. Sales were very slow and a management change at Cinerama in the early months of 1964 would doom the Telcan's prospects in America. There would be a number of attempts at launching home videotape formats and machines in the coming years but nothing would catch on until the launch of Sony's Betamax in the fall of 1975 and JVC's VHS format the following year, and it would take until the '80s for video camcorders to catch on.

*****

On December 14, the *New York Times* ran an article on experiments in the use of hallucinogenic drugs that were taking place on an estate

83

in Millbrook, New York. The "retreat," which had many of the charac-teristics of what would later be commonly known as a commune, was headed by Dr. Timothy Leary and Dr. Richard Alpert, who would lat-er become known as Ram Dass. Their experiments had begun while they were teaching at Harvard University and founded the International Foundation for Internal Freedom. Harvard fired both in the spring of '63 but Billy Hitchcock, one of the heirs to the Andrew Mellon fortune, pro-vided them the use of the Millbrook estate, where they continued their studies of psychedelic drugs.

The week before the *Times* article appeared, Leary and Alpert re-leased a paper dealing with their studies. It concluded, "The LSD expe-rience is so novel and so unique that the more you think you know about the mind, the more intimidated and even frightened you'll be when your consciousness starts to flip you out of your mind. A new profession of psychedelic guides will inevitably develop to supervise these experi-ences." Consider that in December 1963 a decided majority of readers of the *New York Times* likely had no idea what LSD and/or psychedelic drugs were and phrases like "when your consciousness starts to flip you out of your mind" must have been enough to make readers "intimidat-ed and even frightened," indeed. But the following year, Leary, Alpert, and their colleague Dr. Ralph Metzner would co-author *The Psychedelic Experience: A Manual Based On the Tibetan Book of the Dead*, which became the textbook for the psychedelic experiments so many dabbled in over the next few years. Readings from the book, with a sitar music soundtrack by Ravi Shankar, would be released in 1966 as an LP called *The Psychedelic Experience* and would become a prominent part of the late-night sound of the early progressive rock FM radio stations of the late '60s.

The Psychedelic Experience would find its core audience among the children of the post-World War II "baby boom," the oldest of whom were reaching college age by late 1963. In early December, the US Office of Education announced that college enrollment in the US had broken all records for the 12th straight year. Just over 4.5 million degree-seeking students were enrolled at the nation's 2,140 colleges and universities, up 7.7% from the enrollment in 1962 and more than twice the college enrollment of 1951. By the fall of 1964, the population of 18-year-olds was expected to increase by about 20%, with 7 million baby boomers projected to be college students by 1970. But 40% of Americans aged 18 to 21 were already pursuing higher education by the end of 1963. The largest student populations, not surprisingly, were in the various state university systems, with the overall enrollments of the State University of New York and the University of California each topping 100,000. The UC system, of course, included its original campus at Berkeley, and it was only a year later that the Free Speech Movement would emerge there. So in the last weeks of 1963 the stage was being set and the cast was beginning to assemble for the epic saga that would play out on college campuses all over America over the next several years.

For example, expanding Columbia University was moving into the already overcrowded Morningside Heights neighborhood that bordered the Columbia campus in upper Manhattan. The area was crumbling while Columbia was taking over what park-land was available. Thus, the seeds were being planted for the ideological/generational tensions between the Columbia hierarchy and radical students over the building of a gym in Morningside Park that would boil over into full-scale confrontation in April 1968.

Ironically, the end of November saw scenes of student unrest in the Latin Quarter of Paris that looked eerily similar to the rioting that would break out there in the spring of '68 but with one major difference. The '68 riots and general strike would be fueled by many of the same anti-establishment issues that had been igniting student protests all over the globe. The '63 student and faculty strike that began at the Sorbonne and spread throughout French universities was due to overcrowding at French schools caused by the same baby boom that was in the midst of swelling the populations of American universities. The population of French universities was expected to increase a full third by the fall of '64. The Sorbonne already had a student population of 32,000 on a campus built to hold 10,000. The de Gaulle government was slow to expand facilities throughout France's universities and the '63 disturbances were an early sign that the new generation of French students was unwilling to tolerate impediments to its education, let alone outside agitation that would fuel later student demonstrations.

*****

In mid-December, the New York State Liquor Authority revoked the license of New York City "homosexual haunts." Five-and-a-half years before the Greenwich Village "Stonewall riots" launched the gay liberation movement, the world's largest homosexual population was labeled "the city's most sensitive open secret" by the *Times* in an article that painted a picture of homosexuals as a group that did not deserve to be considered a minority because they were deemed to simply be

85

ill or deviant or worse. NYC police Commissioner Michael J. Murphy commented that "Homosexuality is another one of the many problems confronting law enforcement in the city."

*****

By December, the most detailed pictures of the world's weather had become available via the US's newest weather satellite, Tiros VIII. This satellite's TV camera was capable of delivering a photoelectric picture of about a million square miles of the Earth. The shot lasted for 200 seconds while a scanning device read the picture and transmitted it via radio waves to a ground station operator. The ability to immediately access the picture from Tiros was very important when it came to the approach of severe or dangerous weather and any country with about $32,000 worth of standard components was free to use Tiros' pictures. Indeed, pictures from all the Tiros satellites launched since 1960 had sparked major advances in meteorology, with future satellites expected to yield even more diverse information (cloud patterns, temperature, etc.) via computers. Weather forecasting would always be a crapshoot but meteorologists would now have real-time pictures of all the world's weather whenever they needed it.

*****

The era of the celebrity politician, which would bring, among many others, Bill Bradley and Arnold Schwarzenegger onto the national political stage, really began in the winter of 1963-64, and first on the stage was a '30s/'40s song-and-dance man. George Murphy, former actor and studio executive and a Goldwater conservative, announced on December 23 that he would seek the Republican nomination for the US Senate from California. Murphy's ultimately successful Senate bid would be immortalized in song in 1965 by satirist Tom Lehrer ("Oh gee it's great at last/We've got a senator who can really sing and dance").

Next, Bud Wilkinson, the ultra-successful head football coach and athletic director at the University of Oklahoma and head of the President's Council on Physical Fitness, resigned all three positions to run for the Senate from Oklahoma and changed his party affiliation from Democrat to Republican. Wilkinson's politics were also described as Goldwater conservative, despite the fact that JFK had appointed him to the physical fitness post.

Meanwhile, the man who would lead conservatism to the promised land at the beginning of the '80s was still officially an actor and had recently wrapped filming on *The Killers*, a film in which Ronald Reagan played very much against type, portraying a heavy in an adaptation of an Ernest Hemingway short story. (Reagan always regretted having to do a scene in which he slapped Angie Dickinson, the future TV *Police Woman* rumored to be an intimate of JFK.) Reagan had switched party affiliation in 1962 after many years as a Democrat and a stint as president of the Screen Actors Guild and was prominently in the Goldwater camp by the beginning of '64.

At the same time, Caspar Weinberger, Reagan's future secretary of defense, was the chairman of the Republicans in Reagan's home state of California and was trying to preserve party unity amid the Goldwater-Rockefeller battle for the GOP presidential nomination. But Reagan's increasing popularity with California Republicans did nothing but enhance Goldwater's standing in that state. Reagan would even narrate a Goldwater campaign film that would be shown at that summer's GOP convention in San Francisco, right about the time that *The Killers*, which turned out to be Reagan's last feature film, was debuting in theaters.

On the other side, on January 17 the first American to orbit the earth, 42-year-old John Glenn, left the manned space program to run for the Democratic nomination for the US Senate from Ohio. Ironically, a concussion and inner ear injury suffered in a bathtub fall later that winter would force the former jet test pilot and space pioneer out of the race, and it would be another 10 years before Glenn would win the Senate seat he would hold for 25 years, providing him a platform for a successful lobbying campaign for another trip into space aboard the space shuttle.

*****

Little notice was given to President Johnson's January 3 appointment of Esther Peterson to the newly-created post of special advisor for consumer affairs but it turned out to have long-range ramifications. Peterson had served as assistant secretary of labor and director of the Women's Bureau in the Kennedy administration, specializing in labor laws concerning women. She had long been an advocate for working women's rights, and during '63 was the driving force behind the report of a presidential commission on the status of women and the passage of the Equal Pay Act, two building blocks of the women's movement. Now, LBJ was putting Peterson in charge of this new White House office and she would become an even greater advocate for consumers' rights over the next two decades, in two White House stints and in the private sector. Such routine aspects of the 21st century food shopping experience as nutritional rundowns on product labels, sell-by labels on perishables, and unit pricing would be part of the legacy of Peterson's efforts. She would be awarded the Presidential Medal of Freedom in 1981, among countless other honors.

*****

Bizarrely, the Agriculture Department released figures on smoking (the growing of tobacco being considered agriculture) as 1963 came to an end. For the seventh straight year, Americans set a record for cigarette consumption, smoking 532 BILLION cigarettes, "despite rising prices and the 'cancer scare'," according to the New York Times. Smokers were everywhere. At home. In the office. In doctors' offices. In school bathrooms. At the grocery store. In bars and restaurants. Everywhere.

There had been reports over the previous 10 years on the effects of smoking but they were generally private or academic studies based on anecdotal evidence and were suspected of being agenda-driven. There had been a government-sponsored 1962 Royal College of Physicians study on smoking in England, which had the highest lung cancer rates in the world, that was actually followed by an upward spike in cigarette consumption. Indeed, the four members of the British rock band that was about to conquer America were all heavy smokers and did so in public, very much unlike American pop culture figures of that time. But a US government-mandated study had been commissioned by President Kennedy (himself a cigar smoker) in 1962 and the report, out of Surgeon General Luther Terry's office, was about to be released. Cigarette manufacturers were somewhat nervous but generally confident that there would be no lasting damage. After all, the cigarette industry was a major cash cow, an $8 billion a year business that provided a billion dollars in state tax money and over $2 billion to the federal government. Cigarette manufacturers had an industry-wide advertising budget of $250 million a year. But the TV networks felt the report was significant enough to schedule either live coverage of the report's release to the media on the second Saturday afternoon in January or special prime-time reports that night.

The 150,000-word Surgeon General's Report called for "appropriate remedial action" to lower the American death rate related to smoking. "Possible steps seen include warnings on cigarette packs and control of advertising." Among the report's conclusions: Deaths from lung cancer were found to be nearly 11 times as high among smokers than non-smokers. Smoking was found to be the dominant cause of chronic bronchitis and emphysema. Deaths from coronary artery disease, bladder cancer, hypertensive heart disease, and stomach ulcers were found to be higher in smokers than non-smokers. Tobacco smoke, not nicotine, was found to be the cause of lung cancer in smokers. Smoking was found to be a "psychological crutch" for many of the estimated 70 million American smokers (because of the nicotine, at least in part). Cigars and pipes were judged to be much safer than cigarettes, though that judgment would change in future years, and pipe sales had already increased, including dainty little pipes "made for women." Indeed, Surgeon General Terry himself had switched from cigarettes to a pipe during the course of the study. Terry also commented that the report made no firm judgment on the effectiveness of filters and added that the development of better cigarette filters would open a "positive avenue" in reducing the risks from smoking. Overall, though, the report judged smoking to be a "health hazard."

Naturally, the Tobacco Institute immediately rejected the report, saying that it was not the final word on smoking and health. But a sharp uptick in the number of damage suits against cigarette manufacturers was expected, even though no smoker had ever collected damages at the time the report was issued. The three TV networks immediately said that they would re-examine their advertising standards. The Federal Trade Commission was already considering tightening its regulations relating to cigarette advertising, and shortly after the report's release the FTC announced that it would call for a warning label on cigarette packs and print ads and a change in the upbeat tone of cigarette advertising on TV and radio, particularly ads that would be attractive to young people. The National Association of Broadcasters review board quickly recommended that the industry's code of self-regulation be amended to reflect that change in tone. There would be a prohibition on any claims of healthful physical effects from smoking and unsubstantiated claims that any one brand was less harmful than another. On January 16, two bills were introduced in the House that would empower the FTC to take such action. And the Federal Communications Commission announced that once the FTC's plans were firmed up the FCC would decide on its own regulations.

In the meantime, WMCA in New York, one of the city's three Top 40 radio stations primarily listened to by teenagers, announced on January 28 that it would no longer run cigarette advertising in the prime listening hours of 7 to 11 pm, Monday through Saturday. The next day, the American Tobacco Company, maker of three leading brands of cigarettes, announced that it was pulling its radio and TV advertising from sports events at the expiration of individual contracts so that young sports fans would not be encouraged to smoke. Within the next month, *Saturday Review*, *National Geographic*, and *Parents'* magazines announced that they would no longer accept cigarette advertising. And one of the titans of the advertising industry, Young & Rubicon co-founder John Orr Young, declared in his monthly industry newsletter that "today's cigarette companies and their advertising agencies have had it coming to them," particularly given the industry's pursuit of young people as potential smokers. In a follow-up interview, Young said that he had received no protests from inside the advertising industry regarding his comments.

The immediate fallout from the report caused the Pentagon to ban the free distribution of cigarettes in its 479 hospitals and clinics. The Veterans Administration left a similar ban to the directors of its 168 hospitals. And while the report debuted about a week and a half into January, tobacco sales dropped 8% to 10% from a year earlier. Cigarette tax receipts declined as much as 14% in Illinois and another of the leading tobacco companies, Philip Morris, temporarily went to a three-day work week. Sales would rebound and there would be no rapid downturn in smoking levels. But the days of record cigarette consumption by Americans were over.

While it wasn't addressed in the report, two doctors at the National Cancer Institute commented on a possible link between smoking by pregnant women and premature births and stillbirths. It would take until 1985 for warning labels for pregnant women smokers to be included among the by-then-mandatory warning labels on cigarette packs. Meanwhile, there was a major spike in sales of the leading anti-smoking drugs of the day, Bantron and Nikoban, and small life insurance companies were beginning to offer policies with larger benefits for reformed smokers.

Of course, all the publicity given to the report was too much for politicians to resist. On January 27, Senator Gaylord Nelson of Wisconsin proposed that President Johnson's war on poverty could be financed by increasing the federal tax on cigarettes by 5 cents per pack, though such a proposal was certain to run into heavy opposition from lawmakers in the tobacco-growing states. At that point, the federal tax on cigarettes was 8 cents a pack, plus city and state taxes.

*****

As eerie as it is to see pre-September 11, 2001, photos of the Twin Towers of the World Trade Center, it's perhaps even more unsettling to see the front page of the *New York Times* for Sunday, January 19, 1964. Dominating the page above the fold is a large, close-up, black-and-white photo of those same Twin Towers, several years before they would become reality. The day before, the Port Authority of New York/New Jersey held a press reception at the New York Hilton to formally announce the construction of the World Trade Center in lower Manhattan, complete with a giant scale model of the complex, as designed by Minoru Yamasaki, with a detailed look at the proposed centerpiece of the project. The towers were each to be about 1,350 feet tall and 110 stories and expected to be the world's tallest buildings (a title they would hold very briefly, supplanted in 1973 by Chicago's Sears Tower). That model was nearly identical to the actual towers, except for the huge TV antenna that would top the North Tower beginning in 1978. The estimated cost of the project was $350 million, with construction scheduled to begin in 1965 and be completed by 1970.

The reception followed a prolonged battle by a coalition of lower Manhattan business owners who would be uprooted by the project, many of them inhabitants of the area's longstanding Radio Row of electronics stores. The group pursued legal action against the Port Authority to prevent any move toward condemnation of their buildings and the onset of construction. Their case went all the way to the US Supreme Court, which refused to hear it, effectively ending the coalition's efforts. It would take just over a year, though, for the Port Authority to acquire the land and another year before demolition would begin of the maze of 164 low-rise buildings over the 16 acres that would make up the complex. Ground would be broken for the World Trade Center early in August 1966, while construction of the towers themselves wouldn't begin until the second half of 1968 and the beginning of '69. The North Tower would be completed just before Christmas of 1970, with the South Tower topped off in mid-July 1971, so the original '64 target date of 1970 wasn't all that far off the mark, though the formal dedication would wait until April 1973. And the varied estimates of the final tab for the construction of the World Trade Center would range from $900 million to $1.5 billion, quite a bit more than the $350 million estimate from January 1964.

In their time, the Twin Towers would become a New York City landmark but not a particularly beloved one, due to their modernist architecture. That lack of real affection, of course, would give way to other emotions on Tuesday morning, September 11, 2001. As haunting as that *Times* front page of January 19, 1964 is now, though, it must have looked like something out of science fiction to the readers of that era.

*****

In its January 24 issue, *Time* magazine ran a lengthy cover story several months in the making on "The Second Sexual Revolution." According to the piece, the first sexual revolution took place in the "Jazz Age," the 1920s, the era of flappers and "it" girls. The second was characterized by "a revolution of mores and an erosion of morals" in the US Indeed, the article was sub-headed under "Morals." But if this revolution had been a baseball game, it would have been in about the second inning in January 1964. Sure, the Pill and Helen Gurley Brown's *Sex and the Single Girl* had helped spark the revolution, but this was still pre-miniskirts, pre-"free love," pre-*Hair*, pre-*Bob & Carol & Ted & Alice*, pre-Erica Jong's *Fear of Flying*. So when it came to pop culture signposts of this sexual revolution, *Time* concentrated more on books like Henry Miller's *Tropic of Cancer* and William Burroughs' *Naked Lunch*, described by *Time* as a "an incredible piece of hallucinatory homosexual depravity." In contrast, post-Marilyn Monroe Hollywood "eroticism" was dismissed as "coyly fraudulent" when compared with European films and the supposed upfront sexuality of the Broadway stage. Indeed, *Time*'s piece inferred that a number of Broadway shows with scenes of men and women in bed were deliberately written that way so there would be no doubt that the male was heterosexual—and also that the loud "American Bitch" female leads in Broadway plays were a function of so many plays allegedly being written by homosexuals, then, as mentioned, looked on as sexual deviants.

Of course, much of the "sexual revolution" talk stemmed from the changing attitudes toward sex among young people and even within the non-Catholic religious community. For instance, Wally Toevs, the Presbyterian pastor at the University of Colorado, semi-condoned premarital sex when the couple had a true "covenant of intimacy" while a Protestant theologian privately endorsed a "trial affair" (in other words, living together) as a kind of "little marriage" to see if a "great marriage" could last. And better than 30 years before Monica Lewinsky would come to symbolize the alleged Generation X attitude that oral sex isn't sex, a "student of American vernacular" implied that the word "virgin" didn't always mean what it traditionally did, that "It seems acceptable to consider a girl a virgin if she has had experience with only her husband before marriage, or with only one or two steadies." Virgin or not, a lot of females of that era still opted for marriage, often earlier than they should have, and ended up disappointed and disenchanted by marriage. Thus the high divorce rate among baby boomer couples, much higher than their parents' generation. Still, in the first decade of the Pill, the number of illegitimate pregnancies among teenagers had taken a big upward spike and was even higher among women between 20 and 25.

Interestingly, *Time*'s article reflected the birth pangs of sexual liberation among women and the onset of sexual democracy and equality between men and women, from college coeds' casual attitude toward whether sex would happen on a date to office affairs instigated by young women moving into the business world, as portrayed four-plus decades later in the cable TV series *Mad Men*. Women's liberation in the public sense was still some years away, despite the 1963 publication of Betty Friedan's trail-blazing *The Feminine Mystique*, but women's changing attitudes regarding sex were giving them the ability to be more equal as partners in the sexual dance. Shortly after *Time*'s report was published, Columbia University announced it had authorized an unprecedented student-sponsored plan, scheduled to be implemented as of February 15, that would allow visits by women to males' dormitory rooms from 7 pm to midnight on Saturday nights.

*****

While the sociopolitical climate had not yet really heated up on the nation's broadcast airwaves by January of '64, a Federal Communications Commission ruling late that month had long-range ramifications. The commission ruled that it couldn't censor broadcast organizations for overtly political or provocative programming just because certain people found that programming offensive. That ruling was part of the renewal of the licenses of three listener-supported FM radio stations that had been subject to complaints about "filthy" or "left-wing" programming. The three—WBAI in New York, KPFA in Berkeley, CA, and L.A.'s KPFK—were all run by the Pacifica Foundation, which had been accused in some quarters of having Communist connections. Pacifica, through WBAI station manager Joseph Binns, responded that the FCC ruling was a "reaffirmation of the free speech provisions of the First Amendment," that it was "a vote of confidence for intelligent, sometimes exasperating, sometimes controversial, and always free radio."

In fact, Pacifica's stations pioneered the kind of free-form programming that would bring rock music to the commercial FM airwaves later in the decade. WBAI's programming, in particular, wasn't strictly political. The station ran Shakespearean plays and an annual broadcast of Richard Wagner's *Ring Cycle*. In 1970, WBAI would run a four and a half-day round the clock reading of Tolstoy's *War and Peace*. The station's coverage of the political conventions in the summer of '64 would be staffed by contemporary comedians and members of Chicago's Second City comedy troupe. In other words, it was a mid-'60s version of the kind of political satire that Jon Stewart's *Daily Show* would perfect some four decades later.

But in 1973 the FCC would lock horns with Pacifica and WBAI over a listener complaint about the airing of George Carlin's "Seven Words You Can Never Say On Television" routine and its "Filthy Words" sequel. The FCC would reverse its '64 policy, uphold the complaint, and threaten future sanctions against the station. Pacifica and WBAI would appeal that decision and the case would go all the way to the Supreme Court in 1978, with the high court ruling in the FCC's favor while also establishing the hours from 10 pm to 6 am as a "safe harbor" for airing adult-oriented (but not "obscene") material. That, in turn, would set the stage for the FCC's battles with "shock jocks" like Howard Stern in the latter years of the 20th century.

*****

In an era before professional sports teams had strength coaches and sports clubs and yoga became trendy, the exercising fad of the winter of '63/'64 was isometrics. Vince Lombardi's Green Bay Packers had adopted isometrics in the early '60s and won two NFL championships. "Isometric exercising devices" were flying off the shelves at sporting goods stores, signaling the beginning of the era of weight training. But what made isometrics such a wintertime fad was the idea that business people could exercise right at their desks and not work up a sweat. For instance, inhaling, exhaling, and pushing out and pulling in the abdomen (right out of the basic yoga regimen) six times a day was said to take one to three inches off a paunch in a month. Or six-second pushes of one fist into the other hand was supposed to re-ripple the arm and shoulder muscles. So would simply pressing the palms against each other while keeping the arms outstretched. Those exercises were then and still are completely valid, but the fad of doing isometric exercises in the office would give way to going to the gym or taking yoga classes or, in the '80s, doing aerobic exercising to Jane Fonda's videotapes or Richard Simmons' cable TV workouts.

*****

Some two years before Monsanto/Chemstrand's Chemgrass was installed in the Houston Astrodome and became more popularly known as Astroturf, *Time* magazine ran a short piece about the Forman School in Litchfield, Connecticut, which had installed a vinyl surface for a tennis court that would be covered by a nylon tent. *Time* said that the surface was "made by a Japanese patented process originally devised for doormats" and was said to be "a durable and resilient surface, which is divot-proof, affords better footing and less leg fatigue and keeps both balls and players free from grass stains." In other words, the Forman surface was very similar to the original Astroturf. Tennis luminary Gardner Mulloy tried out the surface and proclaimed it as "about as ideal a surface as you could have for the average player," though he felt that it played a tad slow for top-ranked players. Mulloy didn't anticipate the "rug burn" and heavy-duty wear and tear on legs and feet from which athletes, particularly football and baseball players, would suffer on the early artificial surfaces and the rock-hard bases underneath the carpets. Nonetheless, Mulloy judged it to be "the best indoor court I've ever played on" and schools were already lining up to outfit indoor play areas with the artificial surface or install Forman-style outdoor vinyl playgrounds.

*****

On February 14, the *Times* ran an advertising feature on Jo Foxworth, at that time vice president and associate creative director of the female-oriented ad agency Johnstone Inc. Speaking to students at Florida State University in Tallahassee on "the female economy," Foxworth made the claim that "women now buy 75% of all goods sold in the US," "two-thirds of the nation's wealth is in female hands," and that "women contribute 51% of all adult stockholders and take in $50 billion a year as wage-earners." Foxworth said that women could go far in the advertising world but they had to "act like women," that the "militant feminists" were out-of-date, that "now that women wield the power of the dollar, they no longer need their militancy." Jo Foxworth would go on to be a real-life trailblazer for women in the world of advertising, most famously writing a series of commercials for the New York-based D'Agostino's supermarket chain, and would be inducted into the American Advertising Hall of Fame in 1996. But consider that the comments quoted here were made in the winter of 1964, well before female liberation and/or militancy became much of an issue. Given that her comments were made to an audience of college students, they are, to say the least, quite interesting.

Just a few weeks before Foxworth made that college campus appearance, the January 1964 issue of the *Journal of Marketing* appeared with an article about advertisers who were targeting the "old-age market." A new school of thought was that those advertisers were overestimating the buying power of seniors and overemphasizing the distinctiveness of senior buying habits. This was just one sign of the shift in emphasis toward the youth market, the "now generation," as it would soon be known and the eventual overemphasis, in advertising and in the media, on the young "demographic."

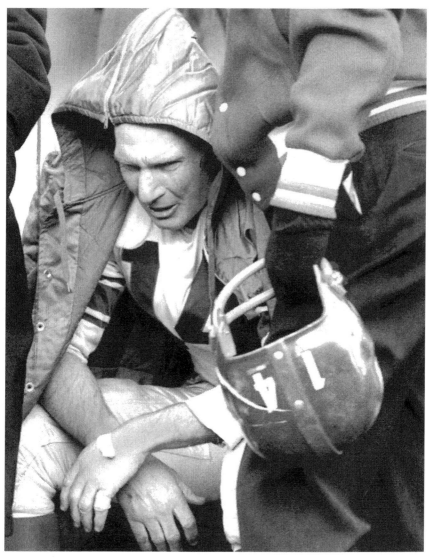

Looking older than his 37 years, New York Giants quarterback Y.A. Tittle on the Giants' bench.

CHAPTER 6

SPORTS: CHANGE TIPTOES INTO THE TOY DEPARTMENT

I n November of 1963, sports was still the world's toy department, the always dependable oasis from the worries of everyday life and the concerns of the world. Oh, there had been some cosmetic changes on the American professional sports landscape as the new decade set in and the new administration arrived in Washington. Indeed, in the spring of 1961 *Sport* magazine had devoted an entire issue to "The New Frontier in Sports." After seven years of franchise moves and the brief threat of a third league to challenge the established National and American leagues, major league baseball had expanded to 10 teams in each league. For the second time in 15 years, a rival professional football league was created to compete with the National Football League, and by '61 the NFL itself had expanded to 14 teams. Even the comparatively young and lean National Basketball Association added a franchise in '61 and had its first real competition for the pro basketball fan's dollar with the birth of the American Basketball League. The ABL folded after little more than one season, though, and the most memorable thing about the league's brief run was that one of the club owners was a young Cleveland-based shipbuilder named George Steinbrenner.

On the field, the games were played much as they had been throughout the 20th century and most players were the traditional strong, silent type. More colorful personalities were generally frowned on by team management or, at the collegiate level, head coaches. Professional players made, on average, more money than the typical American workingman but only the biggest stars made what was considered to be big money in that era and the rank-and-file players usually had to get jobs in the offseason to keep their finances solvent. But all players were legally tied to their teams until they were deemed to be dispensable, with most playing year-to-year on one-year contracts. There was no open market for players and that enabled the owners to keep a lid on salaries. The big money sports were the non-team games. For example, 23-year-old Jack Nicklaus, still in the early stages of what would be an immortal pro golf career, in '63 became the second golfer (following Arnold Palmer) to earn over $100,000 in winnings in one year.

There was still a divide in tournament tennis between pure amateurs and the players on the professional tour. Completely open tournament competition was still some four years away. The Davis Cup matches were the one ongoing international team tennis event during the '60s and that competition had been totally dominated by the US, England, and Australia. The Aussies had won 11 of the last 13, dating back to 1950 while the Americans hadn't won the Cup since 1958. So it was quite the upset in mid-December when the US regained the Davis Cup behind 21-year-old Dennis Ralston and 22-year-old Chuck McKinley, the men's singles champion at Wimbledon that summer. They split four singles matches with future Tennis Hall of Famers John Newcombe and Roy Emerson, then the top-rated player in the world, and defeated Emerson and veteran Neale Fraser in doubles.

The elite professional sports teams were generally the ones that had been elites for years. Baseball's World Series that October had seen the former Brooklyn Dodgers, transplanted to Los Angeles in 1958, win their third world championship in eight years, sweeping the defending champion New York Yankees, winners of 10 World Series since 1947. In early December, Walter Alston, who had managed all three of those World Series-winning Dodgers teams, signed the 11th of what would be 23 one-year contracts with the Dodgers. The National Football League's two longtime glamour teams, the Chicago Bears and the New York Giants, were leading their respective conferences at midseason, with the two-time defending NFL champion Green Bay Packers nipping at the Bears' heels. In the first two months of the pro basketball season, the Boston Celtics had lost just one game and were overwhelming favorites to win their seventh NBA championship in eight seasons, despite the retirement of their playmaking guard, Bob Cousy. And the National Hockey League still had the same six-team lineup it had fielded for decades, with the perennial Stanley Cup champion Montreal Canadiens trailing the Chicago Black Hawks in the early weeks of the 1963-64 season. The highlight of the season came from 35-year-old Gordie Howe of the Detroit Red Wings, who scored the 545th goal of his career in mid-November, a new record for career goals by an NHL player.

Baseball was still considered the national pastime, but with the recent surge in popularity of pro football and the enduring passion for college and high school football the gridiron game ruled the fall. Two players having extraordinary seasons in 1963 at opposite ends of their career paths symbolized the traditional football hero.

Roger Thomas Staubach was the junior-year quarterback for the Midshipmen of Navy. Staubach had first come to national prominence a year before in the 1962 Army-Navy game when, with President Kennedy in the stands, he threw for two touchdowns and ran for another in Navy's 34-14 victory. But Staubach really came into his own in the '63 season. Completing about two-thirds of his passes, Staubach threw for 1,474 yards on his way to becoming just the fourth junior to be awarded the Heisman Trophy as college football's outstanding player of the year and leading Navy to a 9-1 record and a No. 2 national ranking. But the man who would be dubbed Roger the Dodger (before that term would take on a more negative connotation in military circles) was particularly praised for his versatility under fire. As *Sports Illustrated* put it, "It is when Staubach gets into trouble that he is at his very best. Never easy to pull down, he throws with tacklers tearing off pieces of his jersey or clawing at his legs." That, of course, is the image that endures from Staubach's Hall of Fame pro football career with the Dallas Cowboys, but that career wouldn't begin until 1969, following a Navy commitment that would include a tour of duty in Vietnam.

Yelberton Abraham Tittle, in contrast, was in his 16th season as a pro football quarterback. After a college career at Louisiana State, Tittle played for the Baltimore Colts in the last previous attempt at competition for the NFL, the All-American Football Conference. After that league folded in 1950, he signed with the NFL's San Francisco 49ers. After a frustrating decade in which he had to share significant playing time at quarterback but which also included a trip to the NFL championship game in 1957, Tittle was traded to the Giants just prior to the 1961 season. After winning the starting job from about-to-retire Charlie Conerly, Tittle became a New York sensation, teaming with an outstanding receiving corps and a legendary defensive squad to lead the Giants to the NFL title game. In '62, as the no-doubt-about-it starting QB, Y.A. was even better, throwing seven touchdown passes in a late-October game against the Washington Redskins en route to another championship game appearance, albeit a second straight loss to Vince Lombardi's Packers. A soft-spoken 37-year-old Texan who looked a good 20 years older than that, Tittle didn't take to the Big Apple quite as easily as some of his more media-savvy teammates, but New York fell in love with Y.A. and 1963 saw the love affair at full bloom. There was even a record called "I'm in Love With Y.A. Tittle" that got much airplay that fall on WNEW, the radio station that carried the Giants' games. And Tittle reciprocated with his greatest season, completing just over 60 percent of his passes for 3,145 yards, a then-NFL record 36 touchdown passes in just 13 games, and league Most Valuable Player honors.

But the real world suddenly intruded on these autumn heroics on the Friday afternoon before Thanksgiving. Shortly after the announcement of President Kennedy's death, AFL Commissioner (and decorated World War II Marine flying ace) Joe Foss announced the postponement of the league's slate of games for that weekend, as did most colleges and high schools. But NFL Commissioner Pete Rozelle waited to consult the matter with White House press secretary Pierre Salinger. Salinger returned to Washington that night with several members of the Cabinet after the news reached them en route to a trade conference in Tokyo. After talking with Salinger, Rozelle determined that JFK, a scholastic football player and lifetime fan, would want the games to be played, so he announced the NFL's schedule of seven games for that Sunday would be played but without any of the standard game day festivities.

It was a very unpopular choice with both fans and players. For instance, Giants middle linebacker Sam Huff, who had campaigned with Kennedy in the 1960 West Virginia primary, did a regular column for the New York Journal-American during the football season, and in the column that ran that Sunday morning Huff said that he and his teammates really didn't want to play that afternoon. Indeed, the Giants put in a lackluster effort in a 24-17 loss to the St. Louis Cardinals, their only loss in their last nine games of the '63 season. Nearly the usual capacity crowd of around 63,000 turned out at Yankee Stadium but the general mood was solemn and often hushed. A similarly grim atmosphere prevailed at the sites of the other six games, with extra police on hand at Cleveland's Municipal Stadium to ward off any outbursts from Browns fans toward the visiting Dallas Cowboys, then just a fourth-year expansion team but representing the city where the president had been killed.

From a strict pigskin perspective, the Cardinals' victory over the Giants and the Browns' win over Dallas put the Giants, Cards, and Browns into a three-way tie at the top of the NFL's Eastern Conference while the Bears' win over the Pittsburgh Steelers kept them a half-game up on the Packers in the Western Conference after 11 games. The West situation didn't change over Thanksgiving weekend, with the Bears playing a tie with the Minnesota Vikings following another tie in the annual Thanksgiving Day Packers-Lions game in Detroit (regular season overtime in the NFL was still nine years away). With the Browns defeating the Cardinals and the Giants' victory over the Cowboys that Sunday, the Browns and Giants were tied in the East with two games to go.

The Longhorns of the University of Texas preserved their No. 1 national college football ranking with a narrow 15-13 win in their traditional Thanksgiving Day matchup with Texas A&M amid speculation about a possible New Year's Day national championship showdown in the Cotton Bowl with No. 2 Navy. In that era, the entire bowl "season" consisted of the four major bowls on New Year's—the Cotton, Sugar, Rose, and Orange—and a very few second-tier games in the days surrounding January 1. No bloated schedule of corporately sponsored games beginning in mid-December and no BCS/network TV politicking.

The day after President Kennedy's funeral it was announced that the Army-Navy game would be backed up to December 7, an awkward choice since that date was the 22nd anniversary of the Japanese attack on Pearl Harbor. Like the NFL games played on November 24, Army-Navy would be stripped of the usual pomp and celebration. The Midshipmen came away with a 21-15 victory, setting up the national title game with Texas, but the game telecast on CBS featured a peek at the future: the first use of videotape instant replay. Sportscaster Lindsey Nelson, who was calling the game for CBS, had to remind the audience that what they had just seen wasn't the next play but a replay of the last one. The replay showed the same camera angle but the tryout worked just fine. Replay would be a technological novelty at first but it wouldn't take long for it to become an omnipresent part of sports television, on the networks and on local team telecasts. Indeed, by the 21st century replay would become an official part, to one degree or another, of the games themselves.

In early December, the American Football League announced that its championship game would be pushed back a week to January 5. With the AFL completing its fourth season and showing no signs of going away, the two leagues conducted their college player drafts within a few days of each other, right at the end of the college season. The AFL draft was held in Manhattan on November 30, with the first pick quarterback Jack Concannon of Boston College by the Boston Patriots, followed by the Kansas City Chiefs' selection of QB Pete Beathard of the University of Southern California. Concannon was also drafted by the NFL's Philadelphia Eagles and ended up signing with the Eagles for a $50,000 bonus. Beathard was reportedly enticed to sign with the Chiefs by a $20,000 contract, a $15,000 bonus, a new car, and a rent-free apartment. Concannon and Beathard would have respectable but undistinguished pro careers but that AFL draft's big prize would turn out to be the downtrodden New York Jets' selection and quick signing of running back Matt Snell of Ohio State. Snell would immediately become a major offensive threat for the Jets and would score the lone Jets touchdown in their historic January 1969 Super Bowl III upset of the Baltimore Colts.

The NFL draft was held in Chicago on December 2 and the first three picks all would become stars in the league. The first pick was wide receiver Dave Parks of Texas Tech by the San Francisco 49ers. The Eagles then selected offensive tackle Bob Brown of Nebraska, who would go on to a Hall of Fame career. And the Washington Redskins really struck pay dirt with the third pick, halfback Charley Taylor of Arizona State. Taylor would become one of the Redskins' all-time greats and a Hall of Famer, first as a running back and then as a wide receiver.

On the gridiron, the conference races that would set up the December 29 NFL championship game wound down to the final week. With the Bears and Packers winning their next-to-last games on December 8, the Bears needed a win or a tie to clinch the Western Conference title. With the Browns losing and the Giants winning their Week 13 games, though, a bizarre scenario had the Giants and Steelers playing for, in effect, the Eastern Conference championship at Yankee Stadium on the final Sunday, December 15. Even though the Giants had a 10-3-0 record, they technically trailed the Steelers, who had played three ties and were otherwise 7-3. If the Steelers won in New York, they would have a better winning percentage than the Giants and, despite two fewer wins, Pittsburgh would go to the championship game. Fortunately for the NFL brass, the Giants dominated the frigid season finale, beating the Steelers 33-17 to win their third straight Eastern Conference title and sixth in seven years. Meanwhile, the Bears beat the Lions to end the Packers' three-year run as Western Conference champions and set up an old-fashioned Bears-Giants NFL title game two weeks later at Wrigley

Field in Chicago.

*****

On December 9, the American League released its schedule for the 1964 baseball season and it showed the defending AL champion Yankees opening the season at home on Tuesday, April 14 against the Boston Red Sox. The game would be rained out, and when the two teams finally began their seasons two days later, less than 13,000 showed up at Yankee Stadium. For a Yankees-Red Sox game? Well, the legendary rivalry between the two teams was temporarily on low heat by the mid-sixties and the Yankees, despite all their success, were having trouble drawing people to the big ball park in the Bronx. The fact that virtually all of their home games were televised over free TV was a factor but the Yanks also had new competition for the New York baseball fan's dollar. The expansion-born New York Mets, despite losing 231 games in their first two seasons and playing those two years in the crumbling old Polo Grounds, had attracted some two million customers with a scrappy, fan-friendly approach; quite different from the very corporate Yankees. With all of their stars and success and their big ballpark, the Yankees had drawn a little over 1,300,000 fans in 1963, roughly 200,000 more than the mega-losing Mets had attracted on the other side of the Harlem River. The Yankees had garnered gate receipts of $3 million for 68 home dates while the football Giants took in just short of $2.25 million for seven sold out home games that fall at the Stadium

The Mets were slated to move into their new home, Shea Stadium, virtually across the street from the New York World's Fair site in Flushing, for the '64 season and figured to draw big crowds, if only to see the new ballpark. As early as December 17, the Mets and the New York City Parks Department declared that Shea Stadium would be ready for its scheduled opening on Friday, April 17, and the Mets moved their player equipment and offices from the Polo Grounds early in January. But some of the men doing the actual work on the new ballpark were painting a rather different picture. As the winter progressed, shortcuts were taken, particularly regarding the tides from Flushing Bay, which at high tide would cause water to seep into what was to be the outfield and form ice patches in the cold air. An underground pumping system was needed for the water. Indeed, Shea's drainage system in the stadium's first decade or more was abominable. Heavy rains would produce huge puddles in the outfield and affect play. That could have been prevented in the months leading up to the stadium's opening, but with time growing short nothing was done and, indeed, workmen would still be working on the ballpark on opening day.

The Yankees countered the Mets' impending move to their new home by scheduling 24 night games at Yankee Stadium for '64, in an era when teams still played more games during the day, and having six of them begin at 6 pm to attract commuters who worked in Manhattan but lived in the suburbs. In fact, those early-evening matches were billed as "Suburban Night" games. With the two-for-the-price-of-one doubleheader still a baseball fixture, the Yankees were scheduled to play seven Sunday doubleheaders and three twilight/night twin bills, plus doubleheaders added to the schedule as a result of rainouts such as the one that would delay the Yankee Stadium opener until the day before the opening of Shea Stadium.

The Jets, who were slated to become the football tenants at Shea for their 1964 AFL season, played their final game at the Polo Grounds on December 14 and lost to the Buffalo Bills. The final sporting event at the longtime home of the baseball and football Giants drew a tiny audience on a raw, rainy Saturday. With Shea Stadium's completion a year overdue, demolition of the Polo Grounds wouldn't begin until after the formal opening of the new park, and news photos of the demolition would show the old center field clubhouse still standing, topped by the scoreboard that still showed the score of that final football game.

The young man who would lead the Jets to pro football's promised land five years later was a junior quarterback for the Crimson Tide of the University of Alabama in December of 1963. Joe Willie Namath of Beaver Falls, Pennsylvania, had a rifle arm and a riverboat gambler's instincts that made him the centerpiece of coach Paul "Bear" Bryant's offense. He wasn't flamboyant on the gridiron, but was hardly a shrinking violet off it, and at Alabama the Bear ran a tight ship. On December 13, Bryant suddenly announced that Namath was being suspended for the Tide's season finale the next day for "disciplinary reasons." There are various accounts of what those reasons were. One said Namath had simply broken curfew, another that he had been seen drinking after hours, and still another from a biography of Bryant that claimed Namath had been involved in an altercation in a convenience store parking lot and took the fall for teammates who were involved in the same skirmish. Given Namath's long-standing reputation as a great teammate, that third scenario may well be closest to the truth. Nevertheless, the suspension kept Namath out of both the season finale and the Tide's New Year's Day appearance in the Sugar Bowl.

Namath would always defend Bryant's decision as the right thing to do and the Bear would maintain a close relationship with Namath for the rest of his life, always referring to Joe as "the greatest athlete I ever coached." Namath would return for his senior season and lead the Crimson Tide to the national championship but would also sustain the first of the serious knee injuries that would shorten his pro career. After Alabama's Namath-less appearance in the '65 Orange Bowl, Joe would be signed by Jets co-owner Sonny Werblin to a contract with a then unheard of $400,000 bonus. But despite the whole "Broadway Joe" image with the fancy apartment and the girls and the Johnny Walker Red, Namath would never be a disciplinary problem for any of his pro coaches, though old-school Weeb Ewbank would be less than pleased with Namath's public guarantee of a Jets victory in Super Bowl III. Yet that very brashness, which reflected his teammates' supreme confidence that they would win that historic game, would make Namath literally the poster boy for a new breed of nonconformist, nontraditional athletes just as the age of nonconformity was taking off.

The day after Namath's '63 suspension was announced, there was big news from the most famous of all college football programs. The Fighting Irish of Notre Dame had been missing from the game's elite squads for several years, culminating in a miserable 2-7 record in '63. Meanwhile, at Northwestern University Ara Parseghian had coached that school's football team to one of the better records in the school's history over eight seasons, but a falling-out with the head of the school's athletic department caused Parseghian to contact Notre Dame about the head coaching position at South Bend. By mid-December, Parseghian had signed a four-year contract to become the Fighting Irish's 22nd head football coach. What would become known as the Era of Ara would bring a near total reversal of fortune to Notre Dame. The '64 Irish would go 9-1, losing an undefeated season and the national championship in the fourth quarter of the season's final game against USC, giving Alabama its aforementioned '64 national title. But the Era of Ara would bring Notre Dame two national championships and an undefeated season in 1973 before Parseghian's retirement as head coach a year later.

Two days after Notre Dame hired Parseghian, NBC announced that it had bought the rights to the NCAA college football telecasts, previously held by CBS, for the 1964 and '65 seasons for just over $13 million. Given subsequent events that winter, the deal would prove to be a veritable bargain for NBC, especially given the huge nationwide audience for college football. The NCAA released figures on December 18 that showed an increase of about a million over 1962 for attendance at college football games during the '63 season. Despite the losses incurred by the games canceled or postponed on November 23, some 22,377,000 fans came to the stadiums to watch college football in the fall of '63.

*****

The college basketball season began in early December, and while the John Wooden-coached Bruins of UCLA had unexpectedly become the team to watch, the biggest individual story of the young season was a 20-year-old junior at Princeton named Bill Bradley. Already the first basketball All-American in Princeton's prestigious history, Bradley scored 130 points in his first four games of the new season but was hardly a one-dimensional "gunner." As *Time* magazine put it, "He does everything well: dribbles, rebounds, decoys, and sets up plays. Basketball buffs rave about his 'great eye' and 'touch.'" Bradley's shooting accuracy was almost uncanny: 52 percent in those first four games. He was a great believer in self-discipline, a trait that had made him an honor student at the same time that he was scoring over 3,000 points in his high school basketball career. Clearly, Bradley had his sights set on plenty beyond college. Indeed, his career path would lead him to England for studies at Oxford as a Rhodes scholar, then on to a Hall of Fame pro basketball career with the New York Knicks, followed by a return to New Jersey and three terms in the US Senate. Throw in an Olympic gold medal as a member of the 1964 US basketball squad, two NBA championships with the Knicks, and a 2000 run (albeit unsuccessful) for the Democratic presidential nomination and Bill Bradley would far exceed his youthful goal of not becoming simply "Old Satin Shorts Bradley."

Given his sophomore year exploits, the greatness Bradley had shown in the early going of his junior season wasn't a big surprise. UCLA, though, hadn't been expected to be among the nation's Top 20 teams in the pre-season polls. A college team that later would be led at center by Lew Alcindor (the future Kareem Abdul-Jabbar) and then Bill Walton had a 6'5" center, Fred Slaughter. One guard, Gail Goodrich, was listed at 6'1" but looked shorter and the other, Walt Hazzard, was 6'2". Yet, the Bruins were 12-0 by midseason with a run-and-gun offense that gave coach Wooden, not yet "the Wizard of Westwood," the nickname "Mr. Run." Wooden's teams had never had a losing season in his first 15 seasons at UCLA and his 1963-64 squad would finish the regular season 26-0. Tag on four more wins in March's NCAA tournament, including a championship game victory over Duke, and Wooden had the first of what would be a record 10 national championships in his last 12 years as UCLA coach. Meanwhile, Wooden's future center, the 7'1" Alcindor, was a junior at New York's Power Memorial High School in the 1963-64 season. By early February, Power had set a New York high school basketball record with 49 straight wins.

*****

In big-time professional sports in that era, player contracts rarely went beyond one season and that was especially true in baseball. With the onset of winter, the players had begun sending in their signed one-year contracts for the coming season, with some of the game's biggest names signed to five-figure contracts. For instance, Detroit Tigers right fielder Al Kaline, who carried a .309 lifetime batting average after a decade with the Tigers, and Yankees right fielder Roger Maris, who had hit 133 home runs between 1960 and '62 before an injury-plagued '63 season, signed '64 contracts for $60,000 while Maris' Yankee teammate Mickey Mantle was expected to be offered another ultra-premium $100,000 contract. In a comment that might send shudders through 21st century player agents, Mantle said, "I'll sign for whatever the Yankees offer me." The Yankees' total 1964 payroll was estimated at $900,000, down $50,000 from a year earlier, when they were coming off two world championships. Maris' salary had been cut $12,000 while Whitey Ford, after his second 20-plus-win season in three years, was signed for $60,000 to not only pitch but also take on the duties of pitching coach under new manager Yogi Berra. Catcher Elston Howard, the AL's Most Valuable Player in '63, was getting a $10,000 raise to $55,000 while pitcher Jim Bouton, a 21-game winner in his second big-league season, was estimated to be getting a raise up to $20,000.

With Mantle's salary staying at $100,000, the San Francisco Giants made their own superstar center fielder, Willie Mays, baseball's highest-paid player by boosting his salary to $105,000. They also signed slugging outfielder/first baseman Orlando Cepeda to a $52,000 contract. And the Milwaukee Braves signed 42-year-old Warren Spahn, with more career wins than any left-handed pitcher in baseball history, to the largest base salary ever for a pitcher, $85,000.

Players unions in the four major team sports had been formed in the '50s but each had a tough time getting acknowledgment or official recognition from the team owners. For instance, the NBA players had been trying to deal with the owners over the establishment of a player's pension fund since 1957 to no avail. Finally, the players took matters into their own hands and threatened to strike the NBA's showcase event, the midseason All-Star Game, which was being held that year at the Boston Garden, home of the multi-year champion Celtics. At first, the owners and commissioner Walter Kennedy refused to even meet with the player representatives over the issue. It was only after the players refused to leave the locker room for pre-game warm-ups that the owners finally relented and agreed to talk to the union reps. And it was only in the aftermath of this incident that the NBA owners would officially recognize the players association. Meanwhile, with the AFL relatively healthy after completing its fourth year, the league's players announced the formation of their own players union.

*****

While its golden era of the '20s, '30s, and '40s had passed, boxing was still one of the most popular of the non-team sports, particularly in the heavyweight and middleweight divisions that were frequently highlighted on the one remaining network boxing showcase, ABC's Saturday night *Fight of the Week.* For instance, on December 7 veteran middleweight contender Joey Giardello won the title in Atlantic City with a unanimous decision over Dick Tiger. Two weeks later, an ex-con from Paterson, New Jersey, named Rubin "Hurricane" Carter knocked down welterweight champion Emile Griffith twice in the first round of a non-title fight in Pittsburgh, with the referee stopping the fight after the second knockdown. *Ring* magazine, the self-proclaimed "bible of boxing," installed Carter as the third-ranked middleweight contender. It would take nearly a year for Carter and Giardello to fight, though, and Giardello would emerge with a unanimous decision. A year-and-a-half later, there would be a triple homicide in a Paterson bar and so began the epic post-ring saga of the "Hurricane," immortalized in song by Bob Dylan in 1975 ("The man the authorities came to blame but who could have been the champion of the world") and in a 1999 Norman Jewison film.

Another less-than-savory character, Charles "Sonny" Liston, had capped a nearly decade-long post-prison pro boxing career in September 1962 with a first-round knockout of Floyd Patterson at Comiskey Park in Chicago to take Patterson's heavyweight championship. A rematch the following July in Las Vegas lasted four seconds longer but with the same result. The fight-night atmosphere was spiced, though, by the presence at ringside of a brash young contender for Liston's title. Cassius Marcellus Clay of Louisville, Kentucky, had been the light-heavyweight gold medal winner at the 1960 Summer Olympics in Rome before turning pro and moving up to the heavyweight division. By the end of January of '63, the 21-year-old Clay had piled up a 17-0 record but had some problems in his next two fights. In March, Clay won a unanimous but disputed decision over Doug Jones at New York's Madison Square Garden and in June he was knocked down by Henry Cooper before being awarded a fifth-round TKO on cuts to Cooper's face in a fight in London.

Clay's fighting ability had never been disputed. He was 6'3" with a long reach and uncommon speed for a heavyweight and was being trained by Angelo Dundee, a well-known trainer of champion fighters. But Clay's personal style was very different from that of traditional boxers, who tended to be either genial but humble or glowering presences like Liston. Clay instead took a page from the playbook of Gorgeous George, the wrestler who had been one of the stars of TV's early days. Like George, who Clay met at a radio station early in his pro boxing career, Cassius played up his good looks and bragged about his ability—even predicting the round in which he would knock out an opponent and pledging to crawl across the ring and bow to his opponent if he lost—spicing his shtick with bad poetry. Ironically, Gorgeous George, born George Wagner, suffered a heart attack on Christmas Eve '63 and died two days later, just as Clay's self-promotion for his shot at the heavyweight championship was beginning to accelerate.

Having twice knocked out the two-time champion Patterson in little more than the equivalent of one round of boxing, Liston was more than confident that he could beat Clay, who spent a lot of time baiting Liston from ringside at the second Patterson fight. When Sonny signed that fall for a February '64 Liston-Clay fight, he did it for the money, of course, but also for the satisfaction of shutting Clay up. In the meantime, Cassius, now widely known as "The Louisville Lip," went into a recording studio and made an LP, not surprisingly called *I Am The Greatest!*, that was at once comedy and self-promotion.

Heavyweight championship fights were still boxing's glamour events, generally shown on closed-circuit TV hookups in movie theaters, and the Liston-Clay match was expected to be a very hot ticket. But the ratings for boxing's one remaining free TV showcase were in decline and even the recent upheaval among the middleweights didn't help much. So it was not a huge surprise when, just before Christmas, ABC and Gillette, the primary sponsor of the *Fight of the Week*, announced that the series would end with the close of the 1963-64 season. Boxing was already an occasional presence on ABC's Saturday afternoon *Wide World of Sports* series but the sport that was so much a part of TV's early years would never again have an ongoing prime-time place on broadcast network TV schedules. As a consequence of this, though, Madison Square Garden management began thinking about forming a national network to continue the boxing series. This would lead, by the early '70s, to pay/cable telecasts of events at the Garden and then the formation of the Garden's own cable network, though boxing would be come less and less of a presence on the MSG Network and others in the late 20th century and the passage into the new century.

*****

On the same pre-Christmas Sunday on which ABC announced the end of the *Fight of the Week*, the AFL wrapped up its regular season with the San Diego Chargers beating the Denver Broncos to win the Western Division title. In the Eastern Division, the Buffalo Bills and the Boston Patriots finished in a tie and would face each other in a playoff for the division championship the following Saturday, December 28, the day before the NFL title game in Chicago. Just three days before the NFL championship was decided, Vince Lombardi, who had coached the Packers to the last two NFL titles, signed a new five-year contract to stay at Green Bay through the 1968 season. In the first four of those five years, Lombardi would coach the Packers to three more NFL championships and the first two wins in the game that would shortly become known as the Super Bowl, for which he would receive the trophy that within a few years would bear his name.

With the approach of the Bears-Giants title game, Pete Rozelle announced that the game would net the NFL $750,000, counting all revenue. That included a closed-circuit telecast of the game in Chicago. This was the era of the blackout rule, which prohibited telecasts of NFL home games (the AFL, NBA, and NHL had similar rules) within a 75-mile radius of the game site. The rule was meant to encourage fans to become paying customers at the stadiums in cities where attendance had been lagging. In markets like New York, though, where the Giants were sold out for every game, the blackout rule was an autumnal bonanza for hotels and motels north of the city that could pick up the CBS affiliate in Hartford, which carried the games from Yankee Stadium.

With the championship game in Chicago, the blackout rule wasn't a problem for Giants fans back east, but the NBC telecast of the game would be blacked out in Chicagoland, so the same company that had secured closed-circuit rights to the Liston-Clay fight made a deal to show the game via closed-circuit at Chicago's famed McCormack Place and a few other venues signed on in the last days before the game. Meanwhile, the Patriots beat the Bills, 26-8, to win the AFL's Eastern Division and set up a Boston-San Diego AFL championship on January 5.

The Bears-Giants game was a matchup of the NFL's top defense, long a Bears trademark, against the league's top offense, led by Tittle and his 36 touchdown passes. The game, played in frigid (9 degrees at kickoff) Wrigley Field before just 300 short of a sellout crowd, lived up to its billing. Tittle piloted an 86-yard first quarter drive, giving the Giants the lead on a 14-yard TD pass to Frank Gifford, but late in the quarter linebacker Larry Morris hit Tittle as he was throwing. The hit injured Tittle's planting knee and his throwing was compromised for the remainder of the game. Another Morris hit in the second quarter knocked Y.A. out of the game until halftime with what was ultimately diagnosed as a torn ligament in his left knee. Morris had also set up the Bears' first touchdown with a 61-yard interception of a Tittle screen pass. A quarterback sneak by Bears QB Billy Wade tied the game but Don Chandler gave the Giants a 10-7 halftime lead with a 13-yard second period field goal.

Tittle, with his left knee heavily taped and medicated, toughed it out in the second half but had to throw off his right leg, rendering him totally ineffective. He ended up throwing five interceptions, including a third quarter pick by Ed O'Bradovich that set up a second Wade touchdown that gave the Bears a 14-10 lead that held up for the remainder of the game. Late in the fourth quarter, Del Shofner dropped a sure touchdown pass from Tittle in the icy end zone and on the next play Richie Petitbon intercepted Tittle to cinch the Bears' victory. For Bears owner-coach "Papa Bear" George Halas, it was his sixth and final NFL title but the game ball went to assistant coach and defensive specialist George Allen. For Tittle and the Giants, it was their third straight championship game loss and the Giants wouldn't see the NFL postseason again until 1981. The Bears would also go into competitive hibernation and wouldn't make another postseason appearance until 1977.

As for the closed-circuit telecast, owners Dan Rooney of the Steelers and Bill Bidwell of the Cardinals were reportedly quite impressed with the picture quality on the big screen and Rozelle soon encouraged individual teams to consider going the closed-circuit route for blacked-out regular season home games. Three days after the NFL championship game, college football's national title was decided at the Cotton Bowl in Dallas. Playing basically a home game, Darrell Royal's Texas Longhorns clinched the final No. 1 ranking with a decisive 28-6 pasting of Navy. Texas QB Duke Carlisle completed seven passes for 213 yards and rushed for another 54, the game's high on the ground. Roger Staubach was chased all over the field by the swarming Longhorn defense. It wasn't until the fourth quarter that Roger led the Middies to their lone touchdown drive, but he did end up throwing for 228 yards, then a Cotton Bowl record.

In the other New Year's Day bowl games, Steve Sloan was at quarterback for Namath-less Alabama and four Tim Davis field goals gave the Crimson Tide a 12-7 Sugar Bowl victory over Mississippi. Nebraska beat Auburn, 13-7, in what turned out to be the last daytime Orange Bowl game. And in the Rose Bowl No. 4-ranked Illinois beat Washington, 17-7, while a Capitol Records rep reportedly tried to bribe a Washington cheerleader into holding up a sign reading "The Beatles Are Coming!"

By the early '60s, New York's days as a college football hotbed, with big-time teams at Columbia and Fordham, were well in the past, though there was still a sizable "subway alumni" following for Notre Dame. The city's attempt at a December bowl game, the Gotham Bowl, had been a miserable failure, with tiny crowds attending the two games that were played in '61 and '62 at the Polo Grounds and Yankee Stadium, respectively. It was out of the rubble of the Gotham Bowl that on January 7 the NCAA announced the very conditional awarding of a Mayor's Trophy Bowl. The inspiration for the name came from the Mayor's Trophy Game, an annual exhibition between the Mets and Yankees for the benefit of what was then called sandlot baseball in New York. The debut game the previous June had drawn a huge crowd to Yankee Stadium, with the '64 game slated for Shea Stadium. So the debut Mayor's Trophy Bowl was also scheduled for the new home of the Mets and Jets on December 19.

But this was all based on the condition that $100,000 in ticket sales be in the bank by a month before the game. The organization behind the Mayor's Trophy Bowl, which included the Touchdown Club of New York, was headed by Bill Shea, the prominent New York attorney for whom the new stadium was named because of his efforts to bring National League baseball back to New York after the departure of the Dodgers and Giants. But Shea's efforts would be for naught this time. The Mayor's Trophy Bowl never made it beyond the NCAA's announced '64 schedule. The same fate befell a Tobacco Bowl in the Raleigh/Durham/ Wake Forest area of North Carolina, which the NCAA scheduled for the same date as the Mayor's Trophy Bowl. The release just a few days after that NCAA announcement of the surgeon-general's report on smoking and the PR fallout from that doomed the Tobacco Bowl. As for New York, it would have to wait until 2010 for another shot at a postseason bowl game, the Pinstripe Bowl at the new Yankee Stadium, with corporate sponsorship from the New Era cap company, the backing of the Yankees, an unusual four-year licensing commitment from the NCAA, and a sizable first-year turnout. At the outset, at least, quite a contrast from the Gotham Bowl and the stillborn Mayor's Trophy Bowl.

*****

The day after Christmas, Charles O. Finley, the flamboyant owner of the baseball Kansas City Athletics announced that he was moving the A's out of Kansas City's Municipal Stadium in a dispute with city officials over a new lease. Finley's only option for staying in Kansas City was playing in minor league facilities, so by January 6 Finley announced that he had signed a tentative deal for the A's to move to Louisville for the '64 and '65 seasons. The team would be called the Kentucky Athletics and play in the 20,000-capacity State Fairgrounds in Louisville. But Finley's move needed the approval of the other American League owners and, for one, Chicago's Arthur Allyn said that Finley was "a fool and his action is inexcusable." In Finley's defense, the A's had lost over $1 million in his first three years of owning the franchise and, despite all kinds of Charlie O. touches (including a mule mascot, Charlie-O, and dressing his team in green-and-gold uniforms) to liven up the drab ambience of Municipal Stadium, the team had averaged full-season attendance of 694,000 over those three seasons.

A special meeting of the owners was called for January 16 in New York while Kansas City gave Finley a two-week extension to work out the lease dispute. Not surprisingly, the owners voted 9-1 against Finley's move and Charlie threatened to take the matter to court with an anti-trust lawsuit but nothing came of that, despite the encouragement of New York congressman Emmanuel Cellar, who had led a House sub-committee that looked into anti-trust issues in organized sports in the late '50s. So the A's would remain in Kansas City (and at Municipal Stadium) for another four seasons before moving to Oakland for the '68 season, though Finley began talking about a possible move to Oakland within days after the owners had rejected the move to Louisville.

Along with the AL owners giving Finley the back of their collective hand, the owners in both leagues voted unanimously to explore the possibility of a free agent draft for high school and college players. That would short-circuit the ability of rich organizations like the Yankees and Dodgers to snap up all the best prospects by throwing large quantities of money at them. They also voted to look into the viability of a nation-wide weekend afternoon *Game of the Week* telecast. All three networks had carried such a package at various points since the early '50s but only in non-major league markets, which before 1958 was the entire country west and south of St. Louis. Now, with three teams in California and major league baseball having come to Texas and Minnesota, the idea of a completely nationwide weekly TV showcase for baseball made more sense. ABC would begin airing the Saturday afternoon *Game of the Week* with the beginning of the 1965 season and the free agent draft would commence that June.

Another indication of creeping change was the NL's announcement that its teams would play a record 438 scheduled night games in 1964. 77 of those, including 12 Sunday night games, would be played at Colt Stadium in Houston, temporary home of the Houston Colt .45s. The new domed stadium that was rising just across from Colt Stadium wouldn't be ready for another year and the Texas heat and humidity was so overpowering during the summer days that the team received permission to play nearly all its home games at night, when the players would merely have to deal with Houston's immense mosquitoes. The NL season would begin on Monday afternoon, April 13, with the traditional opener at Crosley Field in the city where professional baseball began nearly a century before, Cincinnati, while the AL season would open in Washington with the traditional opener, at which the president usually threw out the first pitch.

In an era in which it seemed everyone smoked cigarettes and kids collected baseball cards with pictures of players with large chaws of tobacco in their cheeks, it was considered just a sad fact of life when a middle-aged former player contracted lung cancer. So it was only mildly surprising when a week before the surgeon-general's report on smoking was released it was announced that 44-year-old Cincinnati Reds manager Fred Hutchinson had been diagnosed with what turned out to be cancer of the lungs, neck, and chest. Hutch, as he was universally known, had been a lieutenant commander in the Navy during World War II, an All-Star-caliber pitcher for the Tigers in the late '40s/early

116

'50s, and a manager with three teams since 1952, including the 1961 National League champion Reds. But he was also a heavy smoker. The announcement, made through the office of his physician brother, Dr. William Hutchinson, said that Hutch would undergo the recent innovation of radiation treatments while continuing to manage the Reds during the '64 season. Hutch would stay at the helm until mid-August, when his weakened condition would force him to turn the reins over to coach Dick Sisler, and he would have to watch from the sidelines the Reds' late-season drive that would result in a second-place tie with the Philadelphia Phillies after the Phils' historic stretch-drive collapse.

Hutch's short battle with cancer would end on November 12, 1964, three months past his 45th birthday. His brother, who had supervised Fred's treatments, would found the Fred Hutchinson Cancer Research Center in the Hutchinson's home city of Seattle, which would become one of the leading cancer research facilities in the world. In 1965, major league baseball would establish the Hutch Award, given annually to the player who best exemplified Hutch's fighting spirit. Among the winners of the award would be players who had fought or were fighting their own battles with cancer or other diseases. Indeed, the 2008 winner, pitcher Jon Lester of the Red Sox, had received chemotherapy treatments for anaplastic large cell lymphoma at the Hutch Center in 2006.

*****

The 1963 pro football season formally ended on January 5 with the Chargers drubbing the Patriots, 51-10, in the fourth AFL championship game while the Packers beat the Browns, 40-23, in the NFL's Playoff Bowl at the Orange Bowl in Miami. The Playoff Bowl (officially named after Rozelle's predecessor as NFL commissioner, Bert Bell) was a game Vince Lombardi would term, among other epithets, "a loser's game for losers." It was sort of a consolation prize for the second-place finishers in each conference and would run through the '60s, ending with the completion of the NFL-AFL merger in 1970.

*****

With the Winter Olympic Games in Insbruck, Austria, fast approaching, the US figure skating championships in Cleveland received more than the usual attention and provided a peek at the future. Fifteen-year-old Peggy Fleming won the women's title and a place on the US Olympic team. The entire US figure skating team, including young Peggy's coach, had been killed in a plane crash three years earlier while en route

117

to the '61 world championships, so not much was expected of the '64 Olympic squad. But Fleming finished sixth in the women's competition and gave viewers a preview of the grace, beauty, and skating ability that would earn her a gold medal at the '68 Games in Grenoble, France. It's been said that America's modern love affair with figure skating began with their first look at Peggy Fleming.

This Winter Olympics was the first one held in the era of videotape, communications satellites, and relatively lightweight equipment. Sylvania had just introduced a cordless, lightweight (less than 30 pounds) portable TV camera with a built-in video transmitter and a rechargeable battery. ABC, which had already begun changing the way sports was covered on TV with its *Wide World of Sports* anthology series, had bought the rights to the Innsbruck Games and began using Sylvania's new cameras in its coverage. The lightweight cameras made it much easier to get the "up close and personal" look at the athletes introduced by ABC Sports executive producer Roone Arledge on "Wide World." With most of the events taking place in the morning in Austria, there was plenty of time to get the raw black-and-white footage transmitted to ABC's on-site studio. The videotapes were then flown to New York, and with no need to process film the tapes could quickly be prepared for broadcast on ABC's prime-time Olympics coverage at night. The telecasts, anchored by Jim McKay and with first-tier sportscasters and experts in each event providing color and analysis, was quite revolutionary when compared with coverage of the Squaw Valley and Rome Olympics just four years earlier. By 1968, satellite transmission of events in color would be possible and ABC would then truly become "the network of the Olympics."

The US wasn't expecting a large medal count at Insbruck and the best hope for gold came from women's skier Jean Saubert, who was the favorite to win both slalom races after winning four events that winter in Europe, including a victory over her primary competition, France's Marielle Goitschel, in the special slalom at the Silver Jag race in Bad Gastein, Austria. But Marielle and her sister Christine would turn the tables on Saubert at Insbruck. Christine won the gold medal in the women's slalom and Marielle snagged the silver, leaving Saubert with a disappointing bronze. Virtually the same thing happened in the giant slalom, with Marielle winning the gold this time.

With the US winning just that one medal in the first week of competition, most of the memorable moments of the Insbruck Games came from non-Americans. 23-year-old Egon Zimmerman of Austria handily won the showcase skiing event, the men's downhill. The Russian husband-wife team of Oleg and Ludmilla Protopopov won the pair's figure skating with a performance that would stay in the memory banks of spectators and TV viewers for decades to come. After being upset for the gold medal by the US hockey team in 1960 at Squaw Valley, the Soviets won seven straight at Insbruck by a combined 54-10 to reclaim the gold. And the top individual performance of the Games came from 24-year-old Russian speed-skater Lidia Skoblikova, who won four gold medals and even exuded a little sex appeal, a rarity for Russian athletes in that era.

But there were some upbeat moments for the Americans in the Games' final week, as they brought their medal count up to six. Fourteen-year-old New Jersey-ite Scotty Allen won the bronze in men's figure skating, making him the youngest medal winner in Winter Olympics history to that point in time. Two 20-year-old American skiers, Billy Kidd and Jimmy Heuga, won silver and bronze, respectively, in the men's slalom, the first men's skiing medals ever for the US And the biggest upset of the Insbruck Games came in the men's 500-meter speed-skating event. A 23-year-old apprentice barber from Essexville, Michigan, named Terry McDermott beat a field that included Russia's world speed-skating champion and record holder, Evgeny Grishin, even besting Grishin's Olympic record for the event. It was the lone American gold medal at Insbruck, and to the Russians McDermott's victory was an upset akin to the Soviet team's hockey loss in '60 and the "Miracle on Ice" US victory at Lake Placid 20 years later. On the way back home to his barber's chair, McDermott did stop off in New York to take a bow on *The Ed Sullivan Show* on February 9 and have a backstage photo op with the shaggy-headed quartet headlining that night's show.

*****

On February 18, that foursome, fresh off their second appearance on the Sullivan show, visited the training camp of Cassius Clay. The Liston-Clay fight was just a week away but the Louisville Lip was only too happy to do a photo op in the ring with his British visitors. Liston had been in the audience at that Sunday's Sullivan show at Miami Beach's Deauville Hotel with fight promoter Harold Conrad and former heavyweight champion Joe Louis, who would be a color commentator on the closed-circuit telecast of the fight. Sullivan introduced both Liston and Louis but the r&b/jazz-bred Liston was none too impressed with this rock 'n' roll band. He referred to them as "bums" and said that his sister

119

Just a few days before he "shook up the world," Cassius Clay stage-managed a photo session at his training camp with the foursome that was already shaking up the musical world.

could play drums better than "the kid with the big nose."

Clay, whose musical taste ran more toward Sam Cooke, a frequent visitor to his training camp, knew of The Beatles primarily because of all of the media attention their visit to America had attracted. During the photo op, he slightly revised his usual patter, saying that The Beatles were "the greatest" and that "the whole world is shook up about you." Cassius also set up most of the shots, almost all of which were arranged to Clay's advantage, and after the Beatle entourage had left the gym, Clay reportedly asked one of his handlers, "Who were those little faggots?" As the '60s progressed, though, there were observers who would look back on that photo op as a meeting of arguably the five most important pop culture figures of the decade.

Meanwhile, in the weeks leading up to the February 25 fight, there weren't a whole lot of people who gave Clay much of a chance against the menacing heavyweight champion. Henry Cooper, whose face had been sliced up by Clay's lightning-fast jabs in their fight the previous spring, had a prescient contrary opinion: "I'll bet Cassius makes him bleed for nine or 10 rounds. This fellow is fast and he boxes from a long distance. I think he'll give him a much harder fight than people think."

Media types, though, had a very different opinion. Jim Murray of the *Los Angeles Times*, one of the most respected sports columnists in the country, said that "the only thing at which Clay can beat Liston is reading the dictionary." With the championship fight deaths of Benny "Kid" Paret and Davey Moore fresh in mind, some were concerned for Clay's safety when he stepped into the ring with the hard-punching Liston. Clay's non-stop bragging, schlock poetry, and verbal abuse of Liston were seen not as self-promotion but a sure sign that Cassius was afraid and would somehow not make it into the ring. As fight day approached, Clay was a 7-1 underdog and most predictions had Liston scoring an early-round knockout while Clay held firm to his prediction, complete with a description set to verse, of an eighth-round knockout.

Clay took advantage of the suspicions that he was fearful of getting in the ring with Liston by putting on a wild scene at the pre-fight physical, shouting at Liston and having to be held back by his handlers. His heartbeat rate was sky-high and observers were convinced that Clay was "scared to death" and would never make the fight. But as soon as the Clay entourage was out of camera/microphone range, Cassius was completely calm and his heartbeat had very quickly returned to normal. As it turned out, Clay's strategy was based on his belief that Liston was nothing more than a bully and bullies were known to be afraid of "crazy people," so along with the wrestling-style self-hype Clay felt that he was getting into Liston's head, that Sonny would be the scared one.

Something else was going on while Clay was training for the fight, though. Malcolm X, the highest profile representative of the Black Muslims despite a December suspension for remarks he had made following the JFK assassination, had been seen numerous times at Clay's camp and rumors were circulating in the media that young Cassius was being courted by the black separatist sect. Since much of white America knew little about the Nation of Islam and was, to say the least, intimidated by Malcolm's rhetoric, the fight organizers and the Clay camp tried to quash any such speculation until after what was expected to be a very big payday for all concerned.

*****

On January 20, it was announced that NBC had bought the rights to the 1965 New Year's Day telecast of the Orange Bowl game in Miami, giving NBC the rights to the Sugar, Rose, and Orange Bowl games while CBS retained rights to the Cotton Bowl game. As well, though, the Orange Bowl was being moved to prime-time, beginning with the

'65 game. That guaranteed a full afternoon and, now, evening of college football throughout the country, most of it on the peacock network.

Four days later came bigger and more far-reaching news for sports on television. With the booming popularity of pro football and with the NFL's latest two-year contract with CBS at an end, Pete Rozelle decided to put the TV rights for NFL games up for bids from all three networks for the first time, rather than just negotiate a new deal with the current rights holder. The winning bid came from CBS, which would pay $28.3 million to retain NFL telecasts through '65. CBS's deal with the NFL for 1962-63 had cost just $9.3 million. Each of the 14 NFL franchises would get an equal slice of this much larger pie, enabling small-to-medium-market teams like the Packers and even the recent expansion franchises in Dallas and Minnesota to be competitive. The new deal also gave CBS the option of providing a late-afternoon West Coast game for certain markets on five or six Sundays during the '64 season. Thus was born the doubleheader telecast, which would be a crucial element in the creation of national fan bases for the Cowboys and the AFL-born Oakland Raiders, because younger fans would see those teams on a semi-regular basis on those late-afternoon games and begin following them with the same fervor that they had previously followed just their local heroes.

The new deal continued the blackout rule so no home games would be carried within a 75-mile radius of the home stadium but the teams did have the option of providing closed-circuit theater telecasts a la the Chicago viewings of the Bears' NFL title game victory.

Less than a week after the new CBS-NFL deal was announced, NBC, runner-up network in the bidding for the NFL games, signed a five-year, $36 million contract to televise American Football League games beginning with the '65 season. To put some perspective on this deal, the final year of ABC's charter deal with the newborn AFL would bring the league just short of $3 million in 1964. Under the NBC deal, each of the eight AFL franchises would reportedly receive about $100,000 a year over the five years of the contract. That infusion of cash would make possible big-money signings like the one that would bring Joe Namath to the Jets a year later and enable the AFL to fully compete in its bidding war with the NFL for high-profile players, which would lead to the merger talks between the two leagues in '66. As it turned out, NBC's deal with the AFL would run for the balance of the league's existence. With the merger going into full effect in 1970, all three networks would have a role in NFL telecasts, with NBC the primary outlet for the games played in what would be the NFL's American Football Conference.

With the ink on the NBC-AFL contract barely dry, the AFL's Houston Oilers pulled off what was thought to be a major victory over the NFL with the signing of Scott Appleton, All-American lineman for national college champion Texas, to a $104,000 contract. Appleton had been voted college football's top lineman of 1963 but would be much less successful in a six-year AFL career, including three unspectacular seasons in Houston. Next, ABC took an unprecedented route into the fray with the announcement that the network would televise five Friday night prime-time NFL games in September and October of '64, with the games beginning at 9 pm, Eastern time. This would mark the first time since the pro football boom began in the late '50s that NFL games would be televised in prime-time and it would mean that ABC would be carrying both NFL and AFL games that fall, since '64 was the final year of ABC's contract with the AFL.

But this plan opened a hornet's nest. Friday night was considered the domain of high school football, with some college football sprinkled in. Friday night high school games were an integral part of the autumnal atmosphere throughout the South and Southwest. The AFL did play some night games but those were generally on Saturday nights, after most high schools and colleges had played their games. Almost immediately, the NCAA challenged the plan and threatened to take it to court, as did organizations representing high school conferences from around the country. At a time when the heads of all four major team sports were lobbying Congress for a blanket antitrust exemption similar to the one major league baseball was awarded in a Supreme Court decision in 1922, the NFL didn't need this kind of adverse publicity and soon backed off the idea of Friday night telecasts, but the concept of a weekly prime-time NFL telecast was certainly something to be worked on. It would take until the NFL-AFL merger was fully consummated, but *Monday Night Football* would debut on ABC, the network that would have carried the '64 Friday night games, in September 1970. It should be added that, in the 21st century, NFL games would be played and televised on Thursday nights, Sunday nights, Monday nights, Sunday afternoons, of course, and Saturdays in December, once the college and high school football regular seasons had concluded. But the NFL would never again try to infringe on the sanctity of college and, particularly, high school football on Friday nights.

Meanwhile, though, baseball decided that this prime-time national telecast idea was a good one and wanted to stake out a similar claim.

What baseball proposed was a pair of regional prime-time games, one for the eastern and central time zones, one for the mountain and Pacific zones. They would be the only two games on the schedule so Monday night would be the logical slot for these televised games, since Monday generally tended to have a lighter schedule. The Monday night series would run for 26 weeks during the season, beginning in 1965, with no blackout restrictions. None of the three networks was interested in a 26-week commitment, since they all had prime-time entertainment shows in first-run until the beginning of summer and a new season of shows beginning in September. And with only the two games scheduled there was the matter of alternative programming if the one game in, say, the eastern half of the country was delayed by rain or postponed entirely. So there was little interest in baseball's proposal and it would take until 1972, after *Monday Night Football* had shown the viability of prime-time sports programming other than the Olympics, before NBC would begin carrying baseball in prime-time on Monday nights.

*****

In the '60s, the term "auto racing" generally meant races featuring the sleek, low-to-the-ground, very-high-speed vehicles that would come to be known as "Indy cars" because they were the type raced in the sport's glamour event, the Memorial Day Indianapolis 500. Stock car racing, including the events put on by the 16-year-old NASCAR, had a much less classy reputation. Many people tended to lump stock car racing in with drag racing, a perception not helped by the fact that some stock car drivers also raced dragsters. With NASCAR based in Daytona Beach, Fla., the stocks were perceived to be a regional pastime so not much national attention was given to the news on February 6 that 26-year-old NASCAR driver Richard Petty had become the first stock car driver to break the 170 mph mark. In a warm-up for a NASCAR event that Saturday, Petty, driving a 1964 Plymouth with a Hemi engine, reached 175 mph. Two weeks later on the same track, the Daytona Motor Speedway, the man who would later be dubbed "The King" of NASCAR racing would win the $33,300 top prize in NASCAR's glamour event, the Daytona 500. For Petty, that would be the first of a record seven Daytona 500 wins.

*****

Two nights after Petty's Daytona 500 win, the long wait for the Liston-Clay heavyweight championship fight finally came to an end. After provoking another wild scene at the weigh-in that morning, Cassius confounded many observers by not quitting in the dressing room at Convention Hall in Miami Beach or on the way to the ring or fleeing the arena entirely. Nonetheless, the fight-time Vegas odds had gone up to 8-1 for Sonny and United Press International's poll of 46 ringside reporters had three giving Clay a chance to win. During the pre-fight instructions from referee Barney Felix, though, Clay countered Liston's baleful stare with a fixed glare of his own.

From the opening bell, Clay hardly stopped moving, his shoe tops barely reaching the canvas as he circled to his left, occasionally to his right, his arms hanging languidly as if to invite Liston to try and hit him. Liston did try to counter the 6'3" Clay's long reach and got nothing but air. Then, late in the round, Clay stopped and let loose a barrage of lightning-fast punches to Liston's head. The supposedly "scared to death" kid could punch with the bully. Liston went on the offensive in Round 2 but his punches hardly landed while Clay's jabs were reddening Liston's face. In the third round, a Clay combination opened a mouse under Liston's right eye and a gash under the left eye, As Henry Cooper had predicted, Cassius was making Sonny bleed, something that had rarely happened before in Liston's fighting career.

Late in Round 4, Clay suddenly began having trouble seeing. A substance on Liston's gloves, perhaps medication for the cut under Liston's left eye or perhaps liniment, had gotten in Clay's eyes. When he got back to his corner at the end of the round, Clay told Angelo Dundee to cut his gloves off, which would have ended the fight and given Liston the win. But Dundee played for time as he wiped water into Cassius' eyes. Dundee got Clay off his stool and ready to fight and told him to run and dance away from Liston until his eyes cleared, which is precisely what Clay did in Round 5. Liston, who hadn't fought very much in the past couple of years, couldn't catch Clay, and when he did his punches were ineffective.

Sensing this and with his eyes now cleared, Clay went after Liston in Round 6. No longer dancing, Clay hit the champion with a flurry of punches that put Liston into a crouch. A try at a knockdown right missed but a series of jabs opened the cut under Liston's left eye again. Two left hooks spun Liston back but didn't knock him down. As the round ended, Cassius could see his prediction of an eighth-round knockout nearly becoming reality as he leaned through the ropes and told the assembled media, "I'm gonna upset the world!"

On the ABC Radio Network broadcast, a New York lawyer-turned-broadcaster named Howard Cosell was providing color for blow-by-blow man Les Keiter, and as Round 7 was about to start, he began screaming, "Sonny Liston's not coming out! Sonny Liston's not coming out! The new heavyweight champion of the world is Cassius Clay!" In what would become an eternal metaphor for losing, Liston quit on his stool. The excuse given later was that Sonny had hurt his shoulder earlier in the fight as he tried to hit Clay, but clearly Liston was being thoroughly beaten and chose to quit rather than be humiliated in the middle of the ring.

Upon seeing Liston spit out his mouthpiece, the new champion leaped to his feet and became a whirling dervish. He pointed to press row and yelled, "Eat your words!" He whooped it up with his handlers, ran from one end of the ring to the other, and could barely be contained for a post-fight interview for the closed-circuit telecast, during which he kept yelling, "I shook up the world! I shook up the world! I'm a bad man!"

In a scenario that would be magnified by the bizarre first-round TKO of Liston in the rematch 15 months later, some writers and fans at ringside immediately suspected the way the fight ended indicated that a "fix" was in, that Liston had taken a dive, a theory that wasn't all that outlandish given Liston's seamy reputation. Clay would have none of that. At the post-fight press conference, he harangued the writers. "Who's the greatest?" he kept asking before murmurs of "Cassius" or "You, you're the greatest" could be heard. The next day, the new champion held another press conference and confirmed the rumors that had been swirling around his training camp. He was joining the Nation of Islam. As well, he was changing his name. For now, he was just dropping the "Marcellus" and had been granted the name Cassius X, a la his friend Malcolm.

A few days later, Cassius headed for New York. On the heels of his *I Am The Greatest!* LP and winning the heavyweight championship, he returned to the Columbia Records studios and recorded a rather off-key version of Ben E. King's 1961 hit "Stand By Me" that would soon be released as a single, with the B-side being a mix of his "I Am The Greatest" poem with an instrumental backing. With an entourage that included Malcolm X, he visited the United Nations, setting off the biggest commotion in that building since Nikita Khrushchev's visit in the fall of 1960. Shortly thereafter, Nation of Islam (or Black Muslim) leader Elijah Muhammad announced that Cassius X was being renamed Muhammad Ali.

Not surprisingly, the overwhelmingly white, middle-aged, male media would have none of this, given their perception of the Black Muslims as a hate group. Only Cosell and veteran boxing broadcaster Don Dunphy would consistently refer to him as Muhammad Ali. For the balance of the '60s, most news stories identified him as Cassius Clay, perhaps with an "aka" or "who prefers to be known as." And once the new champion became a Black Muslim, it didn't take long for the subject of his draft status to come up. In early March, the Louisville Courier-Journal reported that he had twice flunked his pre-induction psychological exam. The legend of Cassius Clay had reached its tumultuous climax. The epic saga of Muhammad Ali was just beginning to unfold.

BEYOND THE FRINGE

October 1962: In the midst of the Cuban missile crisis, the pop-culture British Invasion reaches America with the Broadway debut of *Beyond the Fringe* (clockwise from top left: Alan Bennett – Peter Cook – Jonathan Miller – Dudley Moore).

CHAPTER 7

BROADWAY/BOOKS:
THE BRITISH ARE...ALREADY HERE

On December 10, 1963, the *New York Times* published details of an investigation by the office of New York state attorney general Louis Lefkowitz that had come up with the shocking, shocking news of a black market in the sale of tickets to Broadway shows. This black market was reported to net a conservative estimate of $10 million annually, with the help of employees from the theaters. Ticket brokers would pay "ice" ranging from 50 cents to $7 per ticket for blocks of tickets, which would then be sold for as high as $25 a ticket, even for non-hit shows, with many seats going to high-profile companies.

Of course, for anyone with more than an elementary knowledge of the New York theater scene, none of this was shocking at all. There had been a black market in Broadway and off-Broadway theater tickets for decades but this "revelation" simply illustrated how big the black market and its role in the legitimate theatre industry in New York had become. The story broke in the midst of a rather lackluster theatre season, with no breakout hits as the season neared its midpoint and the onset of winter.

The biggest hit of the season's first half (and the one show that didn't suffer a substantial loss of business in the days following the assassination of President Kennedy) was *Barefoot in the Park*, a Neil Simon-written comedy about the struggles of a newlywed couple, based on Simon's own days as a young married and starring two young acting "comers." Elizabeth Ashley had won a 1962 Tony award for best featured actress in a play for her work in *Take Her, She's Mine* while Robert Redford had won a '62 Theatre World award for his performance in *Sunday in New York* and both were familiar young faces to viewers of early '60s episodic television.

One of the more interesting new arrivals on Broadway, though certainly not a hit, was Dale Wasserman's stage adaptation of Ken Kesey's 1962 novel *One Flew Over the Cuckoo's Nest*. *Time* magazine called the central story "a duel in a loony bin" between the steely, unrelenting Nurse Ratched (Joan Tetzel) and the rule-bending, charismatic patient Randle McMurphy (Kirk Douglas). *Cuckoo's Nest* opened in mid-November and was gone before the end of January. Douglas, though, had obtained the filming rights, with an eye toward starring as McMurphy in a *Cuckoo's Nest* movie, but he would be unable to drum up interest from the Hollywood studios. A decade later, Kirk would pass the filming rights on to his son Michael, who would finally get the film made but (much to Kirk's annoyance) with Jack Nicholson as McMurphy and Louise Fletcher as Nurse Ratched. Their performances would win the best actor and actress Oscars for 1975, 12 years after original Broadway run of *Cuckoo's Nest*.

America was about to be hit with a musical "British Invasion," but there had been a heavy British presence both on and off Broadway and on US movie screens throughout 1963. *Stop The World - I Want To Get Off* had made a star of Anthony Newley, who co-wrote the show's book and musical score (including the show's breakout hit, "What Kind Of Fool Am I?"), along with playing the lead role. Albert Finney, fresh off great reviews (and a forthcoming Oscar nomination) for his onscreen performance in *Tom Jones*, made his Broadway stage debut in the role of religious reformer Martin Luther in *Luther*. Both *Tom Jones* and *Luther* were directed by Tony Richardson, who would become one of the best-known directors in the rising "new wave" in British filmmaking while also compiling a solid resume in stage direction. *Oliver!*, with its book and memorable musical score by Lionel Bart, had numerous standout performances, including Georgia Brown's show-stopping "As Long As He Needs Me" and the work of a young former apprentice jockey from Manchester playing the role of the Artful Dodger. David Jones had been nominated for a Tony for best featured actor in a musical for his first and only Broadway role and would become a teen idol some three years later as Davy Jones and as a member of The Monkees.

And then there was *Beyond The Fringe*.

Beyond The Fringe grew out of the late '50s/early '60s vogue for satirical comedy at a number of English universities, particularly Cambridge and Oxford. Undeniably influenced by the absurdist comedy of *The Goon Show*, but also by the socio/political goings-on of the day, revues like *Cambridge Footlights* had rapidly gained in popularity in the late '50s, especially at the annual Edinburgh International Festival for the performing arts. It was at that festival in 1960 that *Beyond The Fringe* first came to prominence.

All four members of the *Fringe* cast had been university students and had taken part in various revues. Jonathan Miller had already qualified to be a medical doctor. Alan Bennett had a degree in history and appeared to be en route to a career as an academic. Dudley Moore had studied music/composition and performed in the *Oxford Revue* with Bennett. And Peter Cook was rescued from a possible career in the British diplomatic corps by his ability to write and perform comedy.

Following its breakthrough at Edinburgh, it didn't take long for *Beyond The Fringe* to make it to London's West End, the British equivalent of Broadway. Helped greatly by a thumbs-up review from the notoriously-picky Kenneth Tynan, the revue became a London sensation. *Fringe* broke particular new ground with its less-than-reverential treatment of the British effort in World War II, Prime Minister Harold Macmillan's current British government, and even the royal family. This reflected the attitude of the generation of British youth that had been born during the war or in the years surrounding it and grew up with the varied consequences of the war. The success of *Fringe* began what came to be known as a "satire boom" in England that would reverberate through the decade and beyond and spread into the realms of movies, television, and even pop music, with Cook and Moore the boom's symbolic godfathers and a continuing presence through nearly all of it.

Then, the famed Broadway producer/director Alexander H. Cohen brought *Beyond The Fringe* to America. The show's October 1962 Broadway opening took place right in the middle of the Cuban missile crisis and the American audience had little frame of reference for this type of comedy. Nonetheless, *Fringe* became a trail-blazing Broadway hit. A revamped *Fringe*, dubbed *Beyond The Fringe '64*, debuted in January, right about the time that its four stars were appearing on television in a CBS adaptation of Jules Verne's *From The Earth To The Moon*. As well, along with the aforementioned Anglo-bred shows playing on the

Great White Way, a *Fringe*-style show called *The Establishment* debuted off-Broadway in the fall of '63 and a revue called *Cambridge Circus* would spend about 3 weeks on Broadway a year later, with a cast of writer-performers that would include Graham Chapman and John Cleese, both future members of the Monty Python comedy troupe that would arguably be the greatest example of the legacy of *Beyond The Fringe*.

As *Fringe '64* was being prepared for its January rollout, more traditional English fare was also being presented on Broadway in *The Girl Who Came to Supper*, a musical based on Terence Rattigan's 1953 play *The Sleeping Prince* with a book by Harry Kurnitz and a score by the great Noel Coward. The show was set in London in 1911 at the time of the coronation of King George V and starred Jose Ferrer as the Prince Regent of the fictional country of Carpathia and Florence Henderson, at 29 already a veteran of better than a decade on the Great White Way, as an American showgirl. The show had a fine pedigree, since Rattigan's play had been a success on the stage in London and New York and in a 1957 film, *The Prince and the Showgirl*, starring Laurence Olivier and Marilyn Monroe. But, during the pre-Broadway trials for *Supper*, the opening number, "Long Live The King (If He Can)," had to be pulled following the president's assassination. When the show had its Broadway debut on December 8, reviews were tepid at best. What remained of Coward's score didn't have a single breakout song but Henderson received good notices for what turned out to be her final Broadway role. In the coming years, she would become an increasing presence on TV, most notably, of course, in the role of Carol Brady on *The Brady Bunch*.

But the show's best reviews went to a 50-year-old song-and-dance lady from Cardiff, Wales. Tessie O'Shea had been a popular presence in British music halls, cinema, on BBC radio, and on record since the '30s. She was, in effect, a British distillation of Sophie Tucker. Indeed, *Time* referred to O'Shea as "raucous, sentimental, funny and bawdy," terms used for years to describe Tucker's "last of the red hot mamas" on-stage persona. But O'Shea was virtually unknown in the US, having never appeared on an American stage. But Coward created the role of fish-and-chips peddler Ada Cockle specifically for O'Shea and her extended medley of old-time English chestnuts would earn her a Tony for featured actress in a musical. It also earned O'Shea a berth on the February 9 *Ed Sullivan Show*, a British-flavored episode featuring Tessie, the cast of *Oliver!*, and the live American debut of The Beatles, making that show a true British pop culture changing of the guard. O'Shea's performance, which included her theme song, "Two-Ton Tessie From Tennessee," became immortalized because that episode of the Sullivan show garnered the highest ratings for any entertainment program in US television history to that point in time. By the '80s, the multi-generational popularity of The Beatles would be primarily responsible for that episode becoming the most-requested program at New York's new Museum of TV & Radio (later dubbed the Paley Center for longtime CBS head William Paley) and it would belatedly be released for home video in a 2004 DVD set, nine years after Tessie O'Shea's death at the age of 82.

While the first half of the Broadway season was considered to be rather lackluster, help was on the way in the form of two new musicals scheduled to debut in the first two months of '64. *Hello Dolly!*, with music by Jerry Herman and starring Carol Channing in the title role, opened its pre-Broadway trial run in Washington on December 18 with its New York bow scheduled for January 16. And *Funny Girl*, a promising musical based on the life of stage and radio star Fanny Brice and starring Barbra Streisand, very much on the rise due to her club work and a debut turn on Broadway in *I Can Get It For You Wholesale*, was scheduled to hit the Great White Way on February 27 but there were public signs of trouble as early as December, when it was announced that Brice's son-in-law Ray Stark had bought out David Merrick's share of the show's production amid rumors of discord between the two.

Stark had long wanted to produce a chronicle of Fanny's tempestuous life, especially her relationship with noted gambler/con artist Nicky Arnstein, but a book treatment based on Brice's taped memoirs was halted by Stark before publication. He rejected numerous attempts to craft a screenplay for a biopic before, in the very early '60s, he accepted a Isobel Lennart screenplay entitled *My Man*. Stark was ready to accept a movie deal with Columbia Pictures for *My Man* when veteran Broadway star Mary Martin suggested that Lennart's screenplay might work better as a stage musical. Early in 1962, Stark took Martin's suggestion to Merrick, who recommended Jules Styne and Stephen Sondheim as possible composers for a musical score. Sondheim, though, felt that a more ethnic (Jewish) actress than Martin was needed to play Brice. Quickly, though, both Sondheim and Martin bowed out of the project.

Next, Merrick brought veteran producer/director/choreographer Jerome Robbins into the show-building process and Robbins gave Lennart's screenplay to Anne Bancroft, who was offered the title role and accepted, but only if the musical score was right for her. Meanwhile,

Barbra Streisand starring in a musical based on the life of Fanny Brice should have been a fast-track Broadway hit. But that track had some potholes.

lyricist Dorothy Fields turned down an offer to compose the score with Styne so he went ahead and composed a set of melodies that he felt would fit Bancroft's range. Shortly, another noted lyricist, Bob Merrill, came on board and he and Styne completed the score. But Bancroft pulled out because of a past falling-out with Merrill. Are we sensing a fractious trend here?

Eydie Gorme was next approached for the lead role, but she would take it on only if her husband, Steve Lawrence, was given the Arnstein role. Lawrence was judged by Stark, Robbins, and Merrick to not be right for the role so exit Eydie. Carol Burnett was contacted but, echoing Sondheim's sentiments, she felt that Fanny should be portrayed by a Jewish woman. Finally, in the fall of '62, Styne remembered young Streisand, who had become a near-fixture at the Bon Soir in Greenwich Village, and suggested that Robbins see her show. Robbins immediately offered her an audition and, despite her bohemian wardrobe at the tryout, Stark then offered Barbra the part.

Despite finally having a lead actress, though, more trouble ensued. Robbins felt that a writer other than Lennart could better adapt her original screenplay and produce a book suitable for a Broadway musical. Stark sided with Lennart and, in September 1962, Robbins quit the project. With things at a standstill for a considerable time, Merrick brought in Bob Fosse to direct the show. It didn't take long, though, before Fosse quit. Next, Merrick brought in renowned writer/director Garson Kanin, who took over the director's duties in September of '63. Soon after, though, Merrick and Stark had the falling-out that led to Stark buying out Merrick's share of the show.

Inevitably, friction developed between Kanin and Streisand when Kanin suggested that the centerpiece song of the Styne-Merrill score, "People," be cut from the show because he felt that the song didn't fit the Brice character (Robbins and Fosse reportedly had the same inclination). During the stop-and-start process of putting *Funny Girl* together, Streisand had begun a recording career that had taken off practically from day one, with two Top Ten LPs during '63 and a third ready to be released early in '64. She had also made a studio recording of "People" that was slated to be released as a single shortly after the opening of *Funny Girl* so Streisand and Styne protested any attempt to cut "People" from the show, with Styne claiming, "It has to be in the show because it's the greatest thing she's ever done." Kanin relented and decided to let audience reaction decide the song's fate.

Funny Girl was slated to debut at the Winter Garden Theater and was to be preceded there by the return to Broadway of Josephine Baker. Baker was a black singer/dancer/actress who, while born in St. Louis and something of a black pioneer in her early stage work, instead became a superstar in France in the '20s, '30s, and '40s and made that country her home. "La Baker," as she was universally known in France, was a major supporter of and participant in the French Underground and Resistance during World War II and later was a strong proponent of the civil rights movement in her native country, including an appearance at the March on Washington. But she had not performed on Broadway since receiving very negative reviews for her numbers in *Ziegfeld Follies of 1936*. By the '60s, though, Baker had become a cultural muse for numerous singers, actresses, painters, photographers, etc. so her professional return to New York was long-awaited. Her two-week engagement in February was moved to the Brooks Atkinson Theatre and was very successful (even while being somewhat overshadowed by the wild scenes of Beatlemania breaking out just blocks away), so successful and so well-received that La Baker's undeniable star power would require a return engagement of three weeks at Henry Miller's Theatre at the end of March.

Star power has always been good for what ails Broadway and one of its brightest stars of more recent times returned on December 19 with the opening of *Nobody Loves an Albatross*. Robert Preston, who had achieved Great White Way fame in the '50s, most notably as Harold Hill in *The Music Man*, starred as delusional TV producer/writer Nat Bentley, with the entire play staged in Bentley's Beverly Hills living room. As Walter Kerr put it in the *New York Herald-Tribune,* "He just keeps dancing around his living room pretending to be as many other people as possible." It was basically Preston's star power that would keep this not very memorable show running until June of '64.

One new technological option that was thought to enable producers of lower-profile Broadway and off-Broadway shows to showcase their productions was videotaping the shows for telecast via pay TV. For instance, the off-Broadway production of *The Streets of New York* was scheduled to be videotaped and shown on a pay system in Hartford on December 21 and again on Christmas night. The telecast would cost viewers $2 and would be provided by RKO-General Phone Vision. *Spoon River* was slated to be the next play shown via this setup in January, but the show closed before it could be videotaped and the entire concept never developed any momentum, either within the theater business or with the public. But RKO-General's New York free TV outlet, WOR, did carry a videotaped performance from London of Langston Hughes's controversial *Black Nativity* on December 22.

Another potential attention-grabbing option was the advance publication of the script for a Broadway-quality play, a concept that made particular sense when the script's author was no less than Arthur Miller and the script was his first major work since his '50s battles with the House Un-American Activities Committee and his ultimately-failed marriage to Marilyn Monroe. Indeed, *After The Fall* was very much a product of that time and the *Saturday Evening Post*, which had never carried a complete script, leaped at the chance to run *After The Fall* in its February 1 issue.

Miller's close friendship with famed director Elia Kazan was almost permanently ended by Kazan's infamous 1952 testimony before HUAC, in which he implicated several colleagues as members of the Communist Party. By 1963, though, they had at least professionally reconciled to the point where they collaborated on some of the script and direction for *After The Fall*, though Kazan is officially listed alone as director and Miller is listed as sole writer of the play.

After The Fall was the first play produced by the Repertory Theatre of Lincoln Center, which was helmed by Kazan and Robert Whitehead. The play opened on January 23 at the ANTA Washington Square Theatre in Greenwich Village, where it would run as part of the group repertory (including Miller's *Incident at Vichy*) through May 1965. Controversy flared up around *After The Fall* almost immediately because the lead female character, Maggie, was deemed to be too close for comfort to Monroe, only about a year and a half after Marilyn's death. Nonetheless, Barbara Loden's performance as Maggie received very positive notices and, that spring, she would win a Tony for best featured actress in a play while Jason Robards Jr. would be nominated for best featured actor for his performance as the 40-something lawyer Quentin, Miller's thinly-veiled fictional alter ego. A young actress named Faye Dunaway had a bit part as a nurse in *After The Fall* and, a decade later, she would star as Maggie in a television production of Miller's play. Most of the critical reaction, though, centered on the confessional nature of the play. *Time*'s review called *After The Fall* "a memory book of betrayals, a soliloquy with his conscience, an exorcism of guilt, an intimate manual of bad marriages, a chronicle of the birth of a writer, a dirge for the death of love, and underlying all, tormented but intellectualized quest for self-justification."

With the grousing about the state of theatre in general and Broadway in particular midway through the 1963-64 season, more than the normal level of attention was given to the pre-Christmas debut of a new production from Lee Strasberg's Actors Studio. *Marathon '33* was written and directed by June Havoc and starred Julie Harris as a former vaudeville child star (which Havoc, whose sister was the iconic stripper Gypsy Rose Lee, had herself been) in one of the dance marathons that offered quick money fixes in the Depression-era America of the early '30s. Havoc, Harris, and co-star Lee Allen would all be nominated for Tonys for *Marathon '33* but, despite generally good reviews and even though it covered much the same territory as 1969's multi-Oscar-nominated film *They Shoot Horses, Don't They?*, *Marathon '33* was only around for 48 performances and was gone from Broadway by early February.

By the middle of January, *Barefoot in the Park*, having made back all of its production costs and then some, was proclaimed the biggest hit of the 1963-64 Broadway season. That was about to change.

Even during somewhat bumpy out-of-town trials, *Hello Dolly!* gradually took on the look and momentum of a very big hit show. With an estimated $500,000 in advance ticket orders already in hand, producer Merrick was able to announce, three days before the show's January 16 official opening, that he would not be providing tickets for brokers during the show's early run, a sure sign of an out-of-the-box hit.

The first reviews from opening night bubbled over with enthusiasm. Howard Taubman of the *New York Times* praised *Hello Dolly!* for "freshness and imagination that are rare" and composer Jerry Herman's score as "brisk and always tuneful." He proclaimed the show "the best musical of the season." A brief review in *Time* stated that the show had "eye appeal, ear appeal, love appeal, and laugh appeal, but its most insinuative charm is its nostalgia appeal." After all, Thornton Wilder's mid-'50s play *The Matchmaker*, (itself a reworking of Wilder's 1938 play *The Merchant of Yonkers*) with its portrayal of New York in a bygone age, provided the basis for *Hello Dolly!*

The show's star, Carol Channing, received lavish praise, though *Time*'s review cautioned that "the clown in Carol Channing sometimes upstages the actress, but this show thrives on her kind of showoff." The *New York Daily News'* review, though, proclaimed Channing "the most outgoing woman on the musical stage today -- all eyes and smiles." Gower Champion came in for special praise from *Time* for his choreography and "agile, toe-perfect dance company" while the *New York Journal-American*'s John McClain noted, "Seldom has a corps of dancers brought so much style and excitement to a production." And the hard-to-please Walter Kerr in the *New York Herald-Tribune* called *Hello Dolly!* "a musical comedy dream." The public's response to the rave notices could be seen the morning after the show's opening in the lines forming outside the St. James Theater by 10 am. Box office receipts for that day alone were estimated at $25,000. And, of course, those lines made a most inviting high-profile target for the ongoing black-market-in-tickets investigation. Six men spotted on the lines by state investigators were subpoenaed by state attorney general Lefkowitz's office, but only three showed up for questioning.

Hello Dolly! marked Herman's breakthrough as a big-time Broadway composer and Richard Watts Jr. of the *New York Post* commented that Herman's score "is always pleasant and agreeably tuneful although the only number that comes to mind at the moment is the lively title song." Indeed, that title song would take on a life of its own during 1964.

Even as the show's cast album was being quickly recorded and released, the legendary Louis Armstrong recorded the title song and Decca Records' Kapp subsidiary rushed a single out, which debuted on *Billboard*'s Hot 100 singles chart in mid-February, right in the middle of The Beatles' first visit to America. The single would reach the Top Ten by late March and then do the seemingly-impossible in the first full week of May. "Hello Dolly!" would break The Beatles' 14-

week hammerlock on the number one position on *Billboard*'s chart. It would occupy the top spot for just that one week but Louis's recording would spend a very impressive 22 weeks on *Billboard*'s chart, quite a long chart run for a single in that era. By comparison, The Beatles' first two multi-week number one singles that winter, "I Want to Hold Your Hand" and "She Loves You," each spent 15 weeks on the Hot 100. The combination of the title song of the hottest show on Broadway and the multi-generational appeal of this jazz legend and frequent TV variety show guest gave the Armstrong version of "Hello Dolly!" the impetus for a lengthy stay on the hit parade.

The *Hello Dolly!* cast album was recorded just three days after the show's opening, was quickly released by RCA Victor, and began a nearly-two-year run on *Billboard*'s album chart in the last week of February. The cast LP would leap into the album Top Ten in the first week in March and, after spending 12 weeks in the Top Five, would halt The Beatles' 16-week run at number one on that chart by the first week in June. But the cast album would be knocked from its perch the very next week by the rush-released *Hello Dolly!* LP by Armstrong, which would remain at the top for six weeks. Nonetheless, the *Hello Dolly!* cast album would remain among *Billboard*'s Top Ten LPs through the end of October, by which time the title song had become the unofficial theme of Lyndon Johnson's landslide-bound campaign for his own term as president.

The '64 Tonys would confirm the tremendous impact that *Hello Dolly!* had made on Broadway in a very short time. Channing, Herman, and Champion would all win individual Tonys (Champion would win two, for best choreography and best direction of a musical), as would producer Merrick and Michael Stewart, who wrote the show's book, and the show would claim the big award as best musical. All told, *Hello Dolly!* would be nominated for eleven '64 Tonys and would win ten. It would take until the beginning of the 21st century before another show (*The Producers*) would enjoy a better Tony night.

The massive success of *Hello Dolly!* would launch the golden age of the long-running Broadway musical mega-hit. There had, of course, been very successful Broadway musicals for decades but relatively few were long-running classics on the scale of *Oklahoma*, *South Pacific*, or *My Fair Lady*. *Hello Dolly!* would eventually replace *My Fair Lady* as the longest-running musical in Broadway annals, but it would quickly relinquish that title to *Fiddler on the Roof*, which would open just eight months after *Hello Dolly!* debuted. The number of similar mega-hits would grow as the '60s progressed and would really accelerate in the '70s and beyond. Nonetheless, nearly a half-century after its Broadway debut, *Hello Dolly!* would still be among the 20 longest-running shows in Broadway's illustrious history.

On the final Sunday of 1963, almost exactly two months before its scheduled Broadway premiere, a full-page ad for advance tickets for the other much-anticipated new Broadway musical, *Funny Girl*, appeared in the *New York Times*. Advance seat prices ranged from $3 for upper mezzanine matinee seats up to $9.40 for weekend night orchestra seats. *Funny Girl* was scheduled to begin its pre-Broadway run in Boston on January 13 and would move on to Philadelphia February 4-15.

The show's bumpy road to on-stage reality seemed to have finally smoothed out when formal rehearsals began on December 6 with a cast and crew that included a 19-year-old musical prodigy named Marvin Hamlisch, who was serving as Barbra Streisand's pianist for the rehearsals. But nothing seemed to go smoothly for this show. There was dissatisfaction with the script and the musical score throughout the rehearsals. A half-hour had been cut from the show by the time it began its out-of-town trials at the Shubert Theatre in Boston, but the first reviews, which gave Streisand high praise, still indicated that the three-hour show was too long and there were problems with the show's book. Or, as William E. Sarmento of the *Lowell Sun* put it, "It is in rough shape and needs plenty of help." During the Boston run, the second act had been reconstructed and three new songs had been inserted into the score.

By the time *Funny Girl* moved to the Forrest Theater in Philadelphia in early February, Garson Kanin was out as director and Jerome Robbins had returned, this time as "production supervisor." Choreographer Carol Haney suddenly left the show and would die at just 39 years of age that May from pneumonia. Another half-hour had been cut from the show's stage time and songs were being shuttled in and out of the score (Jules Styne biographer Theodore Taylor indicated that some 56 songs were written for the show at one point or another in the show's development). But the first reviews from Philly still indicated that there were problems with Isobel Lennart's book.

It was becoming obvious that *Funny Girl* would not make its scheduled February 27 Broadway opening. Ray Stark would push opening night back five times while Robbins tried to make the necessary repairs as the show moved to Philly's Erlanger Theatre.

Amid all this turmoil, there was no doubt that the show's biggest asset was Streisand (she would make the cover of *Time* in the second week in April) and its musical pivot point was "People." The song that Fosse, Kanin, and Robbins had felt wasn't right for the show was recorded by Streisand in December and rush-released as a single by Columbia Records in January, well in advance of even the original Broadway opening night so the preview audiences in Boston and Philadelphia were becoming familiar with the song through airplay on radio stations with pop standards and/or easy listening formats. With Top 40 radio in the throes of the first wave of Beatlemania, "People" wouldn't reach *Billboard*'s Hot 100 singles chart until the first week in April, ultimately spending two weeks in the Top Five at the beginning of that summer. But, with Streisand's third studio LP also out in the weeks before the opening of *Funny Girl* and the show's cast album released that spring, a *People* album would be held back until the end of the summer, but the strategy would pay off with *People* ending the 12-week number one run of the soundtrack from The Beatles' first film, *A Hard Day's Night*, at the top of *Billboard*'s album chart and remaining there for the entire month of November. By that time, "People" had become Streisand's signature song and would remain so for the balance of the '60s.

Funny Girl would finally reach Broadway for 17 previews before the show's official opening on March 26 and, just over a month after the show's opening, all of the false starts and conflicts and media criticism would pay off with eight Tony nominations to go with a string of sold-out performances. Unfortunately for *Funny Girl*, with the *Hello Dolly!* Tony night juggernaut, *Funny Girl* would go without a win, but the show, even with Streisand leaving at the end of 1965 to star in the London West End production, would remain a Broadway fixture until July 1967.

Just two nights after the Broadway debut of *Hello Dolly!*, more star power came to Broadway with the debut of a new play by Sidney Michaels called *Dylan*. Based on John Malcolm Brinnin's book *Dylan Thomas in America* and Caitlin Thomas' memoir *Leftover Life To Kill*, Alec Guinness starred as the hard-living and ultimately doomed Welsh poet, with Kate Reid as wife Caitlin. Best known to Americans for his Oscar-winning performance in 1957's *The Bridge on the River Kwai* and, more recently, his role as Prince Feisal opposite Peter O'Toole in 1962's epic *Lawrence of Arabia*, Guinness had been a distinguished presence on stage and screen in England since the end of World War II. Most reviews of *Dylan* lavished praise on both Guinness and Reid. *Time* noted the "smoky anguish" in Guinness's eyes, that "Perfectly miming every state of alcoholic disequilibrium, Guinness does a dance of death at ever-varying tempos," and that Reid was "shatteringly good in portraying the kind of woman who marries her author ego." *Dylan* would be nominated for four Tonys, with Guinness winning the award for best actor in a play, but the play itself would have a Broadway run of less than eight months.

Dylan Thomas wasn't the only public figure of recent vintage being portrayed on Broadway that winter. Peter Falk, just beginning to hit his stride as a character actor, took on a portrayal of Josef Stalin, whose reign of Soviet terror had ended with his death just a few weeks short of 11 years earlier, in *The Passion of Josef D.*, a play written and directed by the much-honored playwright Paddy Chayefsky. But Chayefsky's attempt at a portrait of Stalin at the time of the Bolshevik Revolution fell flat, even in the very capable hands of Falk. *Time*'s review praised Falk for portraying Stalin as "a menacing thug with a will of granite," but the same review panned the play as one that "incessantly lectures and never electrifies." What would turn out to be Chayefsky's final Broadway effort played just 11 performances in February.

But that winter's most controversial new arrival on Broadway included a very unflattering portrayal of Pope Pius XII, dead for a little over five years. *The Deputy* was a five-act play by Rolf Hochhuth that had debuted in West Berlin almost exactly a year before a condensed version adapted by Jerome Rothenberg opened on Broadway and had in the interim been performed in several European countries (including an English adaptation by the Royal Shakespeare Company in London). Huchhuth's play accused Pius XII and the Vatican hierarchy of allowing, by saying and doing virtually nothing, the rounding-up of Roman Jews by the Gestapo, who sent them to Hitler's Auschwitz concentration camp and, ultimately, their deaths. The central figure in the play is Father Riccardo Fontana (Jeremy Brett), a Jesuit priest serving with the papal nuncio in Berlin. After learning about Hitler's "final solution" from an SS official, Kurt Gerstein (Phil Bruns), Fontana uses papal connections (his father and a cardinal high in the Vatican command) to get an audience with Pius XII (Emlyn Williams). He tells the pontiff what he's found out about Hitler's plans and implores Pius to publicly condemn Hitler. Pius replies that he's aware of Hitler's already-executed crimes, but he feels that a strong Germany is necessary, given the looming threat of Stalin's Soviets, and has to consider the financial effects on the Vatican if he were to speak out. Pius does dictate a vague, non-committal statement for public release, but Fontana denounces him for having "hid when he was summoned." Fontana then joins the deportees and they're sent to

Auschwitz, where Fontana ultimately dies.

The controversy relating to Pius XII's alleged inaction would endure for decades, as would performances of *The Deputy*. The Rothenberg adaptation of Hochhuth's play, helmed by veteran producer/director Herman Shumlin, would outlast the picketing of early performances and have a Broadway run of just over nine months. Shumlin would soon be nominated for Tonys for both best direction and best production of a drama and would win the best producer Tony.

On February 27, the night after the tumultuous opening of *The Deputy*, a much more traditional piece of Broadway fare debuted. *What Makes Sammy Run?* was a musical semi-comedy that had begun life in 1941 as a novel by Budd Schulberg that told the story of Sammy Glick, a Jewish kid from the Lower East Side who was determined to make good in the newspaper business and, later, the Hollywood of the '30s, by any means necessary. Glick's story was told in the novel by newspaperman Al Manheim of the fictitious *New York Record* and Manheim also developed into one of the book's lead characters. Two TV dramatizations of Schulberg's book were produced during the so-called "golden age of TV drama," one in 1949 and a second ten years later. It would take better than four more years before a musical version of *What Makes Sammy Run?* would reach Broadway. Budd Schulberg and his brother Stuart collaborated on adapting the original novel for the stage, Ervin Drake wrote the musical score, and well-known radio//TV/stage writer Abe Burrows quite effectively took over the directorial duties while the show was having its trial run on the road in the last weeks of '63.

Robert Alda, who had starred on Broadway a decade earlier as Sky Masterson in *Guys and Dolls*, deftly handled the Manheim role while Sally Ann Howes ably took on the role of the central love interest, Kit Sargent. But the casting of the lead role was a puzzlement. The role of Sammy Glick went to Steve Lawrence, less than a decade removed from being Steve Allen's resident TV "boy singer" and perhaps best known for having married the Allen show's "girl singer," Eydie Gorme, who then became Lawrence's professional partner in one of pop music's best-known duet acts. Steve & Eydie also had ongoing successful recording careers, together and solo, with each having had major hit singles in the early '60s. But Lawrence had never appeared in a Broadway show, much less starred in one. As noted earlier, when Gorme was approached regarding the lead role in *Funny Girl*, she said she would take it only if Lawrence was given the lead male role, a role for which Lawrence was judged to be not the right fit at all. So casting Lawrence in the starring role in *What Makes Sammy Run?* was considered to be quite a gamble. But his notices in the early reviews were quite positive. *Time* noted that, as Glick, Lawrence "moves with the wary savage grace of a jungle cat." Indeed, Lawrence would gain a Tony nomination for best actor in a musical and *What Makes Sammy Run?* would have a better-than-expected Broadway life, running until June 1965.

Somewhat overshadowed by all the attention given to Channing's starring performance in *Hello Dolly!* and the raves being lavished on Streisand as *Funny Girl* headed toward Broadway was the breakout star of the four-person cast of *Any Wednesday*, a romantic comedy that debuted on February 18. 26-year-old Sandy Dennis already possessed an impressive resume. She had won a 1961 Theatre World award for her work in the short-lived *The Complaisant Lover*, received good notices that same year for her film debut in *Splendor in the Grass*, and was awarded a 1963 Tony for best featured actress in a play for her work opposite such heavyweight acting talent as Jason Robards, Jr. and William Daniels in *A Thousand Clowns*. But Dennis was given the pivotal character role in *Any Wednesday* and was also the pivot point of the show's reviews. For instance, *Time*'s review began, "Any Wednesday has Sandy Dennis. No other play can make a statement half so adorable."

Dennis's performance, as somewhat ditzy mistress Ellen Gordon, made up for the fact that *Any Wednesday* was really a fairly conventional sex comedy. Don Porter, best known to audiences of the day as Ann Sothern's '50s TV boss, played corporate big-shot John Cleves, who had set up Ellen in the tax-write-off East Side Manhattan apartment that is the play's sole setting, while Rosemary Murphy played Cleve's wife, Dorothy. The fourth member of the cast was 34-year-old Gene Hackman, playing small businessman Cass Henderson, who is mistakenly sent to the apartment and ends up falling in love with Ellen. With just the one setting and four characters, the Muriel Resnik-written script was just a shade better than TV sitcom fare. Nonetheless, the raves lavished on Dennis produced enough buzz to propel *Any Wednesday* to a Broadway run of nearly 2-and-a-half years, followed by a 1966 feature film treatment. Murphy, who had been nominated for a '64 Tony for best featured actress in a play, would be the lone member of the original Broadway cast to reprise her role in the film.

Not surprisingly, Dennis would win the Tony for lead actress in a play and appeared to have as much fast-track potential as any young actress on the Great White Way. Indeed, at the beginning of March, *Time* ran a profile of Dennis and Elizabeth Ashley of *Barefoot in the Park* as the leading lights among the young female acting talents on Broadway. Their career paths, though, would ultimately take some radical detours.

Dennis would attain spectacular success on the silver screen over the next several years. She would win the best supporting actress Oscar for her performance opposite Elizabeth Taylor and Richard Burton in *Who's Afraid of Virginia Woolf*, very positive reviews for her work in *Up The Down Staircase* (arguably Dennis's best-remembered film role) and *The Fox*, and a 1971 Golden Globe nomination for her role as Jack Lemmon's harried wife in *The Out of Towners*. But Dennis's very idiosyncratic acting style would fall out of favor in the '70s and her best later work would be done on the stage, in *Same Time Next Year* and, in the early '80s, both the stage and screen versions of *Come Back to the 5 and Dime, Jimmy Dean, Jimmy Dean*. Sadly, Dennis would lose a short battle with ovarian cancer in March 1992, just a few weeks short of her 55th birthday.

After a mid-'60s flirtation with high-profile feature film roles and a turbulent personal life in the '60s and '70s, Ashley would carve out a lengthy career in TV and stage work, including an early '90s stint as part of the outstanding ensemble cast of the *Evening Shade* TV series. But her most memorable roles were on the stage, particularly her performances in the plays of her close friend Tennessee Williams, including her three-decades-apart stints as Maggie and Big Mama, respectively, in Williams' *Cat on a Hot Tin Roof*.

*****

Firmly ensconced at the top of most fiction book best seller lists late in the fall of '63 and through much of the winter was a novel called *The Group*, a semi-autobiographical tale by author Mary McCarthy of a group of 1933 graduates from Vassar College and the paths their lives took through the Depression decade and toward the onset of World War II. McCarthy was already quite well-known from some two decades of fine work as a critic and satirist, as a defender of liberal causes, as an outspoken critic of both (Senator Joe) McCarthyism and Communism while admitting to being a Trotskyite, and as a critically-acclaimed novelist for 1942's *The Company She Keeps*. But *The Group* was a far more adventurous novel, dealing frankly with premarital sex, contraception and abortion, breast-feeding, and lesbianism, topics rarely covered in a work by such a "highbrow" writer. *The Group* would ultimately spend some two years on the *New York Times* best seller list, but all that success would come at a price. Vassar virtually disowned McCarthy, as did several of the women fictionally depicted in the book. And Norman Mailer, hardly a shrinking violet when it came to graphic prose, denounced *The Group* in the *New York Review of Books* as "a trivial lady writer's novel," a view shared by many of McCarthy's literary colleagues and supposed friends. But the social and literary influence of *The Group* would grow over the years and, in fact, outlive McCarthy (who, in an interview shortly before her death in 1989, declared that the success of the book "ruined my life"). In the first decade of the 21st century, an episode from the 1963-set third season of the *Mad Men* TV series showed Betty Draper, the then-wife of the show's lead character, reading a copy of *The Group* while relaxing in a bubble bath and the book would also get a mention in the November '63-set premiere episode of the Dick Clark-produced *American Dreams* series in 2002.

More significantly, though, as Elizabeth Day of *The Observer* would point out in a November 2009 piece in the British newspaper *The Guardian*, shortly before the book's reissue, "It had a lasting impact on subsequent generations of female writers." Claire Tomalin, a biographer by trade, told Day, "She (McCarthy) opened a further door into brutal frankness. There was something so crisp and clever and bold about her writing." The foreword to that 2009 reissue of *The Group* would be written by Candace Bushnell, the author of an early '90s collection of essays that were intended to be "the modern-day version of *The Group*," as Bushnell's editor first called the book that would become *Sex and the City*. Bushnell would write in the reissue's foreword, "*The Group* reminds us that not much has really changed. It's a book I prize, not only for its blistering satire, but for its technical elements, including McCarthy's brilliant use of the soliloquy, her pacing and razor-sharp descriptions." The sisterly connection to McCarthy's works would even fast-forward another generation beyond Bushnell's with the 2012 arrival of the HBO series *Girls*. Lena Dunham, the primary creative force behind and star of *Girls*, would acknowledge to the *New York Times* the influence of not just *Sex and the City*, but also both *The Group* and *The Company She Keeps*.

Just behind *The Group* on the fiction best-seller list that November was *Publishers Weekly*'s biggest-selling book of 1963, Morris West's Cold War novel *The Shoes of the Fisherman*. Interestingly, the book's central character was a Pope from the Communist bloc, some 15 years before the papal election of the Polish-born-and-bred Karol Wojtyla, who would take the name John Paul II. *The Shoes of the Fisherman* would be made into a film in 1968, starring Anthony Quinn, who would star a decade later in the film treatment of another book that was high on the best seller lists in the fall of '63, James Michener's *Caravans*. Like so many of Michener's books, *Caravans* was set in an exotic, mysterious locale, in this case one that was little-known to many Americans of the early '60s-Kabul, Afghanistan.

Another fixture on the list since its publication that April was the latest of Ian Fleming's James Bond novels, *On Her Majesty's Secret Service*. Fleming's Bond books had sold steadily but unspectacularly since the publication of Fleming's first Bond novel, *Casino Royale*, in 1953. But sales in America, at least, ratcheted up considerably when it was learned that JFK was a fan of the books and really took off in '63 with the success of the film treatments of *Dr. No* and *From Russia With Love*, which had premiered in Britain that October but wouldn't see US release until April '64. *Her Majesty's...* was the second of three books in which Bond's opponent was Ernst Blofeld, who would become one of the most memorable and most resilient of the Bond film villains. It's also the novel in which Bond marries one of his female conquests, Countess Teresa di Vincenzo (a.k.a. Tracy), who is killed in a Blofeld drive-by shooting after the wedding. *Her Majesty's...* would re-emerge six years later as the sixth "official" Bond film. That would be the one film starring George Lazenby as Bond (with Sean Connery, who had played Bond in all of the previous films, having opted out), future TV *Kojak* Telly Savalas as Blofeld, and Diana Rigg of the popular TV series *The Avengers* as Tracy. *The Avengers*, in fact, had already been in production in England for a couple of years by the fall of '63, with the series' original female lead, Honor Blackman, a soon-to-be "Bond girl" in the hugely-popular film adaptation of Fleming's *Goldfinger*, which would reach movie screens not long after Fleming's death from a heart attack in August '64. The last of the Bond novels that would be published during Fleming's lifetime, *You Only Live Twice,* would also be the last volume of the *Blofeld* trilogy and would reach bookstores just a bit under a year after the publication of *On Her Majesty's Secret Service.*

Espionage was also the theme of Helen MacInnes's *The Venetian Affair*, the tale of a New York drama critic on vacation in Europe who just happens to be a former foreign correspondent and a World War II-era OSS agent. Beginning with having his raincoat switched at customs in Paris, the critic quickly finds himself involved in a plot to make it appear that US operatives had put out a hit on General Charles de Gaulle. Naturally, a Communist spy is the book's chief villain and, even more naturally, the critic is recruited by the OSS's offspring, the CIA, and is assigned to journey to Venice on the Simplon Express, posing as the lover of a beautiful blonde. And, of course, right in the middle of the golden age of secret agent movies and TV shows, MacInnes's book would be made into a 1967 film starring *Man From U.N.C.L.E.* star Robert Vaughn and mid-'60s film sexpot Elke Sommer.

January saw the publication of a new entrant in the espionage book sweepstakes, the third novel by a writer called John Le Carre. *The Spy Who Came in from the Cold* was very different from Fleming's Bond novels or even *The Venetian Affair*, but may have been closer to the reality of Cold War-era espionage. The book's central figure, Alec Leamas, is very far from the dashing Bond. He's a middle-aged veteran of the espionage wars who is perceived by his superiors at the British Secret Intelligence Service (or simply the Circus) to possibly be burned-out. Despite that perception, Leamas is assigned to an elaborate mission aimed at taking down an assassin named Hans-Dieter Mundt, an East German double agent Le Carre created for his first book, *Call for the Dead.* But Leamas's role in the plot is one of conspicuous self-destruction that is meant to get the attention of East German intelligence. How much of this, though, is a ruse and how much is Leamas's personal burnout factor and his uncertainty about his own destiny? Thus we have a book that's much more psychological thriller than simple spy novel. As well, though, we have a novel that paints a very different picture of the tactics and principles of espionage as practiced by the Western bloc countries, tactics and principles just as amoral as those of the KGB-type Communist bloc agencies. In other words, a book with a plot very different from the good vs. bad scenarios of the Bond novels. As *Time*'s original review put it, "In the end Le Carre's secret agents, on both sides, are themselves as ruthless as the acts they perform." Better than four decades later, with *Time* naming *The Spy Who Came in from the Cold* to its "100 Best Novels" list, the book would be termed "a sad, sympathetic portrait of a man who has lived by lies and subterfuge for so long he's forgotten how to tell the truth."

The Spy Who Came in from the Cold raced to the top of the fiction best seller lists almost as quickly as those four other young Britishers had just done on the American pop music charts with "I Want to Hold Your Hand." Like The Beatles, very little was known about John Le Carre in January 1964. It turned out that he was a 32-year-old former schoolmaster at Eton named David Cornwell who had served in the British Foreign Service and had written his first three novels, including *The Spy Who Came in from the Cold,* while still working in the intelligence arena and it was the success of that third book that ended his career in British intelligence. That end, though, would be the beginning of one of the most successful careers in the genre of espionage novels, with a catalog that would stretch into the twenties by the second decade of the 21st century. As well, there would be a number of radio, television, and film adaptations of the Le Carre works, including the 1965 movie version of *The Spy Who Came in from the Cold,* with Richard Burton as Alec Leamas. The most popular Le Carre re-workings, though, would be the BBC-TV adaptations of *Tinker, Tailor, Soldier, Spy* in 1979 and *Smiley's People* in 1981, with Alec Guinness as Le Carre's most popular and longest-running character, Circus agent George Smiley.

John Cheever had been a celebrated writer of long-form short stories since The *New Yorker* had run his first major piece, "The Enormous Radio," in 1947. A decade later, his long-in-the-works first novel, *The Wapshot Chronicle,* became a best seller and won the National Book Award. A follow-up novel, *The Wapshot Scandal,* debuted at the beginning of '64 and had made the Top Ten fiction best seller lists by late January. Since the *Peyton Place*-esque Proxmire Manor, the book's central locale, was identified as being in New York's northern Westchester, *Time* proclaimed Cheever suburbia's "first poet-mythologist" and the book as "a totally original work by a writer who is not yet great, but who is greatly obsessed by his exploration of American life" in its mid-January review. Indeed, *The Wapshot Scandal* was so successful that *Time* would return to Cheever and give him its cover story in late March. That summer, a Cheever short story called "The Swimmer" would appear in The *New Yorker* and, unlike *The Wapshot Scandal,* "The Swimmer" would be tabbed for a film adaptation, which would star Charlton Heston and debut in the spring of 1968.

*****

At the top of the non-fiction best-seller lists in mid-November was a right-wing examination of Ian Fleming's friend and Bond fan Jack Kennedy. *JFK: The Man & the Myth* was written by Victor Lasky, a conservative ideologue who had written an anti-Kennedy book that was published during the 1960 campaign in hopes of derailing Kennedy's drive for the presidency. *Man & the Myth,* though, was double the size of that book and, in the book, Lasky claimed that JFK's popularity was based more on image than on actual accomplishments. He cast doubt on the legitimacy of the World War II PT-109 story, which had been one of the major components of Kennedy's resume when he ran for

Congress after the war and had recently been made into a Hollywood movie starring Cliff Robertson. Lasky ridiculed Kennedy's record as a congressman and senator and criticized his dealings with Cuba and the Soviet Union as those of an appeaser to Communists. Interestingly, there was nothing in the book about Kennedy's reckless personal life, particularly his numerous affairs with women, a sure sign that virtually no one outside of the JFK inner circle knew of these affairs at the time. After all, what was a best-selling book would have been a blockbuster had it included allegations of White House hanky-panky, especially on the level of later revelations. Nonetheless, *JFK: The Man & the Myth* topped most non-fiction best-seller lists that appeared in Sunday newspapers on November 24, as preparations were being made for the public viewing of the assassinated president's coffin in the Capitol rotunda.

Rather ironically, an expose` of the funeral home industry, *The American Way of Death* by British-born journalist/left-wing activist Jessica Mitford was right behind Lasky's book that morning and would finish the year at the top of the non-fiction lists. Not surprisingly, Lasky's book nearly disappeared, both from bookstore shelves and on the best seller lists, in the weeks following the assassination but would regain sales momentum during the winter. Both Lasky and Mitford would continue to write for their quite different constituencies. Mitford would write extensively about the anti-Vietnam war movement and the American prison system and would even teach a college course on what she saw as the roots of the Watergate abuses in Senator Joe McCarthy's Communist witch hunts of the early '50s. Lasky, after writing an examination of Robert Kennedy that would cover much the same ground as his JFK book, would write his own thesis on Watergate, *It Didn't Start With Watergate*, in which he would claim that the abuses that led to Watergate weren't solely the work of Richard Nixon and his boys but began during Democratic administrations, particularly those of Franklin Roosevelt, Lyndon Johnson, and, yes, John Kennedy.

Another writer whose politics were about as far removed from Lasky's as one could get was Norman Mailer, whose epic 1960 article on Kennedy for *Esquire*, "Superman Comes to the Supermarket," was one of the first examples of what came to be known as "The New Journalism." That piece was included in a collection of Mailer's work from the New Frontier years called *The Presidential Papers,* which, like Lasky's book, hit bookstores during what turned out to be the last weeks of the Kennedy presidency. While several of the "presidential papers" dealt with JFK, his administration, and Mailer's impatience with both, another long Esquire essay was included, this one dealing with the first one-round Sonny Liston-Floyd Patterson heavyweight championship fight in Chicago in September 1962.

There were two other significant books on those same pre-Thanksgiving non-fiction best-seller lists. James Baldwin's *The Fire Next Time* was his, in effect, manifesto on the state of black America as the civil rights movement was gaining momentum. Most of the book had appeared in two lengthy pieces in The *New Yorker* earlier in the year, which resulted in a mid-May *Time* magazine cover story on the already-world-famous writer/playwright. The essays supported the principles of non-violent protest and conciliation and cooperation with the white race that were the hallmark of the movement in the early '60s and Baldwin was one of the higher-profile celebrities at the March on Washington. Baldwin also took a very hard line against black separatist religion, particularly the Nation of Islam, its leader Elijah Muhammad, and its then-chief spokesman Malcolm X. Baldwin felt that the incendiary rhetoric of the Black Muslims was no better than that of white racists. The essays were soon turned into book form as *The Fire Next Time* and the book would be looked on as a mandatory read for those looking to understand race relations in the pre-"black power" years.

David Ogilvy's *Confessions of an Advertising Man* quickly gained a reputation as a virtual textbook for anyone venturing into the world of advertising. A very successful copywriter, Ogilvy broke down every aspect of the business without loading the text up with a lot of jargon, with individual chapters devoted to every major step along the way to becoming a success in the business, including one on "How to Be a Good Client." Forty-six years after the publication of *Confessions of an Advertising Man* and a decade after Ogilvy's death at 88, his book would become a plot device in the third season of *Mad Men*, a series set in the '60s advertising world, and would be represented by a page on the show's Internet website.

Come January and February, though, the biggest-selling non-fiction book in America was JFK's Pulitzer Prize-winning mid-'50s examination of eight courageous US senators, *Profiles in Courage,* first in the printing already available and, then, a mid-winter reissue with a new foreword by Robert Kennedy. The nearly-seven-year-old controversy over whether Kennedy had actually written the book or if his chief speechwriter Ted Sorensen had done the lion's share of the writing, first brought up by controversial columnist Drew Pearson and perpetuated by Kennedy critics like Lasky, was seemingly forgotten in the post-assassination wave of sentiment for the fallen president. Indeed, by the end of February, *Profiles in Courage* had been followed onto the best seller lists by *Four Days,* a United Press International/American Heritage mostly-photo chronicle of the events of November 22-25. Even Lasky's decidedly-non-reverential *JFK: The Man & the Myth* had gained a sales comeback and was still high on the best seller lists at the end of February, a first indication that the public's fascination with all things Kennedy would include more critical examinations and that fascination, both pro and con, would lead to books on JFK, his assassination, and the Kennedy family being a frequent presence on both fiction and non-fiction best seller lists well into the 21st century.

The Kennedy White House lobbied for the making of this drama about a domestic military plot that premiered less than three months after JFK's assassination.

CHAPTER 8

MOVIES/TV—WINDS OF CHANGE

On December 8, 1963, the El Dorado County Sheriff's Office reported that two men had abducted Frank Sinatra, Jr. from his room at Harrah's Lodge in Stateline, Nevada, along the border with California. Young Sinatra had been appearing at Harrah's Lounge in Lake Tahoe. This was in the midst of an effort to break the nearly 20-year-old Frank Jr. as a re-creation of his father's young self, complete with having him sing with a newer version of the Tommy Dorsey Orchestra, the big band with which the elder Frank first reached stardom two decades earlier. The kidnapping, which took place in the middle of a blizzard, was instantly a major story, if only because of the magic of the Sinatra name.

Twenty-six FBI agents and some 100 California and Nevada sheriff's deputies searched the Lake Tahoe area for any trace of the kidnappers. The elder Sinatra didn't hear from the kidnappers until the next day but it took several calls for them to make an actual ransom demand, the first indication that these kidnappers weren't exactly hardened professionals. He offered them a million dollars but, bizarrely, they only asked for $240,000 in unmarked bills. After another round of phone calls, the ransom drop was made by an FBI agent between two parked school buses in West Los Angeles shortly after midnight on December 11. Frank Jr. was released about two hours later, on the eve of his father's 48th birthday.

Thanks to one of the kidnappers, it took FBI agents and police only three more days to capture the culprits and get back most of the ransom money. John Irwin, a 42-year-old Hollywood area house painter, had already taken his share of the money and was on his way to New Orleans. He stopped off to see his brother in San Diego and confessed that he had been in on the Sinatra Jr. kidnapping. Irwin's brother contacted police and Irwin was quickly in custody, along with his accomplices, the two men who had actually abducted young Frank from his room. They were two L.A. underachievers, Barry Keenan, the ringleader of the plot, and Joe Amsler. Both were far younger than Irwin and had attended University High School in L.A., along with Nancy Sinatra and Jan Berry and Dean Torrance of the hit music duo Jan & Dean. Indeed, Keenan had asked Torrance for money to help finance his caper. Torrance was never implicated in the plot, but according to Torrance's liner notes for a 1972 Jan & Dean compilation LP, his friendship with Keenan cost Jan & Dean an on-screen role in the film *Ride the Wild Surf.*

When the three went on trial in February, they were defended by the flamboyant Southern California attorney Gladys Towles Root and she built a defense that Sinatra Jr. had engineered his own kidnapping as "an advertising scheme" to jumpstart a career that was not taking off. Root had virtually no evidence with which to support this claim but tried to use it to put some doubt in the minds of the jurors. The ploy didn't work and the three were quickly convicted.

*****

By the early '60s, Thanksgiving week had become a big one for the movie industry, with a handful of high-profile films opening on the day before Thanksgiving. So the Sunday newspaper supplements for November 24, which had gone to press as President Kennedy was beginning his two-day swing through Texas, were full of ads for new films that would be debuting that week or had just opened, many of which were chock-full of personalities with whom the general audience had become familiar via television. For instance, there was Jerry Lewis's newest comedy vehicle, *Who's Minding The Store?*, which also included in its cast Ray Walston, the star of CBS-TV's *My Favorite Martian*, Nancy Culp, regularly appearing as Miss Hathaway on the small screen's No. 1 hit, *The Beverly Hillbillies*, and veteran actress Agnes Moorehead, who would soon take on her most popular role, as Endora on a new situation comedy called *Bewitched.* In *Who's Minding The Store?*, Moorehead played the mother of Lewis's love interest in the film, played by a 23-year-old actress named Jill St. John, who was rapidly gaining a reputation for her ability as a comedienne, but also for her sizzling on-screen sex appeal.

Also debuting that week was an Army-set sort-of romantic comedy called *Soldier in the Rain*, starring the unlikely combination of Jackie Gleason, Steve McQueen and Tuesday Weld. The newest film from Walt Disney was *The Incredible Journey*, an adventure about two dogs and a cat trying to get home from 250 miles away through scenic but rough Canadian terrain. Unlike the computer-generated, celebrity-voiced animal adventures of the 21st century, the stars of *The Incredible Journey* were real animals. And going into general release was *Palm Springs Weekend*, a *Where the Boys Are*-esque spring break flick starring a number of the young stars of recent Warner Brothers-produced TV shows. The cast included Andrew Duggan from *Bourbon Street Beat*, Ty Hardin from *Bronco*, Connie Stevens and Robert Conrad from *Hawaiian Eye*, and 21-year-old Stefanie Powers, a relative newcomer who three years later would star as *The Girl From U.N.C.L.E.* and two decades later would star in her best-known role opposite Robert Wagner in *Hart to Hart*. The star of the film was tall, blond Troy Donohue, who had starred in both *Surfside 6* and *Hawaiian Eye* and was arguably the biggest film/TV teen heartthrob of the moment.

Already in general release and one of the top moneymakers of that fall was *The VIPs*, a potboiler set in the VIP lounge at what was then called London Airport. The movie's main hook was that it was the second film of the year (following the epic *Cleopatra*) starring the gossip-page couple of the year, Elizabeth Taylor and Richard Burton. But the film's best notices went to another Briton, 28-year-old Maggie Smith, then in the early stages of one of the modern stage and screen's most varied and distinguished careers, which would feature her playing everything from Desdemona in *Othello* (opposite Sir Laurence Olivier) to the Oscar-winning title role in *The Prime of Miss Jean Brodie* to 21st-century fame with a new generation via the roles of Professor McGonagall in the *Harry Potter* films and Violet Crawley in the TV series *Downton Abbey*. Even as *The VIPs* was playing in American movie theaters, Smith was starring in a London West End production of the recent Broadway hit *Mary, Mary*, for which one critic fittingly called her "a gem of an actress."

Two more young Brits received raves for their performances in *Billy Liar*, which reached American theaters in mid-December. The film's title character is a clerk in an undertaker's office in the North of England

157

who creates a fantasy world for himself in which he's the "king of Ambrosia." Tom Courtenay, who had first grabbed filmgoers' attention in 1962's *The Loneliness of the Long Distance Runner*, had played Billy on the stage at the Cambridge Theatre in '61, taking over the role from Albert Finney. *Loneliness...* was directed by Tony Richardson, who shortly thereafter directed Finney in the film sensation of '63, *Tom Jones*. Courtenay noted at the time that he and Finney "both have the same problem, overcoming the flat, harsh speech of the North." Of course, that accent would soon become very popular, thanks to The Beatles and other pop bands and singers hailing from the North of England.

Billy Liar was directed by John Schlesinger, another of the leading "new wave" British filmmakers, utilizing hand-held cameras and documentary-style techniques. Billy's primary love interest in the film was played by 22-year-old Julie Christie, who *Time* magazine called "an actress so brimful of careless charm that she parlays a few brief scenes into instant stardom." Some two years after *Billy Liar*, Schlesinger would direct Christie in her first starring role as the amoral London model Diana Scott in *Darling*, for which she would win a best actress Oscar and Schlesinger would be nominated for best direction. Soon after, Courtenay and Christie would work together again in David Lean's *Doctor Zhivago*, a much bigger film (both in scope and box office) than either *Billy Liar* or *Darling* and for which Courtenay would earn a best supporting actor Oscar nomination. So Oscar night 1966 would be an important one for Courtenay, Schlesinger, and especially Christie, one worthy of the fantasies of the "king of Ambrosia."

But for sheer mass of star power no movie of '63 equaled or even approached *It's a Mad, Mad, Mad, Mad World*. Directed by Stanley Kramer and clocking in at just over three hours, *IAMMMMW* starred Spencer Tracy, Jimmy Durante, erstwhile "Mr. Television" Milton Berle, fellow early TV icon Sid Caesar, Buddy Hackett, Ethel Merman, Mickey Rooney, Phil Silvers, Edie Adams, Jonathan Winters and Dorothy Provine (yet another Warner Bros. TV personality, from *The Roaring Twenties*)- and others in a story about the mass pursuit by car of $350,000 in stolen money. Very expensively filmed in 70mm "Ultra Panovision" and single-lens Cinerama, *IAMMMMW* was billed as "a comedy to end all comedies" but *Time* magazine called it a "relentless overstatement." In subsequent years, *IAMMMMW* would be looked on by some as a comedy classic and by others as a bloated misfire.

In the last weeks of a year in which the Roman Catholic Church and its ceremonies had been very much in the public mind, given the death of Pope John XXIII, the election of a new pope, the resumption of the Second Vatican Council, and even the administering of the "last rites" to the assassinated first Catholic president, it was entirely fitting for a new film dealing with the Catholic Church to premiere. Producer-director Otto Preminger's *The Cardinal* was based on a 1950 Henry Morton Robinson novel and starred Tom Tryon, previously best known as the star of Disney's *Texas John Slaughter* serial, as Stephen Fermoyle, a young priest who rises from a Boston parish in the 1930s to become a prince of the church. Along the way, Fermoyle encounters many of the hot-button topics of the era: infanticide, the conversion of Jews to Catholicism, racism, the Nazi blight in Europe. And, of course, there were the eternal issues that would lead to the Catholic Church's early 21st century crises: sexual temptation and celibacy. In *The Cardinal*, though, the temptation comes not from adolescent boys but from hot young actress Romy Schneider as a sexy Viennese fraulein. Somehow, Preminger also shoehorned in a song-and-dance number featuring Robert Morse of the Broadway hit *How to Succeed in Business Without Really Trying* and famed director John Huston, in one of his occasional acting roles, played a larger-than-life Boston cardinal who is Fermoyle's connection to the Vatican hierarchy. Preminger promoted the film during the fall '63 session of Vatican II but an American bishop commented, "The picture makes clerical life a lot more exciting than it really is." If he only knew (or perhaps did and wasn't letting on)...

In a tradition that went back 30 years, New York's Radio City Music Hall presented a 30-minute Christmas show during the holiday season featuring the Rockettes, paired with a family-friendly movie. In 1963, that film was a frothy romance-mystery called *Charade*, which featured an instantly hummable (and ultimately Academy Award-nominated) Henry Mancini/Johnny Mercer title song and two stars known for their box-office appeal almost as well as their acting ability. Audrey Hepburn was just two films removed from her career-defining role as Holly Golightly in *Breakfast at Tiffany*'s while 59-year-old Cary Grant was still playing debonair male lead roles usually given to actors considerably younger than he. It all made for perfect holiday fare, especially in tandem with the Radio City Christmas show. By 1979 and the beginning of the age of home video, though, Radio City would end its days as a movie theater and would concentrate on concerts and other events, the biggest of which would be the expanded-to-90-minutes *Christmas Spectacular* that would bring large crowds to Radio City Music Hall every holiday season.

Romantic comedies with a hint of sex had long been a successful formula in Hollywood but the success of the Doris Day-Rock Hudson films like *Pillow Talk* and *Lover Come Back* had made the early '60s a true golden age of bedroom comedy. Three such films debuted on Christmas Day. *Move Over, Darling* had the queen of the genre paired this time with James Garner and a ridiculous plot that had Day's character returning home after five years on a desert island following a plane crash. Her presumed widower (Garner) has had her declared legally dead and has just remarried (to TV game show and commercials fixture Polly Bergen). Day, on finding this out, heads for Monterey to let the honeymooning couple know she's back. Despite that grim premise, lighthearted comedy ensues. As for Doris' best-known screen partner, Hudson's next film vehicle, *Man's Favorite Sport* (debuting in late February), would have a plot nearly as far-fetched as *Move Over, Darling*, with Rock playing a salesman for Abercrombie & Fitch (back in the days when that chain sold sporting goods and not hip-hop culture street wear) drafted into a fishing tournament by the company publicist (and his ultimate love interest in the film), played by Paula Prentiss.

Who's Been Sleeping in My Bed? had Dean Martin starring as a TV doctor (in the era of *Dr. Kildare* and *Ben Casey*) engaged to soon-to-be *Bewitched* star Elizabeth Montgomery but romantically pursued by the wives of his poker night friends, played by, among others, Carol Burnett and Jill St. John (the aforementioned love interest of Martin's erstwhile partner, Jerry Lewis, in *Who's Minding The Store?*). And Dino was also a star in *4 for Texas*, more a Rat Pack vehicle than a romantic comedy, but with sexpots Anita Ekberg and Ursula Andress replacing Sammy Davis, Jr. and Joey Bishop alongside Frank and Dean, who, according to the film's flimsy script, compete to open a floating casino in Old West Galveston while being pursued by a posse of outlaw thugs led by a youngish Charles Bronson. Robert Aldrich reportedly directed *4 for Texas* without ever speaking to Sinatra for the entirety of the filming while also squeezing in a cameo by The Three Stooges. Even in the lightweight annals of Rat Pack comedies, *4 for Texas* would never reach the status of *Robin and the 7 Hoods* or the original *Ocean's 11*.

With all of the bedroom hijinks in these comedies and the escalating amount of semi-nudity in many Hollywood films, veteran actor Dana Andrews, recently elected president of the Screen Actors Guild, criticized actresses who allowed themselves to be filmed in the nude or in what were for the time graphic sex scenes (Carroll Baker's already notorious scenes in the not-yet-released *The Carpetbaggers* being a timely example) and blamed this growing trend on the greed of the studios and producers and the competition from television for the audience's attention.

Ironically, Andrews made these comments even as one of the original '50s European cinema sex kittens, Brigitte Bardot, returned to the American screen, often sans clothes. *Love on a Pillow* was originally released in France in September 1962 and was directed by Bardot's first husband, Roger Vadim, who had directed her breakthrough film, *And God Created Woman*, in 1957. *Love on a Pillow* was ostensibly based on a French novel, *Warrior's Rest*, but Vadim mainly used it as a showcase for Bardot and her sexuality, since much of the film is devoted to bedroom scenes involving Bardot and her co-star, Robert Hossein. Indeed, the promotional material for the film merely showed a barely-clothed Bardot. As he would spectacularly show in his films with Jane Fonda later in the decade, subtlety was not part of Vadim's cinematic vocabulary.

In another popular film genre, the tone of movies set during World War II, especially those made by non-American filmmakers, was beginning to change. The traditionally noble portrait of war was being countered by a grittier, more cynical view of war as a brutal endeavor in which nobody really wins. This was the point of *The Victors*, a three-hour "personal statement" by writer-producer-director Carl Foreman, who had written the screenplay for *Bridge on the River Kwai* and wrote and produced *The Guns of Navarone*, both of which had been largely turned into "feel good" war films by Hollywood. With *The Victors*, Foreman attempted to show what war really does to the people who fight it and those most directly affected by it. There were no sweeping battle scenes filmed a la *The Longest Day*. Battle footage was all taken from newsreels, as was footage of the American home front. Foreman instead concentrated on the toll the war took on a US Army squadron during the war in Europe. In *The Victors*, war turns young men into cynical, amoral, predatory warriors, capable of amusing themselves by shooting a puppy belonging to another GI on a bet or just watching as two Southern racists beat up a pair of black soldiers. And women, already victims of the ravages of the war in Europe, are simply part of the spoils of war, merely to be used and discarded.

The scene that attracted the most attention in reviews of *The Victors*, perhaps because the film opened in American theaters just before Christmas, was one centered on the Christmas Eve execution by firing squad of a young American deserter, obviously modeled on the execution of Eddie Slovik in January 1945. A crowd of GIs is trucked to a snowy, desolate field to witness the shooting and the scene is punctuated by a soundtrack of Sinatra's wartime version of "Have Yourself A Merry Little Christmas," followed, after the shots are fired, by a recording of "Hark the Herald Angels Sing." The film's climactic scene takes place in the bombed-out Berlin of the last days of the war in Europe, as an American GI (played by George Hamilton) picks a fight with a Russian soldier (the ubiquitous Albert Finney). They end up killing each other with knives and the camera pulls back to show their bodies lying in the shape of Winston Churchill's "V for Victory," which would become the peace sign for Vietnam war protesters just a few short years after this decidedly-anti-war film debuted.

Despite the film being Foreman's "personal statement" on war, *The Victors* had plenty of star power. Along with Hamilton and Finney, the cast also included George Peppard, Eli Wallach, Michael Callan, Vincent Edwards from TV's *Ben Casey*, and young Peter Fonda, then primarily known as Henry's son and Jane's brother. And there was a strong cast of European-born actresses for the roles of the women who are generally romanced/exploited by the soldiers, including Jeanne Moreau, Romy Schneider, Melina Mercouri, Senta Berger and Elke Sommer.

Somewhat more traditional holiday fare was *Love With the Proper Stranger*, a romantic dramedy starring Natalie Wood as Macy's salesgirl Angie Rossini and Steve McQueen as Rocky Papasano, a jazz musician with whom she has a one-night summer fling. Angie soon finds out that she's pregnant and, after finding Rocky, he agrees to pay for a backroom abortion (a decade before Roe v. Wade would make abortion legal), but the abortion doesn't happen when the abortionist turns out to be a sleazy midwife. Once Angie decides to see her pregnancy through, the film becomes more of a typical love triangle involving Angie, Rocky, and Angie's boyfriend, Anthony. The role of Anthony marked the film debut of Tom Bosley, at 36 already a TV and theater veteran who would become a TV star in the '70s as Howard Cunningham (aka Mr. C.) on *Happy Days*. In *Proper Stranger*, Bosley was part of an excellent supporting cast that included Edie Adams as the typical Hollywood version of a good-hearted stripper and Herschel Bernardi and Harvey Lembeck as Angie's domineering brothers. Befitting a film released on Christmas Day, the climactic scene with Angie and Rocky takes place outside of Angie's workplace, the iconic Macy's in Herald Square.

The "feel good" movie of the '63 holiday season was *Lilies of the Field*, an adaptation of a 1962 William Edmund Barrett novel about an unemployed handyman (Sidney Poitier) who befriends a group of East German refugee nuns he meets on an Arizona farm after his car overheats. After helping the nuns with some odd jobs, the nuns, particularly their strict mother superior, believe that he has been sent to them by God and that he will help them build a chapel for their new settlement. The fact that the man, Homer Smith, is black is a non-factor for the nuns or for the townspeople, who soon help Smith with the building of the chapel, and Smith shares some of his Baptist traditions with the European Catholic nuns, including music. One of the film's best-remembered scenes involves Smith teaching the nuns the gospel tune "Amen" and that word replaces "The End" onscreen at film's end.

Lilies of the Field would be nominated for five Academy Awards, including best picture and a best supporting actress nod to Skala. Poitier would win the best actor Oscar, the first won by a black in a competitive category. Poitier was already an accomplished actor, widely recognized for his talents within the acting community, but his Oscar win would be looked on by the general public as the tearing down of another barrier in the name of civil rights. And a march-tempo adaptation of "Amen" by the gospel-bred R&B group The Impressions would be released on their "Keep on Pushin'" LP in the spring of '64 and become a hit single by year's end.

Walt Disney's contribution to the roster of Christmas Day '63 releases was, not surprisingly, an animated feature. *The Sword in the Stone* was an adaptation by Bill Peet of a novel by T.H. White that eventually morphed into *The Once and Future King*. It all revolves around a forgotten sword encased in a stone in London and an orphan named Wart who is destined to become King Arthur and is tutored by Merlin the Magician. Highlighted by the kind of dazzling animation that had long been a Disney hallmark, *The Sword in the Stone* would never become a Disney classic, but would turn out to be well-respected among longtime observers of the studio's animated films, and Merlin would become one of the live characters appearing at the various Disney theme parks.

In early January, *Time* ran a short profile of a rapidly up-and-coming actor the magazine branded as a "canny Scot." Thirty-three-year-old Sean Connery had been a film and TV presence in Britain and America since the mid-'50s, including a brief stint with Disney (*Darby O'Gill and the Little People*) in '59. But Connery's big break came in 1962 when he was selected for the role of British secret agent James Bond for the first big-screen treatment of one of Ian Fleming's Bond novels, *Dr. No*. The author himself was rather skeptical about the former bodybuilder and footballer's fitness for Fleming's profile of Agent 007 but *Dr. No* and *From Russia With Love* (released in Britain in October 1963, with a US bow coming in the spring of '64) showed the Scot to be more than up to the task. Steely, controlled, seemingly irresistible to women, with just the right amount of wry humor, Connery appeared tailor-made for the role of Bond and, a half-century later, would still be considered the best of all of the actors who have taken on the role.

But, even at this early stage of the Bond era, Connery refused to be artistically pigeonholed and continued to take on a wide variety of roles. At the time of the *Time* article, he was in the midst of filming the Alfred Hitchcock-directed *Marnie* and had ruffled some Hollywood feathers by asking to read the script before accepting the co-starring role opposite Tippi Hedren. This was not considered normal form for a Hitchcock project but it was an early example of Connery's against-the-grain personal and professional style. He also was keeping Hollywood at arm's length, even while admitting that it had "a very seductive atmosphere." He rented a $1,000-a-month Bel Air house while filming *Marnie*, but would return to England soon after filming wrapped to prepare for his third outing as 007 in the film that would launch Connery and Bond into the pop culture stratosphere, *Goldfinger*.

On January 10, an entertainment industry trade paper called *Film Daily* announced the results of a poll of movie reviewers and commentators that named Paul Newman and Shirley MacLaine, who were slated to co-star that spring in *What a Way to Go*, the top film performers of 1963. Newman, in particular, had a very big '63. *Hud* would soon receive seven Academy Award nominations, including a best actor nod for Newman. He would lose the Oscar to Poitier but co-stars Patricia Neal and Melvyn Douglas would snag the best actress and best supporting actor prizes, respectively. Next, Newman and wife Joanne Woodward teamed up for *A New Kind of Love*. And Christmas Day saw the opening of an espionage thriller set at the Nobel Prize ceremonies in Stockholm. Based on a best-selling novel by Irving Wallace, *The Prize* starred Newman as a Nobel laureate with writer's block, a drinking problem, and an eye for the ladies. He finds himself investigating the suspicious behavior of a German-American physicist played by gangster movie icon Edward G. Robinson while also pursuing his assistant from the Swedish Foreign Office, played by Elke Sommer, that winter's movie sexpot du jour.

Thrillers like *The Prize* and the Connery-starring Bond films put a glamorous, fantasy-based face on the ideological chess game being primarily played between the United States and the Soviet Union. Two films that had been ready for release in the last weeks of 1963 but were pushed back in the wake of the JFK assassination approached the Cold War from very different stylistic places while dispensing with the froth. January 29 saw the delayed premiere of *Dr. Strangelove or: How I Learned to Stop Worrying and Love the Bomb*, a dark comedy about nuclear war which Stanley Kubrick directed, produced and co-wrote (with Terry Southern). According to the plot, a maniacal general, Jack D. Ripper (Sterling Hayden), suspects a Communist plot to contaminate the American water system, so he orders his arsenal of B52s to leave their fail-safe positions and cross into Soviet airspace. The news of Ripper's order reaches the Pentagon's "war room" as Gen. Buck Turgidson (George C. Scott) briefs President Merkin Muffley (Peter Sellers) about Ripper's putting into effect Wing Attack Plan R.

Kubrick and Southern's screenplay (based on Peter George's 1958 novel *Red Alert*) paints a portrait of an out-of-control US military. Besides the paranoid Gen. Ripper, Turgidson is a virulent Commie-hater who recommends a full-scale first strike on the Soviets to get an edge on them and even grapples with the Soviet ambassador in front of President Muffley in the war room. Indeed, Scott's over-the-top portrayal of Turgidson has some elements that he would later bring to his Oscar-winning portrayal of Gen. George S. Patton. Sellers gives one of the greatest performances of a stellar career, in three separate roles, as the egg-headed Muffley, as the one sane military authority figure, British exchange officer and Group Captain Lionel Mandrake, and in the title role, a wheelchair-bound weapons expert turned science advisor stolen away from the Nazis.

In the hands of Kubrick and Southern, the Soviet premier and ambassador are duplicitous buffoons whose literal ace in the hole is a "doomsday device," a cluster of bombs that will detonate if the Soviets are attacked. Dr. Strangelove is the chief proponent of an American "doomsday" option, but is overruled by a think tank.

Eventually, those US planes that haven't been shot down once they entered Soviet airspace are turned back. One plane, though, ends up in limbo, unable to return to base and with a punctured fuel tank and bomb release. Its mission climaxes with the plane's commander, Major T.K. "King" Kong (cowboy film veteran Slim Pickens), riding a nuclear bomb, rodeo-style, to detonation below. Minutes later, as Dr. Strangelove explains a re-population scheme that sounds suspiciously like the Nazi "master race" strategy, he becomes so inspired he steps out of his wheelchair just as the "doomsday device" sets off a chain reaction of detonations all over the world, to a soundtrack of Vera Lynn's World War II hit, "We'll Meet Again."

The critical response to *Dr. Strangelove* was very positive upon its release and the film would soon be considered a cinema classic. In a typical review, *Time* called the film "an outrageously brilliant satire; the most original American comedy in years and at the same time a supersonic thriller." Just over a year later, *Dr. Strangelove* would receive four Academy Award nominations, including best picture, a best director nod for Kubrick, and a best actor nomination for Sellers for his trifecta of classic roles. As it happened, the movie version of *My Fair Lady*, which would be released at the end of '64, would sweep those three categories. But *Dr. Strangelove* would take on legendary status with the passage of time. For instance, famed Chicago-based movie critic Roger Ebert would proclaim it "arguably the best political satire of the century" while the American Film Institute, in its end-of-century surveys of great films, would recognize *Dr. Strangelove* as the 26th greatest film and third greatest comedy of the 20th century.

Seven Days In May, which premiered in Washington on February 12, would never reach the critical heights of *Dr. Strangelove* and had none of that film's dark comic outrageousness, but it grew out of the same tense Cold War atmosphere. Filmed less than a year after the Cuban missile crisis and during a time when the US and the Soviets were negotiating a nuclear test ban treaty, *Seven Days in May* ventured into the very touchy territory of a possible military coup led by an ego-driven general. Given that President Harry Truman's confrontation with Gen. Douglas MacArthur during the Korean conflict was little more than a decade in the rear-view mirror, along with the recent far-right activities of Gen. Edwin Walker, the film's plot was not totally far-fetched. Indeed, a military-fueled plot was just one of the scenarios that would be put forth in the coming years by the proponents of a conspiracy of some sort behind the assassination of President Kennedy. Ironically, the Kennedy White House had supported the filming of *Seven Days in May*. JFK had read the original novel by Fletcher Kriebel and Charles W. Bailey II and thought that the plot was very believable. Interestingly, the Pentagon was against a possible film version of the novel but Kennedy, through his Hollywood connections and press secretary Pierre Salinger, got the word out that he was very much in favor of the making of such a film and would even make the area outside of the White House gates available for filming exteriors.

Two Hollywood heavyweights, director John Frankenheimer and actor-producer Kirk Douglas, were most responsible for bringing *Seven Days in May* to the silver screen. Frankenheimer already had a distinguished track record, including a recent socio-political thriller in 1962's *The Manchurian Candidate*. Douglas was one of Hollywood's most box-office-friendly stars and had his own production company. Armed with the encouragement from the Kennedy White House, famed screenwriter and *Twilight Zone* creator Rod Serling did the screenplay and Frankenheimer and Douglas assembled a superior cast that included Douglas' long-time colleague Burt Lancaster, Fredric March, Edmond O'Brien, Martin Balsam and Ava Gardner.

The film's plot centers on the unpopularity of President Jordan Lyman (March), who has just negotiated a nuclear disarmament treaty with the Soviet Union, and the rising popularity of Air Force Gen. James Mattoon Scott (Lancaster), chairman of the Joint Chiefs of Staff, in the aftermath of a circa-1970 Korea-style conflict in Iran. One of Scott's underlings at the Pentagon, Marine Corps Col. Martin "Jiggs" Casey (Douglas) is suddenly and accidentally made aware of a plot involving Scott and the other Joint Chiefs and certain congressional allies to stage a military coup and remove Lyman from power in exactly seven days.

Casey contacts Lyman's inner circle about the Scott-led plot and thus begins a tense race against time. The film was highlighted by excellent performances by O'Brien as a Georgia senator and personal friend of Lyman's who has seen his best years and has a drinking problem, Gardner as a vulnerable former mistress of Scott's from whom Casey obtains incriminating evidence, Balsam as a presidential aide who obtains a confession of knowledge of the plot by the commander of the 6th Fleet (played by John Houseman) only to die in a plane crash on the way back to Washington, and March as the put-upon but resolute president. And, of course, there's Lancaster and Douglas, two classic Movie Stars in roles that fit each like a glove.

Media reaction to *Seven Days in May* was generally positive, but not nearly as rapturous as the reviews for "Dr. Strangelove." For example, *Time* called it "the kind of fast-paced melodrama that is made to order for a rainy Saturday afternoon," but pooh-poohed "its patently fictional view of Washington" as "more far-fetched than a campaign promise." A year later, though, O'Brien would be nominated for a best supporting actor Oscar and would win a Golden Globe in the same category.

*****

The cast of the original UK *That Was The Week That Was* on October 26, 1963. From left to right: David Frost - William Rushton - Millicent Martin - Roy Kinnear - Lance Percival

The times were indeed a-changin' in the fall of 1963 and, as was the case on Broadway stages, the silver screen and, very soon, the pop music charts, the winds of change for television were blowing not from the American TV networks, but from England.

The British TV sensation of 1963, the BBC's *That Was the Week That Was*, wrapped up its second season on December 28 with a series finale that included many of the show's best moments. The roots of *TW3*, as the show was popularly known, grew out of the same university-based "satire boom" that had produced *Beyond the Fringe*, with a writing staff and core cast of (mostly) young men steeped in the same pointedly irreverent brand of humor. And they could not have asked for more made-to-order material than Britain's two biggest political stories of '63 -- the rocky relationship between the UK and Charles de Gaulle's France and the John Profumo-Christine Keeler sex-and-espionage scandal. Add a dash of Beatlemania, and *TW3* had plenty of ripe-for-satire material to take it into 1964. But, with a British national election campaign looming, it was felt that a televised weekly vehicle for socio-political satire would be inappropriate, a position that would seem ridiculously quaint within just a few years. Besides, the show's central cast member, 24-year-old

David Frost, was becoming a frequent flier between London and New York as an American version of *TW3* was taking shape in advance of its January 10 debut on NBC. Frost and *TW3* creator Ned Sherrin would oversee the US edition and Frost was slated to make at least three on-air appearances in the early going with announced regulars Elliott Reid, Henry Morgan and American "TW3 girl" Nancy Ames, who would each week sing the topical theme song, done by Millicent Martin each week on the UK edition.

The pilot for the US *That Was the Week That Was* had aired on NBC on Sunday night, November 10. Henry Fonda was the host, with Morgan, a ubiquitous figure on game shows and late night talk shows since TV's early years, also on board, so it became clear from the get-go that the American version wouldn't have quite the youthful edge of its UK forebear. Two weeks later, NBC ran the British show's hastily-put-together November 23 program, which was a sincere, non-mawkish tribute to President Kennedy.

Frost and Sherrin would be the only tangible links between the UK and US versions of *TW3*. The American show would be produced by stage, screen and TV veteran Leland Hayward, with a writing staff headed by actor-turned-writer Robert Emmett and a cast that included such familiar faces to American viewers as the aforementioned Morgan, Orson Bean, Phyllis Newman and puppeteer Burr Tillstrom (of *Kukla, Fran, & Ollie* fame). But the evolving cast also included younger performers such as Alan Alda, son of veteran actor-singer Robert Alda. The younger Alda began his performing career with a late '50s stint in the Compass Players, much the same kind of university-spawned (in this case the University of Chicago) comedy revue that produced much of the cast and writing staff of the British *TW3*.

In fact, a number of alumni of the Compass Players (the troupe that planted the seeds for the considerably more famous Second City comedy proving ground), including Bob Dishy, Sandy Baron and the already iconic team of Mike Nichols and Elaine May, would spend at least some time working on the American *TW3*. So would Buck Henry, a writing/performing alumnus of Steve Allen's envelope-pushing syndicated late-night show. In fact, even while he was working on *TW3*, Henry was also working with Mel Brooks on the creation of the secret agent satire series *Get Smart* and would bring two of the *TW3* writers, Gerald Gardner and Dee Caruso, with him to the *Get Smart* team. The resident *TW3* songwriter was mathematician-turned-satirist Tom Lehrer, who contributed songs about changes in education ("New Math"), the Catholic Church

("The Vatican Rag"), and relations between the races ("National Brotherhood Week"). Unfortunately, NBC's censors often made changes to the lyrics of Lehrer's songs before they could be performed on the live *TW3* shows. So, following his tenure with the show, Lehrer recorded an album of the unexpurgated songs he had written for the show and, not surprisingly, titled the LP *That Was the Year That Was*.

Critics were, for the most part, not impressed with the January 10 premiere episode. *Time*, for instance, pronounced the American *TW3* "bland and unfunny, full of toothpicks masquerading as rapiers." In reality, while not as edgy as its British predecessor, the American *TW3* was undeniably irreverent, especially when it came to politics, and that would be the show's undoing. Despite mediocre ratings, the show would remain in its Friday night perch until July, when it would go on hiatus for the summer and the political nominating conventions. But it would be moved to Tuesday night upon its return for the new season, opposite the popular sitcom *Petticoat Junction* on CBS and the pioneering prime-time soap opera *Peyton Place* on ABC. As well, *TW3* would be frequently preempted that fall for paid political programming. By November, with the election campaign over and the audience having deserted for the trendy competition, the show's ratings would go into a steep decline and *TW3* would fade into history by May 1965, as would social or political satire in prime time. It would be some two years before *The Smothers Brothers Comedy Hour* would revive the genre and it would be more than a decade before NBC's New York studios would be the home for a live show that featured this brand of comedy, albeit in a late-night time slot. That, of course, would be *Saturday Night Live*, a show whose roots went back to the same kind of local comedy troupes that produced a number of the members of the creative teams behind both the British and American versions of *That Was the Week That Was*.

On Saturday, November 23 in Britain, the same evening that *TW3* presented its JFK tribute, the BBC presented the premiere episode of a new science fiction series called *Doctor Who*. The premiere nearly didn't make it to air. The Beeb had devoted much of its broadcast time since the news from Dallas reached Britain on Friday evening to coverage of the JFK assassination, not an easy endeavor since these were the very early days of satellite transmissions. As well, there were a number of power blackouts at various British locales that interfered with BBC transmissions. So the debut of *Doctor Who* began shortly after its scheduled 5:15 p.m. air time and, since a number of people were unable to watch, the episode was repeated the following Saturday, just before the

Dr. Who

SATURDAY'S serial begins when two teachers (**Jacqueline Hill** and **William Russell**) probe the mystery surrounding one of their pupils (**Carol Ann Ford**)—and meet the strange Dr. Who

An advert from the UK's Radio Times for the November 23 debut of *Doctor Who* on BBC-TV, nearly derailed by power outages and Beeb coverage of the JFK assassination.

airing of the second episode.

Brits who did catch either showing of the premiere of *Doctor Who* saw a fairly bizarre science fiction cliffhanger, the first episode of a four-part serial. The debut episode dealt with the curiosity of a pair of schoolteachers, Barbara Wright (Jacqueline Hill) and Ian Chesterton (William Russell), about a very precocious but mysterious student of theirs, Susan Foreman (Carole Ann Ford). The teachers follow Susan home after school one day, but end up in a junkyard and hear her voice coming out of a blue London police call box. That box would become the symbol of the *Doctor Who* series, known as the TARDIS (Time and Relative Dimension in Space). The teachers open the call box and suddenly find themselves in a dark room, but much bigger than that call box looks from outside. The lights come on and Susan confronts the teachers, along with her quite unfriendly grandfather. This marks the first appearance of the Doctor (William Hartnell). The confrontation escalates into a struggle between the Doctor and Ian within what looks like the interior of a very primitive spaceship. The episode ends with the Doctor having launched the TARDIS, with the teachers and Susan on board, en route to the Stone Age.

That humble, rather low-tech episode marked the beginning of what the *Guinness Book of World Records* would call the longest-running and most successful science fiction television series of all time (yes, even more so than the *Star Trek* television franchise). That first four-part serial, which also introduced the Doctor's longest-running adversaries, the Daleks, would lead to a run of 26 seasons (plus two mid-'60s feature films starring Peter Cushing as the Doctor) that would end in December 1989, to be followed by a 1996 TV movie and, beginning in 2005, a new series still ongoing as this is written.

Unlike *TW3*, though, there would be no attempt at an American version of *Doctor Who* so it would take quite some time for the US audience to become aware of the Doctor in any form. Journalist Bill King of the *Atlanta Journal-Constitution* (also longtime publisher of *Anglofile* and *Beatlefan* magazine) and author Walter Podrazik (who, with Harry Castleman, has written several books, including the essential season-by-season television history *Watching TV*) each recall getting a comic book adaptation of the first of the Cushing *Doctor Who* movies, 1965's "Doctor Who and the Daleks." But neither recalls seeing episodes of the BBC series until PBS stations around the US began running them in the '70s. It would be in the era of the two '70s Doctors, Jon Pertwee and Tom Baker, that a cult following would develop around the show in America, despite the delay of several months between the Beeb telecasts and the US showings. By the time of the first stirrings of the *Doctor Who* cult, the series had been on the air in England for a decade or more and it would be understandable for the show's new followers to be curious about the early episodes of the show and the first two Doctors, Hartnell and Patrick Troughton. By comparison, though, the '60s *Doctor Who* episodes would look very low-tech by even '70s standards and, besides, they were all in black-and-white. The Chicago-bred Podrazik points out, "I do not think I ever saw more than ONE rotation of the black-and-whites (at least in Chicago). Clearly, the flaws (cheesy production, black-and-white) remained, even with a dedicated fan base." As well, a large number of episodes from the '60s would either be destroyed (the same fate that befell many non-filmed American TV programs of the same era) or the tape quality would quite visibly deteriorate within the BBC archives. Those that would survive had been transferred to film-on-video (not unlike the American kinescopes of live or videotaped programs), which would make for difficult viewing for audiences of future decades. Nonetheless, even with the gaps in the history of the Time Lord, *Doctor Who* would become one of the most-honored-and-influential ongoing parts of the pop culture of Great Britain.

No such claims would ever be made about the shows on the fall '63 prime time schedules for the three major American TV networks. With *The Beverly Hillbillies* the highest-rated of all network series, those schedules were loaded with situation comedies of wildly varying quality. Even with the vogue for Westerns having largely faded, there were seven running in prime time in the fall of '63, headed by the still-very-successful veterans *Bonanza* and *Gunsmoke*. There were plenty of pretty male faces in prime time, too, several of them certified teen heartthrobs. There was Richard Chamberlain of *Dr. Kildare*, Vince Edwards of *Ben Casey*, James Franciscus of *Mr. Novak*, and George Maharis of *Route 66*. All four were regular presences on the pages of the American teen magazines, though that was about to change. *Route 66*, in fact, would finish its first-run prime time tenure in the spring of '64 and the cancellation ax also fell on the show that had begun the "prime time pretty boys" trend.

77 Sunset Strip was the first of the glossy, scenic, humor-tinged Warner Brothers-produced detective shows that highlighted ABC's prime time schedule at the tail end of the '50s and the early '60s. It was the show that made a star of Efrem Zimbalist Jr. and a pompadoured, comb-waving teen idol of Edd "Kookie" Byrnes. But the show's ratings had declined sharply in the '62-'63 season so *77 Sunset Strip* was reconstructed in the fall of '63, with the no-nonsense Jack Webb and William Conrad at the helm as executive producer and director, a new musical theme, and only Zimbalist held over from the show's longtime cast. His character, Stu Bailey, was turned into a more serious, solo private investigator and the show was moved to the beginning of ABC's Friday evening lineup. The changes didn't work, to say the least, and *77 Sunset Strip* was canceled before mid-season. And, in an interesting turn of the page in the annals of pop culture, the final first-run episode of *77 Sunset Strip* was telecast on Friday evening, February 7, 1964, as The Beatles were spending their first evening in America.

Of course, The Beatles were in New York principally to make their live American debut that Sunday night on what was still TV's No. 1 variety series, *The Ed Sullivan Show*. Variety shows were a significant part of the network TV schedule and a major story line as the '63-'64 season began was the arrival of three new variety shows, each helmed by a major star "of stage, screen and television," as it was so often put in that era.

By far the most successful of the three would be *The Danny Kaye Show*. Kaye had established himself as a multi-talented star on radio, the stage, and in family-friendly films in the '40s and '50s, and as a good-will ambassador on behalf of UNICEF (United Nations Children's Fund). He was something of a latecomer to television, but his guest spots on variety shows and a few early '60s starring-vehicle specials convinced CBS that Kaye would do quite well as the host of a variety series. He was offered the Sunday night 9-10 p.m. time slot for the '63-'64 season, following the Sullivan show, but Kaye knew that he'd be going up against NBC's *Bonanza* and flatly turned down the offer. But CBS then offered Kaye the Wednesday night 10-11 pm position. This time, Kaye said yes.

The Danny Kaye Show debuted on September 25 and generally adhered to the variety show template, with an emphasis on musical numbers and comedy skits to take advantage of Kaye's talents as a singer, dancer, and comic actor. Reviews for the show were mostly favorable, if not total raves, and ratings throughout the season would be respectable, though not spectacular. The Kaye show would finish as the 30th highest-rated series of the season, with a 21.5 rating, and would win an Emmy award for best variety series. The Kaye show would run for another three seasons, bowing out in June 1967, having won three more Emmys and a Peabody award. Kaye would move on from regular TV work to concentrating on his ambassadorial pursuits for UNICEF and theater work while semi-regular cast member Harvey Korman would quickly transition in the fall of '67 to a new CBS variety hour hosted by Carol Burnett, which would be Korman's vehicle to comic stardom.

In contrast, Jerry Lewis had a much longer relationship with television than Kaye. After (Dean) Martin & Lewis became the hot young comedy team of the late '40s, they appeared on the June 1948 premiere of Sullivan's variety show, then called *The Toast of the Town*, and became, along with Eddie Cantor and the team of Bud Abbott & Lou Costello, hosts of NBC's *Colgate Comedy Hour*, which competed with Sullivan on Sunday nights in the early '50s. With the coming of coast-to-coast video connections in 1951, Dean & Jerry and Bud & Lou headlined the West Coast feed of the Colgate show from the El Capitan Theater in Hollywood, quite convenient for Martin & Lewis, who were by then in the early stages of a manic filmmaking regimen for Paramount Pictures that would last until the duo's breakup in July 1956.

Aside from guest shots and his growing annual telethon for the Muscular Dystrophy Association, Lewis's blossoming film career had pretty much eliminated the chance for regular TV work by the early '60s. But Jerry did a short stint hosting *The Tonight Show* in the spring of 1962,

174

in the interim period between the departure of Jack Paar as the show's host and the arrival of Johnny Carson behind the host's desk, and found that he liked the format of the show and the pace. Indeed, Lewis was reportedly quite disappointed when Carson was tapped as the show's new regular host.

The following year, hot on the heels of Lewis' big-screen success as *The Nutty Professor*, ABC made Lewis what was a mega-offer for that era—a five year, $40 million contract—to do a weekly variety/talk show and even bought the old Martin & Lewis stomping ground, the El Capitan Theater, renaming it the Jerry Lewis Theater and making it the show's home.

Years later, in an interview for the Archive of American Television, Lewis would say that he had insisted that the show be live and two hours long, admitting, "I'm responsible for that. I put it right where it went, in the toilet, and I even flushed it. It was a very big mistake."

Part of the problem with *The Jerry Lewis Show* was that ABC scheduled the show for Saturday nights following two hour-long music programs (aimed at two very different audiences), *Hootenanny* and *The Lawrence Welk Show*. In that era, the networks' prime-time schedule began at 7:30 pm, Eastern time, so the Lewis show wouldn't begin until 9:30 on Saturday night. That meant that the late network and/or local news would be pushed back a half-hour every Saturday night. And the combination of the live two-hour format and Lewis' ever-growing creative ego made for a chaotic mess, a bloated attempt at combining a variety show with a late-night talk show. One show was billed as an "old-time vaudeville show," another had Jerry and five comic colleagues discussing their craft, while a third was basically a two-hour promotion vehicle for *It's A Mad, Mad, Mad, Mad World*, five days before the film's premiere. Counting Lewis, 17 members of the film's cast appeared on that one episode.

By early December, ABC realized that it had indeed made "a very big mistake." *The Jerry Lewis Show* limped to the end of a 13-week run, finishing up on December 21 with Sammy Davis, Jr. and tap-dance legends the Step Brothers reprising their appearances on the vaudeville episode. The network paid off Lewis' gargantuan contract, but ABC was now stuck with the Jerry Lewis Theater. So the theater was given yet another facelift and re-christening over the holidays. By January 4, it had re-emerged as The Hollywood Palace and a Sullivan-style hour-long variety show of the same name debuted that night, hosted by the always dependable and bankable Bing Crosby. Indeed, while there would never be a permanent host for *The Hollywood Palace*, Bing would be the show's good-luck charm, hosting it more often than anyone else during its 6-and-a-half-season run. Guesting on the premiere *Palace*, along with a puppet troupe, acrobats, an illusionist, and a musical clown act, were Mickey Rooney, Bob Newhart, jazz-pop vocal stylist Nancy Wilson, clean-cut folk group The Young Americans, and Bing's son and frequent duet partner Gary. Much more memorable would be the final show of the first half-season of *The Hollywood Palace* on June 13, 1964, with host Dean Martin throwing insults at the series' first British rock band guests, The Rolling Stones.

The third of the big-name variety series that debuted that fall was a calculated gamble from the start by CBS. Judy Garland had been a star in movies, radio, TV and on records for nearly three decades. Over the same period, though, she had gotten a not-always-deserved reputation for erratic behavior and a lack of dependability. But a series of triumphant concerts and tours all over the world had also branded Garland as one of the most dynamic onstage performers in all of show business. To many, the greatest moment of Judy's performing career was her legendary concert at Carnegie Hall on April 23, 1961. On the heels of ecstatic concert reviews, Capitol Records released a two-LP *Judy at Carnegie Hall* package that July. It spent more than two years on *Billboard*'s album chart, was No. 1 for 13 weeks in the fall of '61, and won the Grammy for album of the year a few months later.

Off that huge success, CBS, despite a stormy past relationship with Garland and her then-husband, Sid Luft, signed Judy to a contract for a series of specials, beginning in 1962. The first one, with Frank Sinatra and Dean Martin the primary guests, was so successful that CBS, despite the misgivings of company President James Aubrey, then offered Garland a $24 million deal to do a weekly series. Needing money for various reasons, including a decade-old tax issue, Garland accepted CBS' offer of a four-year contract in December 1962. Thirty-year-old George Schlatter, who would be one of the creators of the revolutionary *Rowan and Martin's Laugh-In* some four years later, was named executive producer of the Garland series, Mel Torme was recruited as musical arranger and composer of special material, and Jerry Van Dyke was brought in as the series' resident comic.

With Kaye having turned down a time slot opposite the mighty *Bonanza*, the Garland show was given that unenviable time slot, but it was scheduled immediately following *The Ed Sullivan Show*, so the thinking was that at least some of Sullivan's large regular audience would stick around for Judy rather than switch over to NBC and the Cartwrights. Show taping began on June 24, 1963, with Mickey Rooney almost naturally (and at Garland's request) being the first guest and the format being the usual mix of music and comedy (though that first show didn't air until December 3). Some six weeks later, though, Aubrey fired Schlatter and much of the writing staff, replacing Schlatter with Norman Jewison, who set out to put more of a sketch comedy element into the show and to de-glamorize Judy. Van Dyke's role was increased and Garland became the target of jokes that perpetuated the shakier aspects of her reputation and her career. That bizarre direction was mercifully short-lived and Bill Colleran was brought in as the show's third producer in less than half a season. Colleran de-emphasized the comedy and played more to Garland's strength as a concert performer. Indeed, Van Dyke was gone from the show after the tenth episode taped, though that show wouldn't air until March 1.

By the end of November, though, the shows were being taped much closer to their eventual air dates and, while there was comedy from guests, the emphasis was now very much on music and, particularly, Garland's magnetic solo performances. Judy herself had received very positive notices for her work on the series, but the erratic format and Van Dyke in particular came in for much criticism. And, of course, the Garland show was walloped in the ratings by *Bonanza*. Even though the quality of the shows had greatly improved by January, CBS was ready to cancel the series. But Garland's contract stipulated that the network couldn't unilaterally cancel the show. That call had to come from Judy and it came on January 22. CBS issued a statement, supposedly from Judy, that she was ending the series because she wanted to spend more time with her children. The seven shows taped following the Garland announcement were all *Judy Garland in Concert* shows, four with guests and the other three solo Garland showcases. The final CBS *Judy Garland Show* would be taped on March 13 and would air on March 29.

While those three high-profile variety series were the big television story as the 1963-64 season began, no one could have imagined what ultimately became the biggest TV events of that season. Those who saw the radio-with-pictures coverage in the first hours after the shooting in Dallas had to be impressed with the way the three network news departments rose to the occasion to cover that weekend of public mourning and ceremony, but also the events in Dallas that culminated in the murder of the accused assassin. Some two and a half months later, the already venerable *Ed Sullivan Show*, which had an estimated weekly audience of about 35 million viewers, had the two highest-rated episodes in its entire 23-season history. The numbers for the February 9 and 16 Sullivan shows were, for all intents and purposes, double that customary 35 million estimate and the 73 million estimate for the February 9 show made it the most-watched entertainment program in television's still-rather-young history. The headline attraction on those two shows was not any of the show business giants one was accustomed to seeing on Sullivan's show, but a British rock 'n' roll band that the majority of Americans had never heard of on New Year's Day, 1964. The February 23 Sullivan show, with The Beatles featured via a pre-taped performance, didn't come close to the numbers from the previous two weeks, but they were still above the Sullivan norm.

Beginning with the appearance of The Dave Clark Five, hyped by the media as Beatles "competitors," rock 'n' roll, which had been featured rather sporadically on Sullivan's show, would now become a nearly-weekly featured element of the show, with the first wave of British Invasion bands getting particular emphasis in the coming months. Soon, the other major variety series and even situation comedies would begin featuring both British and American rock acts, followed that fall by the first weeknight primetime network rock 'n' roll showcase, *Shindig!*

WLS

The bright sound of Chicago Radio

THIS WEEK	JANUARY 17, 1964	WEEKS PLAYED

* 1.	There I've Said It Again ....Bobby Vinton — Epic	11
* 2.	Drag City ....Jan & Dean — Liberty	10
3.	Surfin' Bird ....The Trashmen — Garrett	6
* 4.	California Sun ....Rivieras — Riviera	8
* 5.	You Don't Own Me ....Lesley Gore — Mercury	6
* 6.	Popsicles & Icicles ....The Murmaids — Chattahoochee	8
* 7.	Hey Little Cobra ....The Ripchords — Columbia	5
* 8.	Dumbhead ....Ginny Arnell — MGM	12
* 9.	Daisy Petal Pickin' ....Jimmy Gilmer — Dot	9
*10.	Java ....Al Hirt — RCA	8
*11.	What's Easy For Two ....Mary Wells — Motown	8
*12.	Forget Him ....Bobby Rydell — Cameo	10
*13.	Slippin' and Slidin' ....Jim & Monica — Betty	8
*14.	A Letter From Sherry ....Dale Ward — Dot	4
*15.	Long Tall Texan ....Murry Kellum — MOC	10
*16.	In The Still Of The Night ....The Reflections — Tigre	6
*17.	Since I Fell For You ....Lenny Welch — Cadence	8
*18.	Whispering ....Nino Tempo & April Stevens — Atco	6
19.	The Gorilla ....The Ideals — Cortland	7
*20.	Baby I Love You ....The Ronettes — Philles	5
*21.	Tell Him ....The Drew Vells — Capitol	7
*22.	I Have A Boyfriend ....The Chiffons — Laurie	7
*23.	When The Lovelight Starts Shining ....The Supremes — Motown	9
24.	For You ....Rick Nelson — Decca	2
*25.	Stay With Me ....Nick Noble — Chess	5
*26.	I Can't Stop Talking About You.........Steve & Eydie — Columbia	8
*27.	Anyone Who Had A Heart ....Dionne Warwick — Scepter	4
*28.	Bless 'Em All ....Jane Morgan — Colpix	9
*29.	As Usual ....Brenda Lee — Decca	5
*30.	Wow Wow Wee ....The Angels — Smash	2
*31.	Girls Grow Up Faster Than Boys ....The Cookies — Dimension	4
32.	Little Boy ....Tony Bennett — Columbia	2
33.	True Love Goes On and On ....Burl Ives — Decca	1
*34.	Somewhere ....The Tymes — Parkway	5
*35.	A Fool Never Learns ....Andy Williams — Columbia	4
*36.	Todays Teardrops ....Rick Nelson — Imperial	4
*37.	Boy You Ought To See Her Now ......Kevin & Greg — Assoc. Artist	4
*38.	See The Funny Little Clown ....Bobby Goldsboro — UA	4
*39.	Um Um Um ....Major Lance — Okeh	2
*40.	I Want To Hold Her Hand ....The Beatles — Capitol	2

FEATURED ALBUMS
GORME COUNTRY STYLE — EYDIE GORME — COLUMBIA
THE WONDERFUL WORLD OF ANDY WILLIAMS — COLUMBIA

Bernie Allen

12:30—3:00 P.M. 12:00—3:00 P.M. Saturday
Monday—Friday 12:15—3:00 P.M. Sunday

WLS • DIAL 890 • 24 HOURS-A-DAY
ABC RADIO IN CHICAGO

This survey is compiled each week by WLS Radio/Chicago from reports of all record sales gathered from leading record outlets in the Chicagoland area. Hear Bob Hale play all the SILVER DOLLAR SURVEY hits daily from 3:00 to 6:30 P.M. *Denotes record first heard in Chicago on WLS.

"I Want to Hold Your Hand" had been No. 1 for better than a week on WABC in New York, but hadn't yet caught fire on its ABC Radio cousin, Chicago's Top 40 giant WLS.

CHAPTER 9

POP MUSIC: NOT SUCH A BAD ROAD
AFTER ALL

A s the '60s were coming to an end, the emerging first generation of rock critics realized that rock 'n' roll had a history that was worth chronicling. Over the next few years, a number of books, films, and radio documentaries on the history of rock music debuted and a myth grew out of these accounts of rock's history. According to the oft-repeated story, after the first golden era of rock 'n' roll in 1956 and '57, the music then entered a dark age that stretched from, take your pick, either Elvis Presley's induction into the US Army or the plane crash that killed Buddy Holly right up to the release of The Beatles' breakthrough hit in America, "I Want to Hold Your Hand." One radio documentary series even named this period after a Duane Eddy instrumental hit from that time, "Forty Miles of Bad Road." According to this version of the music's history, that period was dominated by teen idols, novelty records, and dance crazes, and it took The Beatles and the subsequent musical British Invasion to bring rock 'n' roll back to musical credibility.

Now, let's give the benefit of the doubt to these critical accounts regarding 1959 and '60. During those two years there were a bumper crop of teen idols of varying ability, novelty records of varying types, and, thanks largely to daily national TV exposure on *American Bandstand*, a number of popular dances, topped off by Chubby Checker's original number one success with his version of "The Twist." But there was hit music of more lasting quality during those two years as well, and an increasing amount of quality material over the next three years, 1961-63.

During this period, there were great records coming out of New Orleans (Chris Kenner, Ernie K. Doe, Huey "Piano" Smith, the songwriting and production work of Allen Toussaint), Detroit (the first hits from what eventually became the Motown empire), Chicago (great R&B/ blues from the Chess and Vee-Jay labels), Philadelphia (hits from the Cameo/Parkway and Swan labels and continued national exposure via *Bandstand*), Norfolk (Frank Guida's atmospheric production work on the hits of Gary US Bonds), Memphis (the last gasp of Sun Records and the first stirrings of what would become Stax), Los Angeles (the development of what became known as "surf music") and particularly New York. The bumper crop of great songs coming from the Brill Building songwriters was just one aspect of the New York pop-rock-R&B scene in the early '60s. There were timeless records being produced by Jerry Leiber and Mike Stoller with The Drifters, Leiber/Stoller semi-protégé Phil Spector's first efforts as a producer, the Peppermint Lounge twist hits of Joey Dee & the Starlighters, and Bob Crewe's successful transformation of a struggling New Jersey doo-wop group into one of the biggest hit vocal groups of the era, The Four Seasons. Hardly "Forty Miles of Bad Road."

1963 yielded even wider-ranging musical riches than '61 or '62. It was the year of the girl group and the girl singer and the slightly mad king of this genre was Spector, who had moved his Philles Records to Los Angeles. There, with instrumental backing by the team of session players later dubbed The Wrecking Crew (backing that just got bigger and bigger, as Spector constructed his "wall of sound") and session singers that included The Blossoms and that group's de facto leader, Darlene Love, and two girl groups Spector had brought out from New York, The Crystals and The Ronettes, Spector created some of the greatest records of the decade. In the first 10 months of '63 alone, he turned out "Da Doo Ron Ron" and "Then He Kissed Me" by The Crystals, "Today I Met The Boy I'm Going to Marry" and "Wait 'til My Bobby Gets Home" by Love, "Why Do Lovers Break Each Other's Hearts" by a studio singer assemblage Spector dubbed Bob B. Soxx & the Blue Jeans, and "Be My Baby" by the exotic-looking Ronettes and their sultry-voiced lead singer, Veronica "Ronnie" Bennett. And, through the year, Spector used the same cast of players and singers to create the first real rock 'n' roll Christmas album, *A Christmas Gift for You from Philles Records*, which had reached distributors in mid-November.

The L.A. surf music scene had largely been all-instrumental, lots of twangy guitars and bubbling basses, emulating Duane Eddy and the first rock instrumental group to sell large quantities of LPs, The Ventures. But then came a group from Hawthorne, California, that blended that surf guitar sound, the anthemic rock of Chuck Berry, and the vocal harmonies of The Four Freshmen. The group was called The Beach Boys and their sound originated in the creatively-fertile brain of the band's bass player and principal writer, Brian Wilson. The band had its first hit single, "Surfin' Safari," in the fall of '62, followed by their first LP. A year later, The Beach Boys had become a pop-rock sensation, the first self-contained rock band to have major hit albums and two double-sided surf-and-hot-rod-themed hit singles, "Surfin' USA."/"Shut Down" and "Surfer Girl"/"Little Deuce Coupe." A third double-sided hit, the school spirit anthem "Be True to Your School" and the more-introspective ballad "In My Room" was headed for the upper reaches of the charts by mid-November.

The Beach Boys' *Surfer Girl* LP included a track called "Surfers Rule," with a coda that proclaimed, "Four Seasons, you better believe it/ Surfer's rule," complete with a falsetto vocal similar to that of Four Seasons lead singer Frankie Valli by Brian Wilson. Despite that challenge from the striped-shirted Californians, though, the Seasons had chalked up their third straight number one single in March with "Walk Like A Man," followed in the summer by the Top Five success of "Candy Girl."

Folk music had enjoyed a revival in recent years, thanks largely to the success of The Kingston Trio, who were still having hits in '63 ("Reverend Mr. Black" and "Greenback Dollar"), and the exposure provided by ABC-TV's Saturday night folk showcase *Hootenanny*. But there was also a new, more topical form of folk music that was largely absent from *Hootenanny* because of its event-charged social commentary and its ties to blacklisted folk elders like Pete Seeger. The most successful of the topical folk acts was the Greenwich Village-based trio Peter, Paul & Mary, who had scored three Top 10 singles during '63, including "Puff The Magic Dragon," written by group leader Peter Yarrow and the subject of much controversy in later years. The other two, "Blowin' in the Wind" and "Don't Think Twice, It's All Right," were written by the new folk's boy king, a baby-faced, tousle-haired young man from Hibbing, Minn., who called himself Bob Dylan. "Blowin' in the Wind," in particular, became one of the anthems of that summer's civil rights movement. Indeed, Peter, Paul & Mary, Dylan, and the queen of the new folk, Joan Baez, all performed at the March on Washington. Meanwhile, right in the midst of the drive for more equitable treatment of blacks throughout the nation, Berry Gordy's Detroit-based collection of labels under the Motown corporate umbrella was gradually becoming the most successful black-run record company in the US, with Top 10 pop hits during '63 by The Miracles, Marvin Gaye, two by Martha & the Vandellas, and topped off in August with a number one single, "Fingertips-Part 2," by a blind multi-instrumentalist and vocalist dubbed, by Gordy, Little Stevie Wonder.

At the beginning of 1963, the No. 1 single in the US was actually by a British band, a group called The Tornadoes, with an instrumental called "Telstar," inspired by the communications satellite launched by the US the previous summer. The record had a otherworldly, very space-age sound provided by producer Joe Meek, and was the first single by a British band to reach No. 1 in America since the beginning of the rock 'n' roll era. But the handful of UK imports that had become American hits in recent years was more in the realm of novelties than mainstream pop-rock. For instance, that summer, England-based native Australian Rolf Harris had a Top 10 hit with the very Aussie-flavored novelty "Tie Me Kangaroo Down, Sport." Meanwhile, a number of American acts made their customary treks to England and Europe and came home talking about what was going on in England: the growing phenomenon of The Beatles and the large number of bands that were creating great excitement throughout the UK Philly teen idol Bobby Rydell even recorded a single in England that was written and produced by Tony Hatch, who would achieve international fame in the coming years for his work with, among others, Petula Clark. The song was called "Forget Him" and was originally packaged as an extra with an LP of Rydell's covers of hits of '63 and released early that fall. Soon, though, "Forget Him" was released as a commercial single on its own and was beginning to gain chart momentum in mid-November, on its way to becoming one of the bigger American hits of that winter. But "Forget Him" would also be Rydell's last significant hit in the US

Gene Pitney, who had become a consistent hit maker as both a singer and songwriter, came back from a summertime trip to Britain with a more visual example of what was going on there. When he appeared at New York deejay Murray the K's multi-act show at the Brooklyn Fox Theater at the beginning of September, he had combed his hair forward, though the fringe only reached about mid-forehead. Still, he was giving the New York audience an advance peek at the hairstyle that would conquer the world over the next year.

Tommy Roe, who had scored his first major hit late in the summer of '62 with the Buddy Holly-esque "Sheila," had toured England with Chris Montez the following spring and got an early look at the rising popularity of The Beatles, who were on the same bill and, by the time the tour ended, were getting the greater crowd response. That fall, Roe released a single that he said was his interpretation of the new sound that was on the rise in the UK "Everybody" was an acoustic guitar-driven tune with an infectious chorus. Even though the American audience wasn't yet aware of the song's roots, it was tailor-made for radio airplay and had reached the national Top 5 by early December.

Along with the British import No. 1 at the beginning of the year, 1963 also saw two foreign language singles become multi-week No. 1's, a very rare occurrence in America. The first was a record by Japanese singing-acting star Kyu Sakamoto, which had been a hit in England early in the year in an instrumental treatment by Kenny Ball. The record's original Japanese title roughly translated to "I Look Up When I Walk," but Pye Records (whose owner, Louis Benjamin, had heard Sakamoto's original while on a visit to Japan) opted to go with a title that would be Japanese, but recognizable for the Anglo audience. In a later era, the choice might have been "sushi" or a brand name like "Sony" or "Honda." But Pye's choice was "Sukiyaki." Then, in a scenario quite similar to one at year's end that would greatly contribute toward the breakthrough of The Beatles in America, Rick Osborne, a nighttime disc jockey at a small radio station in the state of Washington, was able to obtain an imported single of Sakamoto's original vocal recording of Ball's UK hit. (In December, it was airplay of an imported copy of "I Want to Hold Your Hand" by Carroll James, a nighttime deejay in Washington, D.C., that accelerated the building momentum that would finally break The Beatles in America in the first weeks of '64.) Airplay of the original "Sukiyaki" began to spread through the upper Northwest and Capitol Records (also the unwitting beneficiary of the December scenario) got the rights to Sakamoto's record and released it with Pye's title from the Ball version. Ironically, the Capitol executive who gave the go-ahead for Capitol to release Sakamoto's record was Dave Dexter, who was responsible for screening EMI's international releases for possible American release on Capitol and spent much of the year giving the thumbs-down to releases by the increasingly-popular (in England and Europe) Beatles. In any event, by '63's midpoint, "Sukiyaki" was America's No. 1 single.

Then, late in the year, another foreign language single topped the American charts. An LP by a Belgian nun, accompanied by just a guitar and backing vocals from four other nuns, that had been recorded in Brussels and released in Europe by Philips Records, credited to "Sister Sourire" (in English, Sister Smile), had subsequently been released in the US under the title "The Singing Nun." Then, it was decided that one of the tracks on the album, "Dominique," should be released as a single. The song was a tribute to St. Dominic, founder of the Dominican order, and was written by the record's vocalist, Sister Luc-Gabrielle (real name: Jeanine Deckers).

"Dominique" took off like a rocket upon its release as a single and was already in the national Top 20 by mid-November. In New York on November 20, "Dominique" was the No. 2 song on WMCA, one of the three Top 40 radio stations in the Big Apple, and was number one on WABC, which was already on its way to becoming the biggest Top 40 station in America. In the following week's issues of the leading music business trade publications, *Cashbox* and *Billboard*, dated November 30 but based on chart data from the previous week, "Dominique" was at No. 1 in the former and No. 2 in the latter magazine.

Those facts directly contradict another long-held myth, that "Dominique" owed its success to the assassination of President Kennedy. Indeed, those who buy into that myth point out the number of ballads and "softer" songs that were major hits during the last weeks of '63 and contend that, because of the emotional pall cast over the nation by President Kennedy's death, the dominant hits were softer tunes. The facts are that there have always been periods when lighter material tended to dominate the upper reaches of the pop charts and the latter weeks of 1963 were indeed an example of that. But that trend had begun in October, when the hottest record in the US was the decidedly soft-rock "Sugar Shack" by Jimmy Gilmer & The Fireballs. Among the biggest records of the coming weeks were the folk-flavored instrumental "Washington Square" by The Village Stompers, Nino Tempo & April Stevens' interpretation of the standard "Deep Purple," and Dale & Grace's country-tinged "I'm Leaving It Up To You." (the latter two preceded "Dominique" as national No. 1 songs in November, previous to JFK's trip to Texas).

Conversely, the second-hottest record in the US throughout December was the soon-to-be-iconic rocker "Louie Louie" by The Kingsmen, a band straight out of the upper Northwest hotbed of young rock bands that had also produced Paul Revere & The Raiders (who, in fact, had also recorded "Louie Louie" earlier that year). The fact that "Louie Louie" never became No. 1 on the industry standard *Billboard* Hot 100 (and this was months before all the nonsense about the supposedly "dirty" lyrics in the song became a cause celebré) may have had more to do with the middle-aged males who put together the charts for *Billboard* in that era and who may have felt that the moment wasn't right for a rocker to be the nation's top-ranked song, though "Louie Louie" did top *Cashbox*'s singles chart for two weeks in January. In Top 40 radioland, it was quite a different story. In New York, for example, "Louie Louie" was number one for the final three weeks of '63 on both WABC and WMCA, weeks before it topped *Cashbox*'s national chart.

In a bizarre confluence of fate, or bad karma, the lives of both Kyu Sakamoto and Jeanine Deckers would end prematurely, within five months of each other in 1985. On March 29, Deckers, whose story of being ripped off by her record company and deserted by her former religious order would read like an episode of the 21st century TV series *Behind The Music*, would commit suicide with an overdose of barbiturates in the wake of accelerating financial troubles and several failed comeback attempts. On Aug. 12, Sakamoto would be one of 520 souls who would perish when Japan Airlines Flight 123 crashed into the side of a mountain, one of the worst airline disasters in aviation history.

The musical year of 1963, at least in America, will be primarily remembered for the bumper crop of hits by girl groups and girl singers. The Chiffons, who had one of the biggest hits of the spring (and one of the best-remembered girl group records of the era) with "He's So Fine," were nearly as successful during the summer with Gerry Goffin and Carole King's "One Fine Day," and finished the year with a third national Top 40 single, the joyous "I Have A Boyfriend," primarily written by Jeff Barry and Ellie Greenwich. The Angels reached No. 1 in the fall with the classically sassy "My Boyfriend's Back." The Shirelles, the most successful girl group of the early '60s, had their last two Top 10 singles with the Doris Day cover "Everybody Loves a Lover" and Howard Greenfield and Helen Miller's "Foolish Little Girl." Fifteen-year-old Peggy March became the youngest artist to that point in time to reach No. 1 in the spring with "I Will Follow Him," an American-ized version of the French hit "Chariot." Skeeter Davis, at 31 a young veteran country hitmaker, had a multi-genre Top Five hit that spring with "The End of the World" and followed it up in the fall with the Goffin-King-written Top 10 hit "I Can't Stay Mad at You." But the biggest success story among the girls of '63 was that of a 17-year-old high school junior from Tenafly, NJ.

Lesley Gore was something of a musical prodigy when she was signed to Mercury Records, while still singing in the chorus at the Dwight School for Girls, and was placed under the wing of the label's New York head of A&R, the great Quincy Jones. Out of a large stack of demos that Jones brought to her parents' home one night late in the winter of '63, Lesley selected a teenage melodrama called "It's My Party," which had very recently been recorded by England's most popular teenage pop vocalist, Helen Shapiro. While Shapiro's version of the song waited months to be released by her record company in the UK, Gore's version, with a superb arrangement/production by Q, raced up the US charts and was No. 1 by the end of May.

A literal sequel to the triangle saga in "It's My Party," "Judy's Turn to Cry," also reached the national Top 5 in August. But Gore's first LP, *I'll Cry If I Want To*, was a very different affair. Here, the jazz leanings that Gore and Jones shared predominated over the teen tearjerkers, with renditions of "Cry Me A River," "Misty," "The Party's Over," and Anthony Newley's "What Kind of Fool Am I?"

A third Gore single, "She's a Fool," and a second LP, *Lesley Gore Sings of Mixed-Up Hearts*, followed that fall and the single became her third straight Top 5 hit early in December. Once again, the LP contained Gore's interpretations of pop standards like "Fools Rush In" and "Young and Foolish," but it also contained three major hit singles (including "She's a Fool") and a very popular B-side.

"The Old Crowd" was a Goffin-King tune that was the b-side of "She's a Fool." It's a nostalgic look back at high school friends and the "good old days." Given the generational demarcation line and what many would feel was the end of the "good old days" that was just weeks away when the single was released in October, it's a very interesting nugget from that moment in time.

"You Don't Own Me" is different from virtually any of Gore's major hits. It's a rather stark, brooding song of female emancipation (written, of course, by two men, John Madara and David White). Less than a year after the publication of Betty Friedan's *The Feminine Mystique* and several years before the drive for female liberation gained momentum, a song that proclaimed, "Don't tell me what to do/Don't tell me what to say/And please when I go out with you/Don't put me on display" was quite different from the usual boy-adoring fare from the young girl singers and groups. (Indeed, Gore's next single, "That's The Way Boys Are," was exactly that kind of let-boys-be-boys song.) Nonetheless, "You Don't Own Me" became a very big hit in the early weeks of 1964 and, if it had been nearly any other time, it would have equaled or bettered the success of "It's My Party." On Lesley's home turf, New York, "You Don't Own Me" spent three weeks in late January/early February at No. 3, behind "I Want to Hold Your Hand" and "She Loves You," on WABC's survey and, nationally, it spent three weeks in February at No. 2 behind "I Want to Hold Your Hand."

"Sunshine, Lollipops, and Rainbows," which immediately preceded "You Don't Own Me" on *Lesley Gore Sings of Mixed-Up Hearts*, was just about the musical polar opposite of "You Don't Own Me." A short, bouncy piece of pop confection, written with Howard Liebling by 19-year-old Marvin Hamlisch (the same young prodigy who was Barbra Streisand's rehearsal pianist for *Funny Girl*), it would remain an album track until the spring of 1965, when it would be used in the beach party variation flick "Ski Party" and subsequently would become a Top 20 hit that summer. It would be Gore's seventh and next-to-last Top 20 single and Hamlisch's debut hit as a composer, the beginning of a historic career.

Nearing the end of what would be the most successful year of his career as a producer, Phil Spector was ready to unleash a big musical one-two punch: The Ronettes' follow up single to "Be My Baby," "Baby I Love You," and the Christmas LP that he and his stable of artists and session players had been working on much of the year. The two releases had far less immediate impact than Spector was expecting. "Baby I Love You" barely made the national Top 25 while *A Christmas Gift for You from Philles Records* failed to make much of an immediate impression. In future years, the mythologists, this time led by Spector, would again lay the blame for the immediate commercial failure of Spector's Christmas album with the JFK assassination and the alleged pall it cast over so much of the nation, including Top 40 radio.

In reality, Spector's Christmas LP, which would become a revered collector's item by decade's end, was a very unusual release, a full-on pop-rock Christmas album with virtually no precedent and without the promotional power of a major record label. Phil's claim of a November 22 release date for the album may very well be apocryphal since, even in that era, the week before Thanksgiving was very late for the release of a Christmas album. Then again, there were no radio stations playing nonstop Christmas music beginning Thanksgiving week in those days. Nonetheless, it would take time for the Spector Christmas album to gain its legendary status. The LP would be reissued as *The Phil Spector Christmas Album* during Spector's early '70s days at Apple

Records, with numerous reissues right into the iTunes era. Decades after the original album's release, Darlene Love and Ronnie Spector (the former Ronnie Bennett would carry her married name well after she escaped her difficult marriage to Phil) would make annual Christmastime concert appearances, featuring their best-known moments from *A Christmas Gift for You*. The Ronettes' take on Leroy Anderson's "Sleigh Ride" would become an omnipresent part of those 24/7 all-Christmas radio formats. And Love would make an annual pre-Christmas appearance on *The Late Show With David Letterman* to sing "Christmas (Baby Please Don't Go)" well into the 21st century, despite the feeling of many that that song isn't even her best moment on the album (her version of "White Christmas" may well be a more iconic performance).

As for "Baby I Love You," that single would also gain stature with the passage of time. It would never be looked on as a classic on the level of "Be My Baby," but certainly a highlight of Spector's Philles years and a great piece of Brill Building pop primarily written by Barry and Greenwich. Indeed, in 1969, Barry would release a cover of "Baby I Love You" by his new professional collaborator, Andy Kim, on Barry's own Steed Records and Kim's version, while not nearly as memorable, would outperform the Ronettes' version, reaching the Top 10 that summer.

A more immediately-successful Christmas release than Spector's ambitious LP was a new single by The Beach Boys. The Chuck Berry-esque "Little Saint Nick" was a natural for Top 40 radio Christmastime airplay and would become a much-covered rock 'n' roll holiday standard in decades to come. At the same time, "Be True to Your School" spent all of December in the Top 10 and the sun-and-surf-dominated *Surfer Girl* LP was a Top 10 album at the same time. Then, the all-car-songs *Little Deuce Coupe* collection spent all of January in the album Top 10. That gave The Beach Boys three Top 10 albums in less than a year, an unprecedented run of success for a rock band. But then, as Brian Wilson would later term it, "It was, like, kwompf!"

That "kwompf" was the sudden breakthrough of The Beatles in America. Their huge success and the fact that the first US Beatles hit single, "I Want to Hold Your Hand," was released on The Beach Boys' recording home label, Capitol Records, once again brought out the competitive spirit in Brian. The first Beach Boys single of 1964 was arguably their best to date. "Fun Fun Fun" had all the elements of a great pop-rock single – a great, Chuck Berry-inspired guitar intro, a driving beat, an infectious hook, and even a soaring climax powered by Brian's

Apart from Top 40 radio, the first and—in the opinion of many— greatest of all rock 'n' roll Christmas albums received little attention upon its release in late November of '63.

falsetto. "Fun Fun Fun" entered the national singles charts in the middle of February, while The Beatles were in the midst of their first visit to America, and hit the Top 10 by the beginning of March. "Fun Fun Fun" would peak at number six in those Beatles-heavy Top 10s, but it made the point that The Beach Boys weren't going to let the English upstarts completely dominate. Indeed, their next single, "I Get Around," would become the band's first No. 1.

Brian had also been creatively collaborating with Jan Berry of Jan & Dean, the "clown princes" of surf and hot rod music. Together, they had written the duo's No. 1 hit from the summer of '63, "Surf City." With L.A. disc jockey Roger Christian, rapidly becoming the poet laureate of hot rod music, they wrote "Drag City," which reached the national Top 10 in January. Utilizing many of the same ace L.A. session players both Brian and Spector had been using, "Drag City" had a much "bigger" sound than "Surf City," complete with sound effects of revved-up engines and squealing tires and sounded great on a car radio. Then, Berry, Wilson, Christian, and longtime Berry colleague Artie Kornfeld collaborated on the melodramatic "Dead Man's Curve," which had, if anything, even a denser production than "Drag City." This ended up being a double-sided hit, with "The New Girl In School," a cleaner, more polished re-write of a Wilson-Berry collaboration called "(When Summer Comes) Gonna Hustle You," reaching the Top 40. "Dead Man's Curve," which would reach the Top 10 in April, would take on near-legendary status in years to come after Jan was nearly killed in a car crash, some two years after "Dead Man's Curve." That accident would have some eerie parallels with the song and leave Jan with physical and mental damage that would be with him for the rest of his life. Indeed, "Dead Man's Curve" would be used as the title song of a 1978 TV movie about Berry's slow recovery from the crash, with Richard Hatch and Bruce Davison starring as Jan & Dean.

Even as the Liverpudlian tsunami approached American shores, the California surf-hot rod sound was having a major presence on the charts in the first weeks of 1964, including hits by acts based nowhere near southern California. The Minneapolis-based Trashmen struck pay dirt with "Surfin' Bird," a reworking of The Rivingtons' 1962-63 hits "Papa-Oom-Mow-Mow" and "The Bird's The Word." The Rivieras, from South Bend, Ind.. reached the Top 5 with "California Sun." Closer to the actual California sun, a Long Beach-based instrumental surf group called The Pyramids had a Top 20 national hit with "Penetration" while an assemblage of mostly session instrumentalists called The Marketts reached No. 3 with "Out of Limits," a surf-sound variation on the theme for *The Outer Limits*, a TV show with an intro a little too-close-for-comfort to the *Twilight Zone* theme for that show's creator, Rod Serling. And right behind "Out of Limits" was a car song, "Hey Little Cobra," by a southern California group called The Rip Chords. This record is particularly significant because the lead vocals on "Hey Little Cobra" were done by producers Bruce Johnston and Terry Melcher. Johnston would later make a name for himself as writer of the mid-'70s Barry Manilow hit "I Write The Songs" and an off-and-on association with The Beach Boys that would continue into the 21st century. Melcher, son of Doris Day, would become a prominent producer for Columbia Records, achieving particular success in the mid-to-late-sixties with The Byrds and Paul Revere & The Raiders.

Meanwhile, in New York The Beach Boys' East Coast competitors, The Four Seasons, also rose to the challenge from England. The Seasons had left the financially-shaky Vee-Jay Records at the end of '63, amid a legal wrangle over royalties and a further dispute over new recordings that the group had made with producer Bob Crewe and had

given to their new label, Philips, which just happened to be distributed by Mercury Records, like Vee-Jay headquartered in Chicago. One
of the new songs was a composition by the Seasons' Bob Gaudio and
Brill Building songwriter Sandy Linzer called "Dawn (Go Away)." The
recording had all of the best elements of the group's Vee-Jay hits: an
instantly-accessible hook, a powerful lead vocal by Frankie Valli, and
a bright, atmospheric arrangement by Charlie Calello. Like "Fun Fun
Fun," "Dawn (Go Away)" was a virtually-instant smash hit, debuting
the first week in February, leaping to just below the Top 10 two weeks
later, and then spending the last two weeks of February and the first
week in March at number three, behind "I Want to Hold Your Hand"
and "She Loves You." By the third week in March, *Billboard*'s Top
Five singles would be three Beatles releases (with Vee-Jay's reissue
of "Please Please Me"), "Dawn," and "Fun Fun Fun." The following
week, "Dawn" would round out the Top Five below four Beatles songs,
followed by the historic April 4 *Billboard* Hot 100 with the all-Beatles
Top Five singles (and top two LPs). Nonetheless, like their West Coast
rivals, The Four Seasons had shown that they could compete quite well,
even in the midst of the blitz of multi-label Beatles releases. Indeed,
the Seasons' next Philips single, "Ronnie," would peak at No. 6 that
spring and its follow-up, "Rag Doll," would be a nearly-instantaneous
No. 1 song on New York Top 40 radio early that summer and a national
chart-topper in short order.

Meanwhile, Vee-Jay, quite busy trying to exploit its small inventory
of Beatles masters in every possible way while also battling Capitol Records, The Four Seasons, and various and sundry creditors in numerous
legal actions, would be able to gain a pair of moderate Four Seasons
hits with a cover of Maurice Williams' 1960 hit "Stay" that spring and
a Seasons version of The Shepherd Sisters' 1957 hit "Alone" that summer. In the fall, Vee-Jay would cap its relationship with The Beatles and
The Four Seasons by releasing a double album package of its already
multi-packaged *Golden Hits of The Four Seasons* and *Introducing The
Beatles* as "The International Battle of the Century" before fading into
the mists of music and litigation history.

On the album charts, the dominant group of the fall of '63 was un-
doubtedly Peter, Paul & Mary. In its 79th week on *Billboard*'s album list
and a year after a seven-week run as the No. 1 LP in the country, the
group's 1962 debut LP returned to the top of the chart, only to be ousted
a week later by their third album, *In The Wind*, which rocketed to No. 1
in just its second week on *Billboard*'s list and spent the last week in Oc-

tober and all of November at the top of the list. By that time, Peter, Paul & Mary's second album, *(Moving)*, had been on *Billboard*'s list for over 40 weeks so there were three LPs by the trio among the Top 10 albums for most of November.

In The Wind contained both of Peter, Paul & Mary's '63 hit singles written by Bob Dylan, who played a number of high profile gigs in the fall, including prestige shows at New York's Carnegie Hall and what was then called Philharmonic Hall at the city's new Lincoln Center for the Performing Arts. He had also wrapped up recording sessions for his third album, which would showcase the young king of topical folk music's take on the issues of the time and include songs that Dylan had been performing in various venues throughout the country since the spring. Most of these new songs would deal with civil rights, the downtrodden, and the Cold War, but the album's title song and lead-off track would be an attempt by Dylan to write "a song with a purpose…a big song." The song was called "The Times They Are A-Changin'" and it would become an anthem of change that would echo through the decades and never lose its relevance, despite its author's often ambivalent public comments on it.

Ironically, *The Times They Are A-Changin'* album would be released in mid-January 1964, just a few weeks after the ultimate moment of change for Dylan and his musical constituency. In typical Dylan fashion, he would give out very mixed signals regarding his reaction to the assassination of President Kennedy, but, within months, Dylan would totally turn away from songs of social commentary and turn within for inspiration for his new songs and those songs would become more and more layered and complex. By the fall of '64, Dylan would re-label "The Times They Are A-Changin'" as not a statement: "It's a feeling."

Dylan was back on the road when the *Times They Are A-Changin'* LP was released and it was right about that time that he first heard "I Want to Hold Your Hand." He was impressed with The Beatles' "weird chords" and was particularly impressed with the refrain in the song's middle-eight, words that he heard as "I get high," instead of the actual "I can't hide." By the end of that summer, Dylan would meet The Beatles in New York and turn them on to pot. The following year would see each of their careers turn in quite unexpected ways. For Bob Dylan and The Beatles, the times would indeed be a-changin'.

Half a century before Berry Gordy's somewhat sanitized version of the Motown story would become a hit Broadway "jukebox musical," Gordy's empire was still experiencing growing pains. Marvin Gaye followed up his debut Top 10 single, "Pride and Joy," by just missing the national Top 20 with "Can I Get A Witness" while The Miracles followed their Top 10 success with "Mickey's Monkey" by not even making the national pop Top 30 in the early weeks of '64 with "I Gotta Dance to Keep From Crying." Martha & the Vandellas, after racking up Top 10 hits in '63 with "Heat Wave" and "Quicksand," fell short of the Top 40 early in '64 with "Live Wire" and Stevie Wonder wouldn't gain another national hit single for some 2½ years after "Fingertips." But two groups that would be among the greatest contributors toward establishing the Motown musical dynasty had their pop breakthroughs between the last weeks of '63 and the spring of '64. The Temptations, after a lengthy period of personnel transition and lack of commercial success, had their pop hit debut with "The Way You Do the Things You Do." It was written and produced by The Miracles' lead singer and principal writer, Smokey Robinson, as would be virtually all of the first two years' worth of hits by this multi-talented group that emerged from a pair of Detroit vocal groups, one of which was known as the Primes.

A group of local girls called The Primettes were the Primes' sister act but, when the girls were signed to Motown and made their professional debut as The Supremes, the trio had little success for the better part of two years, even with Smokey and Gordy overseeing their early work. The closest The Supremes got to a hit record was singing backup for Gaye on "Can I Get A Witness." Shortly thereafter, the writing/production team of Eddie and Brian Holland and Lamont Dozier, who were on a hit-making roll with those recent hits by Gaye and Martha & the Vandellas, took on The Supremes and their first collaboration, "When the Lovelight Starts Shining Through His Eyes," was recorded and released in October of '63. It took until December for the record to gain real momentum, but it ultimately reached the pop Top 20 in *Cashbox* (and #2 on that magazine's R&B chart), peaking at #23 in *Billboard*. Interestingly, under Diana Ross's lead vocal on "When the Lovelight Starts Shining Through His Eyes," the backup vocals were done by not just the other two Supremes, Mary Wilson and Florence Ballard, but were augmented by another male Motown vocal group, The Four Tops. It would be the massive success of The Supremes, The Temptations, The Four Tops, and the production and songwriting work of Holland-Dozier-Holland that would enable Motown to become America's most consistently successful music entity during the peak of the British Invasion and the success story that Gordy would chronicle for the stage a half-century later.

Meanwhile, in Memphis, what would become known as "the Stax/

Volt sound" was also beginning to take shape. One of the early musical architects of that sound, Rufus Thomas, whose daughter Carla had one of the label's earliest hits (even though it was nationally released on Atlantic) in 1961 with "Gee Whiz," reached the Top 10 at the end of November with "Walking the Dog." And, in late January, Otis Redding, who would become Stax's greatest star before his death in a plane crash in December 1967, made his first appearance within *Cashbox*'s Top 50 pop singles with "Pain in My Heart," the same week that "I Want to Hold Your Hand" first topped *Cashbox*'s chart.

In Chicago, The Impressions, a gospel-doo-wop-based R&B group founded by Jerry Butler and Curtis Mayfield in the late '50s, had their single biggest hit of a lengthy career in the fall of '63 with Mayfield's "It's All Right," reaching No. 4 on both *Cashbox* and *Billboard*'s pop charts and No. 1 on each magazine's R&B chart in November. "It's All Right" was the first of seven Impressions singles, most written by Mayfield, that would reach at least the national Top 15 between the fall of '63 and the spring of 1965, including Curtis's first two great social anthems, "Keep On Pushing" and "People Get Ready," and their Christmastime '64 reworking of "Amen." As well, Mayfield had a brief run of great success as a writer and producer for childhood friend Major Lance. "The Monkey Time" was a very popular dance tune (a hit at the same time as The Miracles' "Mickey's Monkey") that hit the national Top 10 in September of '63. The very similar-sounding "Hey Little Girl" reached the Top 15 in the fall and a third Mayfield tune, "Um, Um, Um, Um, Um, Um," was the most successful, reaching the Top 5 by the second week in February.

Doo-wop, the musical form in which Mayfield first worked as a professional, was certainly fading from the mainstream, but hadn't completely disappeared. Even as The Beatles were conquering America, a two-year-old record called "Rip Van Winkle" by a by-then-disbanded New York vocal group called The Devotions was reissued on Roulette Records and reached the national Top 40. Jersey City's Duprees had their last significant hit in the last weeks of '63 with the Top 20 success of "Have You Heard." Naturally, both records did even better on home turf New York Top 40 radio. In Philadelphia, The Tymes, who had racked up national Top 10 hits during the summer of '63 with the near-acapella "So Much In Love" and the Johnny Mathis cover "Wonderful Wonderful," reached the Top 20 for a third time in the year's last weeks with "Somewhere." And Patti LaBelle, who would have a mid-'70s No. 1 R&B-pop hit with "Lady Marmalade," reached the national Top 40 with her first group, the Blue Belles and the doo-wop-flavored "Down The Aisle (Wedding Song)" along with their re-working of "You'll Never Walk Alone."

Indeed, in the early morning hours of February 7, 1964, just hours before The Beatles were scheduled to arrive in New York, Bob Lewis, the deejay who called himself Bobaloo, was playing a lot of doo-wop oldies on his overnight show on WABC. Presumably, he was playing them from the station's normal pre-arranged playlist, but a listen to his show from that night does give one the feeling that, subconsciously, someone was aware that one chapter of pop music history was closing and a new one was about to begin later that day.

The most immediate casualties of this musical sea change were a number of hitmakers of the late '50s/early '60s, who suddenly became out-of-fashion. As mentioned, Bobby Rydell had his last major hit during this time with "Forget Him," though he would soon record a cover version of Peter & Gordon's No. 1 single that spring, the Paul McCartney-written "A World Without Love." Dion DiMucci, a teen idol going back to his late '50s days with The Belmonts, reached the Top 10 in the last weeks of '63 with his cover of The Drifters' mid-'50s R&B hit "Drip Drop." It would be nearly five years before he would have a bona fide hit single again, with "Abraham, Martin, and John," and none after that. Rick Nelson, despite his weekly network TV exposure on *The Adventures of Ozzie & Harriet*, had his first Top 10 single in just over a year with "For You" and had just one more, "Garden Party," in the fall of 1972, for the remainder of his career. Bobby Vee was already a year removed from his most recent Top Five hit, "The Night Has a Thousand Eyes," and would have only one more, "Come Back When You Grow Up" in the summer of '67. Bobby knew what was coming, though, and recorded a very Beatles-like single, "I'll Make You Mine," with backing by The Eligibles, but it failed to reach even the national Top 50 late in the winter of '64.

Johnny Tillotson reached the Top 10 at the beginning of January with the country-flavored "Talk Back Trembling Lips," but would never have a significant pop hit again. Brenda Lee, the most successful female vocalist of the early '60s, reached the Top 15 with "As Usual" and would have another couple of Top 20 entries over the next couple of years while transitioning into a lengthy career as a country hitmaker. Neil Sedaka reached the Top 40 in the last weeks of '63 with "Bad Girl" and, while he would have occasional hits as a songwriter, Sedaka wouldn't have another US hit single as a performer until 1974's "Laughter in the Rain." Chubby Checker had parlayed his 1962 Top 5 success with the Caribbean-flavored "Limbo Rock" into a Top 20 double-sided hit in '63's last weeks with "Loddy Lo"/"Hooka Tooka." That spring, the erstwhile "King of The Twist" would reach the national Top 25 with "Hey Bobba Needle" (with a great folk-flavored b-side, "Spread Joy"), but that would be his last significant hit as a featured artist. And Roy Orbison, who also knew what was coming, having toured with The Beatles and Gerry & the Pacemakers in England in the spring of '63, had a double-sided hit with "Mean Woman Blues" and "Blue Bayou" that fall and would have two of the biggest hits of his career in '64 with "It's Over" and his single biggest hit, "Oh, Pretty Woman."

As for Elvis Presley, he still had enough superstar clout that "Bossa Nova Baby" became a Top 10 hit in November and the movie soundtrack that yielded that single, "Fun in Acapulco," reached the album Top 10 in February. The theme from The King's next movie, *Kissin' Cousins*, would barely make *Cashbox*'s Beatles-heavy Top 10 and just miss *Billboard*'s in mid-March. But those movies were becoming increasingly awful and, while they were moneymakers, they weren't producing major hit singles. Between "Bossa Nova Baby" in November of '63 and "In the Ghetto" late in the spring of 1969, Elvis would have just one other Top 10 single, his recorded-in-1960 cover of The Orioles' "Crying in the Chapel," at the beginning of the summer of 1965. That would be the most successful of a slew of out-of-the-vaults singles that would be released during 1964-66 to compensate for the quickie junk ("Do the Clam," "Long Legged Girl (With the Short Dress On)") that songwriters were submitting for the soundtracks of Elvis's current cinematic fare.

Speaking of songwriting, the team of Burt Bacharach and Hal David, whose star had been steadily rising during '63, finished the year and began 1964 with a trio of hits: the Jack Jones-sung movie theme "Wives and Lovers," Gene Pitney's dramatic "Twenty Four Hours From Tulsa," and "Anyone Who Had A Heart," the first Top 10 hit by the lady with whom Bacharach and David would have the most chart success as songwriters, Dionne Warwick.

David Gates was an Oklahoma-bred but L.A.-based songwriter, producer, and session player who had his first major hit as a composer in the last weeks of '63 and the beginning of '64 with "Popsicles and Icicles" by a one-hit wonder girl group called The Murmaids. Despite its easy-listening sound, "Popsicles and Icicles" was produced by Kim Fowley, a major presence/legendary character in the L.A. rock scene for years and the man who would manage The Runaways to hard rock stardom in the '70s. Gates, who turned 23 as "Popsicles and Icicles" was climbing the charts, would continue his very successful behind-the-scenes career through the balance of the '60s and, in the '70s, would become a star as the lead singer and principal songwriter for the easy-rock band Bread.

As detailed earlier in this chapter, there was plenty of easy-rock on the charts during this time, including such one-hit wonders as "I Wonder What She's Doing Tonight" by Barry and the Tamberlanes and "Midnight Mary" by Joey Powers. But there were also a goodly number of songs that, in retrospect, would be looked on as quite interesting in later years, but were also good listens on the radio at the time. There was Shirley Ellis's first pop hit, "The Nitty Gritty," and Nino Tempo & April Stevens' follow-up singles to "Deep Purple," similar-sounding covers of the pop standards "Whispering" and "Stardust." There were the unlikely successes of a '40s big band-era ballad, "Since I Fell for You" by Lenny Welch, and a French ballad from the same era that was rewritten with English lyrics as "I Wish You Love" and became a Top 30 hit for Gloria Lynne. Both songs became '60s pop-jazz standards. Sam Cooke began what turned out to be the final year of his life with the soulful "(Ain't That) Good News" and the bluesy "Little Red Rooster" (which would be covered just months later by The Rolling Stones). Jackie De-Shannon's composition "When You Walk in the Room" was released in November as the b-side of her single "Till You Say You'll Be Mine" but radio airplay of the flip caused that to become the record's plug side and, while the DeShannon version made little impression on the national charts, it would soon be recorded by The Searchers and become something of a rock standard, covered by a wide variety of artists in decades to come.

One of the star acts of what would become the Southeastern US musical genre called "beach music," The Tams, had their lone national hit with "What Kind of Fool (Do You Think I Am)" while one of the country music stars of the day, Bobby Bare, had his only pop hit under his own name (he had a hit as Bill Parsons in 1959 with the Elvis-based novelty "The All American Boy") with an adaptation of the folk ballad "500 Miles from Home." Meanwhile, country superstar Johnny Cash crossed over to the pop Top 40 with a No. 1 country hit. "Understand Your Man" was a Cash original, but with liberal parts of the melody nicked from Dylan's "Don't Think Twice, It's All Right." It would also be one of the last songs Cash would ever perform in public, at a function at the Carter Family Ranch just over two months before the Man in

Black's passing in September 2003.

The musical democracy that was the hallmark of Top 40 radio in the '60s enabled one to be able to hear, perhaps side by side, high energy rocker Freddy Cannon's "Abigail Beecher," New Orleans trumpeter Al Hirt's "Java," Bobby Goldsboro's country-tinged pop number "See The Funny Little Clown," and Tommy Tucker's 12-bar blues "Hi-Heel Sneakers." One might also have heard Diane Renay's Bob Crewe-produced debut hit, "Navy Blue," Bob & Earl's uptown R&B "Harlem Shuffle" (covered decades later by The Rolling Stones), R&B hitmaker Betty Everett's "You're No Good" (a hit single a decade later for Linda Ronstadt), Eddie Holland's Holland-Dozier-Holland-written "Leaving Here" (later covered by a number of hard-rocking British and European acts), and Sammy Davis, Jr.'s "The Shelter of Your Arms." That latter song was performed by Sammy on *The Ed Sullivan Show* on February 2, one week before the live American debut of The Beatles, and it was written by a New York-based songwriter-producer named Jerry Samuels. Some two and a half years later, Samuels would achieve brief popularity as Napoleon XIV with the best-forgotten novelty "They're Coming to Take Me Away, Ha-Haaa." And, of course, getting lots of airplay was Bobby Vinton's second straight No. 1 single (and third in less than two years), "There! I've Said it Again," which topped *Billboard*'s pop chart for almost all of January before being ousted by "I Want to Hold Your Hand."

One of those semi-easy-listening hits of the last weeks of 1963 was a pop re-working of Ernest Tubb's '50s country hit "You Don't Have to Be a Baby to Cry" by a girl group called The Caravelles. While the record was in the Top 5 that December, no one took much notice of the fact that The Caravelles were from England. It was also in December that a record called "I Only Want to Be With You" by a big-voiced girl singer called Dusty Springfield was given airplay as the "Good Guys Sure Shot" on WMCA in New York. It took better than a month for that single to appear on the national charts, by which time "I Only Want to Be With You" was already in the Top 20 on both WMCA and WABC; surveys already topped by "I Want to Hold Your Hand." By the second week in February, with Beatlemania having seized the East Coast, "Glad All Over" by Tottenham's Dave Clark 5 and two records by two other bands from Liverpool, "Hippy Hippy Shake" by The Swinging Blue Jeans and "Needles and Pins" by The Searchers, had all made those same New York radio surveys and began to make some impression on the national charts by the end of the month. Even Cliff Richard, England's biggest pop star of the late '50s/early '60s but never a hitmaker in the US, reached the mid-20s on the national charts for the first time in mid-February with his cover of the Tommy Edwards '50s hit "It's All in the Game." By the end of the month, though, "I Only Want to Be With You" had already peaked and missed the national Top 10 while "Glad All Over" had not yet really taken off. Indeed, when The Dave Clark 5 arrived at Kennedy Airport for their first visit to New York and their March 8 appearance on *The Ed Sullivan Show*, there were none of the scenes of mass fan hysteria that had greeted The Beatles upon their arrival three weeks earlier.

The Beatles' two-week first visit to America had already become the stuff of legend. Along with the thousands who showed up at Kennedy Airport for their arrival, large crowds of fans paralyzed the area around the Plaza Hotel. The group's two live appearances on the Sullivan show attracted the largest viewing audiences for an entertainment program, to that point in time, in television's still-young history. Their debut American concert at the Washington Coliseum and their two historic shows the next day at Carnegie Hall were wildly successful. By the time The Beatles returned to England on February 21, they had three of the five most popular songs on New York's two main Top 40 stations and the top two singles and two of the top three albums on the charts of the two major trade magazines. Such huge, rapid-fire dominance would not be repeated by any of the British acts that would be following The Beatles to America in the coming weeks and months.

Nonetheless, The Dave Clark 5's debut appearance on the March 8 Sullivan show, which highlighted their dapper on-stage suits and Dave Clark's movie star good looks, was quite successful and, at Ed's on-air request, they returned for a second appearance the following Sunday, eventually appearing on Sullivan's stage more than any of the British rock acts of the decade. That following week, "Glad All Over" would begin to really catch fire, though it wouldn't reach the national Top 10 for nearly another month. By that time, though, The Beatles had demolished all previous marks of popularity by having *Billboard*'s five top national singles and top two LPs. No other British act of that era would remotely approach that kind of dominance.

Thus, The Beatles have to be considered a phenomenon up at their own rarefied level of historic success and massive popularity. That means that the DC5's March 8 live American debut with Sullivan is really the beginning of what came to be known as the British Invasion (at least, the musical portion) because they showed that other British acts could make a real impression in America, something that no Anglo performer or band had been able to do beyond a one-off hit like "Telstar." During 1964, the DC5 would have seven singles that would, at minimum, reach the national Top 15, though none of them would reach No. 1. But then came the support troops from Liverpool—Swinging Blue Jeans, Searchers, Gerry, Billy J—and the Invasion was on...

The Beatles on stage at Carnegie Hall on February 12, 1964, complete with prime on-stage seats. Imagine such seating arrangements for Beatles shows just six months later...

CHAPTER 10

THE BEATLES—IT WASN'T JUST KENNEDY

The story of The Beatles' conquest of America in the early weeks of 1964 has been told and retold ad infinitum over the past half-century. The definitive chronicle of the yearlong struggle to break the group in the US is Bruce Spizer's The Beatles Are Coming! *(498 Productions, LLC, 2003) and that story has figured to no small degree in the story I've tried to tell in the previous chapters in this book. So, rather than redundantly go over the same facts covered so well elsewhere, let's examine why and how The Beatles broke through in America in such a huge fashion and, just to ruffle a few more feathers, pop at least one more myth about why this all happened the way it did.*

From the moment that thousands of teenagers showed up at the International Arrivals Building at the recently renamed John F. Kennedy International Airport in New York on Friday afternoon, February 7, 1964, for the arrival of The Beatles on US asphalt, there seemed to be a need for the US news media to explain why this was happening. That need became more intense when, two nights later, the group's live American debut on *The Ed Sullivan Show* garnered the highest ratings for any entertainment program in television's still-rather-brief history and a second live appearance a week later attracted only slightly less of an audience.

In the mid-sixties, there was no pop music press. There were jazz and folk music critics and publications dedicated to those musical genres (*Down Beat, Sing Out*), but there was no similarly intelligent writing about rock 'n' roll. There were just the teen magazines and the odd radio station freebie carried in record stores. There were the music industry trade magazines, but they dealt less with music than with the business of music. To august publications like the *New York Times*, "music" meant classical music, and rock 'n' roll was hardly considered music. So, with no rock press, The Beatles' first visit to America was covered, for the most part, by general assignment reporters, the vast majority male and middle-aged, whose musical taste, if any, ran to the big bands and classic pop vocalists like Frank Sinatra. Rock 'n' roll was this noise to which their teenage kids listened.

There were highbrow looks at the psychology of what the UK press had dubbed "Beatlemania," including one by celebrity psychologist Dr. Joyce Brothers, but they didn't really get to the gist of why this was happening. The mainstream media felt the need to explain why The Beatles had seemingly appeared out of nowhere and had attained massive popularity so quickly. To their thinking, it couldn't be the music because that was just more rotten rock 'n' roll, and it couldn't be The Beatles themselves because, while they showed themselves to be glib and humorous at that first press reception at JFK, the only one of the four who stood out was the short one with the big nose and the funny name, over whom so many of the girls were going crazy.

No, there had to be a deeper reason for this sudden outbreak of mass hysteria, so, between the media and the professional and amateur psychologists, it was decided that the reason for The Beatles' sudden popularity was that teenagers were so traumatized and saddened by the assassination of President Kennedy, who was a hero for young people, that The Beatles gave them something to laugh about again (as if The Beatles were a group of comedians and not musicians). Despite the fact that this theory had more holes than a well-worn pair of socks, it took hold and many teenagers of that time would buy into this in later years, thus creating a myth that would grow with the passage of time.

The facts are quite different. Yes, the death of President Kennedy was a deep psychic body blow for many Americans, and he was very popular with the youth of the US. But JFK was not universally popular, which is one of the reasons why he made the ill-fated trip to Texas in the first place, and there were teenagers who became Beatles fans from the start who had no particular opinion of Kennedy or didn't care for him.

Also, unless there was a death or a major calamity in one's family, teenagers tended to bounce back from an emotional trauma much quicker than adults. So, by December of '63 most teenagers were going on with their lives and were not in some perpetual state of depression over the loss of JFK. Indeed, it was on December 10, after seeing the postponed Alexander Kendrick report on The Beatles on *The CBS Evening News with Walter Cronkite*, that a Silver Springs, Maryland teenager named Marsha Albert wrote to her favorite nighttime deejay, Carroll James of WWDC in Washington, to request that he play music by The Beatles. A week later, after he had obtained an imported copy of "I Want to Hold Your Hand," James invited Marsha to come on the air and introduce the record. Obviously an anecdotal case, but hardly the actions of a girl wrapped up in depression for the martyred young president.

Top 40 radio played a crucial role in the breakthrough of The Beatles in America. The group's singles released by Vee-Jay and Swan during 1963 had received airplay on a number of stations, but with little listener reaction. That changed as soon as James' audience heard "I Want to Hold Your Hand." With his Washington area request lines going crazy, James made a tape dub of his imported copy of the single and sent it to a deejay friend in Chicago. A station in St. Louis began playing it and, even though Capitol Records hadn't really launched their "The Beatles Are Coming!" campaign, "I Want to Hold Your Hand" began to spread like a prairie fire. On December 26, about three weeks ahead of schedule, Capitol released the domestic single, and that same day it made its New York radio debut on WMCA. On New Year's Eve, WABC's new All American Survey had the record at No. 35 while WMCA's Fabulous 57 list for the next day listed "I Want to Hold Your Hand" as the station's "Sure Shot" for hit potential. One week later, it was No. 1 on WABC and took just one more week to reach the top of the list on WMCA.

Unlike the computerized, genre-specific, personality-neutered contemporary hit radio of the 21st century, '60s deejays, particularly the nighttime personalities, had much more influence in picking the music to be played and more freedom in promoting records or acts they especially liked. Granted, they didn't have the total autonomy that an Alan Freed had in the '50s, thanks to the payola scandal that sank Freed's career. But, for instance, Scott Muni of WABC was enough of an out-of-the-box believer in The Beatles that he was the on-the-air spokes-deejay for the formation of a Beatles fan club before the group's official fan club had the chance to form an American chapter. As well, Muni and Cousin Bruce Morrow, the station's late evening deejay (and, after

Muni's departure from WABC a year later, the prime-time personality), covered the arrival of The Beatles at Kennedy Airport live. In contrast, B. Mitchell Reed, the jazz-blues-loving nighttime WMCA Good Guy, took a wait-and-see attitude toward the group and didn't even go to Kennedy Airport for their arrival. Murray the K, WINS' prime-time deejay, had played "She Loves You" on his "Record Review Board" feature the previous October to mediocre listener reaction and was on vacation when "I Want to Hold Your Hand" took off. He had to be coaxed back to New York to helm the station's Beatles coverage, but Murray knew an opportunity for self-promotion when he saw it and he knew The Beatles brought such an opportunity.

On February 7, Murray went to Kennedy Airport and wiggled his way to the front row of media types for The Beatles' first American press conference, causing one reporter to call out, "Tell Murray the K to cut that crap out!" That got the attention of The Beatles, who (according to Murray) were aware of him and began kibitzing with him. Before long, Murray had made enough of a positive impression that he became a constant companion of the group during their two weeks in America. Despite Murray's ubiquitous presence, The Beatles also recorded station IDs and did interviews for the other two Top 40 stations in NYC, for Carroll James and WWDC, and for Rick Shaw and WQAM in Miami when they flew to Miami for their second Sullivan show appearance. Brian Epstein reportedly even had to put the kibosh on the group calling in to stations to record IDs and request favorite records and was not pleased when Murray began calling himself "the Fifth Beatle."

Meanwhile, the listeners couldn't get enough Beatles music. In January, after "I Want to Hold Your Hand" had taken off, Swan reissued "She Loves You" while Vee-Jay paired the UK No. 1s "Please Please Me" and "From Me to You" for a new single release. Soon, late afternoon back-to-back airplay of the three A-sides became a daily feature on WABC, and by early February the three New York Top 40s were playing the B-sides of the singles as well. They also added both sides of MGM's release of the 1961 single the group had made in Germany as backing for Tony Sheridan, "My Bonnie"/"The Saints," and the not-yet-released-in-the-US Capitol of Canada single of their cover of Chuck Berry's "Roll Over Beethoven." And, in an unprecedented move for Top 40 radio, all three began playing tracks from Capitol's *Meet The Beatles!* LP. By the latter part of the month, the station surveys were as Beatles-clogged as the national charts would be a month later. For instance, in the first week in March, The Beatles held down the top three places on WQAM's survey and three of the four top slots on both WABC and WMCA.

Top 40 radio's embrace of The Beatles was crucially important for both. WABC, with its 50,000-watt signal and a reach that enabled the station to be heard in 38 states at night, would soon begin referring to itself as W-A-Beatle-C and, over the next two years, would use that association on its way to becoming the most important Top 40 station in the country. WMCA didn't have nearly the broadcast reach of WABC, but it used The Beatles' recorded IDs for the station and their endorsement of the Good Guys to establish that group of deejays as one of the most famous in all of radio, even as the personnel changed. About a year later, B. Mitchell Reed would leave WMCA to return to KFWB in Los Angeles (and later become a West Coast FM progressive rock personality counterpart to Muni in New York). He would be replaced by a young deejay from Detroit named Gary Stevens. By that August, Stevens would be among a select group of radio deejays accompanying The Beatles on their second full tour of North America.

In contrast, despite Murray the K's relentless self-promotion and riding of The Beatles coattails, WINS' ratings went into free-fall. Murray would leave the station early in 1965, still trumpeting his "Fifth Beatle" status, and by April WINS had switched to an all-news format, leaving New York with two Top 40 stations to fight over "first and exclusive" debuts of new Beatles releases, which became listener-attracting events for the stations. But The Beatles were also beneficiaries of Top 40's sudden case of Beatlemania. Yes, Capitol Records embarked on a big promotional campaign to introduce America to The Beatles, but it was the December airplay of "I Want to Hold Your Hand" in several major markets that began to build up excitement, and the willingness of a number of East Coast stations (and elsewhere) to give saturation airplay to the group in January and February that was more crucial than record company hype in making it possible for The Beatles to break as a phenomenon so quickly and so hugely. Remember that, even with the airplay "I Want to Hold Your Hand" received in December, on New Year's Day most of America had still never heard of The Beatles. Just over a month later, the group's upcoming live American TV debut on *The Ed Sullivan Show* had become a major event.

The Ed Sullivan Show eventually would be canceled by CBS at the end of the 1970-71 season. Sullivan himself would pass on a little over three years later, and the variety show format would fade into history not too many years later. Thus, much of the 21st century audience would look at YouTube postings and DVD releases of material from Sullivan's show and be quite confused by the seemingly bizarre combination of acts appearing on his show and by the show's round-shouldered, decidedly nonslick host.

Edward Vincent Sullivan was first and foremost a newspaperman, one who had worked for a number of news organizations since the '20s before settling in at the *New York Daily News* in the '30s with a Broadway/New York entertainment scene column called "Little Old New York." That column, while not as sharp-elbowed as the Hollywood gossip columns of Louella Parsons and Hedda Hopper, was the primary New York-based competitor to the *Daily Mirror*'s widely syndicated Walter Winchell. Like Winchell, Sullivan branched out in the '30s into radio and even feature films, though Sullivan wasn't nearly as socio-politically controversial as Winchell.

In 1948, at a time when many show business luminaries were very reluctant to be involved with the still-quite-new medium of television, CBS offered Sullivan the opportunity to host a Sunday night variety show, which debuted that June under the title *Toast of the Town*. Despite his ill-at-ease on-camera demeanor and marble-mouthed vocal delivery, Sullivan's show became instantly popular, particularly because of Sullivan's ability to break hot new talent. For instance, the comedy team of Dean Martin and Jerry Lewis appeared on the very first *Toast of the Town* and that appearance would be generally credited as one of the more crucial steps on the duo's path to superstardom.

The show's title was changed to *The Ed Sullivan Show* for the 1955-56 season, just in time for the rise of rock 'n' roll, but the show was hardly a weekly showcase for rock acts and Sullivan certainly didn't "break" any early rock talent. Elvis Presley's three appearances on the Sullivan show, in the fall of 1956 and January of '57, came only after Elvis had made numerous network TV appearances, going back to early '56. It wasn't until Steve Allen, Sullivan's direct competition on NBC at the time, scored a ratings bonanza with a July 1 appearance by Presley that Sullivan decided that Elvis' swiveling hips were worthy of being seen by the Sullivan audience, though Elvis was shown only from the waist up for his third and final appearance on Ed's "really big shew."

Sullivan was very conscious of making his the ultimate show for the whole family, and most families indeed watched it as a single unit. For much of the Sullivan show's 23-year run, most homes that had a television had just one. It was generally in the living room and the family would watch together. So Sullivan programmed his show for every taste, from middle-of-the-road pop singers, animal acts, comedians of various stripes, the casts of Broadway shows, opera stars and plate spinners to dramatic readings, sports stars, ventriloquists and puppets and rock 'n' roll stars. The formula certainly worked. In its prime years, Sullivan's show was routinely among the Top 10 highest-rated TV programs, with an average audience between 25 million and 35 million viewers.

At the beginning of 1964, the Census Bureau estimated the US population at about 190 million. Not all of those 190 million people owned a television. TVs were still relatively expensive and many people in poorer areas of the country couldn't afford them. And there were others, primarily oldsters, who didn't yet believe in TV and were perfectly happy without a television. Of those who did have TVs, there were some affluent families that allowed the kids to have a TV in their bedroom, but most families had just that one living room television. So there were far fewer than 190 million televisions in use at the beginning of 1964. That's what made what happened on the night of February 9 so remarkable.

According to the legend, Sullivan was at London Airport in late October '63 and saw the huge commotion when The Beatles arrived back in the UK after their first visit to Sweden. Sullivan made a mental note to find out about this group and that's what led to The Beatles being signed in November for two appearances on Sullivan's show in February, with a third, pre-taped, appearance being added to the deal in December. Regardless of how much of that story is true and given that The Beatles had no record of success in America when Sullivan and Epstein hammered out the original deal in November, it was a calculated gamble for both. Once "I Want to Hold Your Hand" began to take off and Jack Paar, no great friend of Sullivan's, plugged The Beatles' live American debut after showing film from a British Beatles show early in January, it became obvious that the gamble was going to pay off.

A month later, a monetary and record sales payoff for The Beatles and a ratings and publicity bonanza for Sullivan had become virtually a sure thing. With Sullivan's news background, he knew that the February 9 show would get some free publicity from the increasing media coverage of The Beatles. But when thousands of kids showed up at Kennedy Airport that Friday and hundreds laid siege to Grand Army Plaza, across from the Plaza Hotel, and the Saturday rehearsal for Sunday's show became a media event, Sullivan knew that this was going to be a "REALLY BIG SHEW."

The February 9, 1964 broadcast was, aside from its lead attraction,

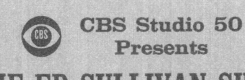

**CBS Studio 50
Presents**

THE ED SULLIVAN SHOW

FEBRUARY 9, 1964

— ADMIT ONE —

The hottest ticket in New York over the second weekend in February, 1964.

fairly typical of the "something for the whole family" formula Ed had been using for nearly 16 years. There was a magician (Fred Kapps) and an impressionist (the future Riddler on the *Batman* TV series, Frank Gorshin). Sullivan introduced a sports star from the audience, Terry Mc-Dermott, winner of the US' lone gold medal at the Innsbruck Winter Olympics. In one of the more bizarre examples of guest placement, a pre-recorded routine by an acrobatic troupe, Wells & The Four Fays, was shown AFTER the climactic second set by The Beatles. Over the years, the show had featured Martin & Lewis, Wayne & Schuster, Burns & Schreiber, and especially Stiller & Meara (with Ed persisting in calling Anne Meara "Mara"), so that night there naturally was another comic duo, Charlie Brill & Mitzi McCall. And there were two examples of the pop culture British Invasion that was already holding forth on Broadway: veteran British star Tessie O'Shea from Noel Coward's *The Girl Who Came to Supper* and the cast of Lionel Bart's *Oliver!* featuring Georgia Brown and David Jones (a future teen idol as Monkee Davy).

But it wasn't that lineup that drew an estimated 73 million people to *The Ed Sullivan Show* that night and Sullivan referenced the media horde that had descended on CBS Studio 50 (later to be renamed the Ed Sullivan Theater). "These veterans agree with me that the city never has witnessed the excitement stirred by these youngsters from Liverpool who call themselves The Beatles," he said. A moment later, after Sullivan introduced The Beatles, amid a wall of screams, there was a quick shot of the audience followed by a pan down toward the group. Their first number was "All My Loving," already a fan favorite from the *Meet The Beatles!* LP and much radio airplay. Paul McCartney and George Harrison very much played to the crowd while Ringo Starr and John Lennon seemed to be spending more time watching the audience reaction as America got its first live onstage look at The Beatles. Indeed, Harrison was grinning at the camera every time he saw himself on the monitor.

(The band's first actual performance before a US audience was the taping for the February 23 show, which was done after the February 9 dress rehearsal and was seen by a different studio audience than that for the live February 9 broadcast.)

In homes across the country, the teenage reaction was only slightly more restrained, while many parents harrumphed about the pudding-bowl hairdos and the jangly rock music. Then came a master move that The Beatles had used when they performed at the Royal Variety Show in London that November. For their second number in America, they performed Meredith Wilson's "Till There Was You" from *The Music Man*, already something of a pop standard and sung by the member of the foursome with the most mom-appeal. While he had been visibly nervous performing the song at the Royal Variety Show, here McCartney was at his charming best. As well, while Paul was singing, each Beatle's name was shown onscreen, with Ringo getting the most cheers, and the addition, under John's name, of "Sorry girls, he's married," which lent a further charming touch to the number. Immediately, any attempts at '56 Elvis-type condemnation of The Beatles were short-circuited. Oh, sure, the next song was "She Loves You" and the kids could go back to screaming and the parents could go back to complaining about the "yeah yeah yeah" refrain. But there would be no strong adult backlash against The Beatles. America was theirs.

The Beatles' second two-song set was one of those moments people would later point to as a moment when they moved from a band that had made it very big very quickly in the US to a pop culture phenomenon. They performed both sides of the No. 1 single in America at that moment in time. First, a high-energy "I Saw Her Standing There," with McCartney wowing the studio and home audience and the band showing, within the sterile confines of a TV studio, just what a great rock 'n' roll band they were. Then came the first notes of "I Want to Hold Your Hand," and if there hadn't been several floors above the studio the crowd reaction would have blown the roof off. All through both sets, there had been reaction shots of girls in the audience, lots of Peter Pan collars and jumpers and flip curls. But at one point during "I Want to Hold Your Hand" the camera focused on a fan who looked much more womanly. She was wearing a dress, earrings, some makeup and her blonde hair appeared to have been teased a little. She looked, if not orgasmic, certainly

213

as if she was really enjoying herself and the group she was watching. It's not hard to imagine the young teen Bruce Springsteen and Billy Joel and Tom Petty seeing that young woman and saying or thinking "I want THAT," meaning not just the girl, but the effect that The Beatles were having on her. A generation of young rockers was born during that hour of television (which Steven Van Zandt of the E Street Band has called "rock 'n' roll's Big Bang") and perhaps during that one song.

After the song ended with that last elongated chord, The Beatles bowed and trotted over to be congratulated by Sullivan and wave to an audience that was showering them with screams and applause. From the perspective of a half-century later, it's obvious something special had just happened, that the heart of American pop culture had just skipped a beat and changed irrevocably. The mere fact that perhaps half of the available televisions in the United States were tuned to that one program, the largest audience for an entertainment program in the medium's young history—and, a half-century later, still one of the largest audiences for an episode of a continuing series—is testament to that.

In case there were people who figured this was a one-time aberration propelled by hype, or doubters regarding The Beatles' ability as performers and as viewer draws, the February 16 *Ed Sullivan Show* from the Deauville Hotel in Miami Beach went far towards putting such ideas to rest. Instead of performing in a television studio, the Miami Beach show was telecast from the hotel's ballroom, with a small stage on which The Beatles were performing closer to each other than they had in the New York studio. The Beatles were literally just months removed from playing ballrooms in England so, not unlike the intimate atmosphere for their appearance on the Swedish TV show *Drop In* the previous October, they were truly in their element. As well, the sound mix, such as it was, had McCartney's bass and Starr's drums dominant, giving their two sets an even more organic, big-beat feel. And Lennon, McCartney and Harrison exhibited their fine three-part harmonies on "This Boy," with the three gathered around one mike, doo-wop style. Two live national TV appearances in, the group had shown itself to be far more than some manufactured teen craze.

The ratings for the second Beatles appearance on the Sullivan show were only slightly lower than the February 9 show, making it the second highest-rated episode in Sullivan's 23-season run on Sunday nights. Their third appearance was taped on February 9, prior to that night's live telecast, and included the centerpiece of the band's onstage repertoire, their rocked-up version of The Isley Brothers' 1962 hit "Twist and Shout," highlighted by Lennon's classic rock lead vocal. However, since it was common knowledge that The Beatles were actually back in England, that third appearance drew a much smaller viewing audience, though still above the norm for Sullivan's show.

Radio and television exposure had contributed much more than record company hype toward the breakthrough of The Beatles in America, but it *still* doesn't really zero in on why they became so very big so very quickly. It boils down, really, to two elements: The Beatles' very fresh, high-quality music and their very appealing individual personalities.

When "I Want to Hold Your Hand" began to catch fire in the latter part of December, The Beatles had released five singles and two LPs in Britain. Yes, "Please Please Me" and "From Me To You" had been UK No. 1 singles in the first half of '63, but it was "She Loves You," with its instantly catchy melody and "yeah yeah yeah" hook, that took the UK by storm and launched Beatlemania. "I Want to Hold Your Hand" had the same attributes, along with a "big" sound unlike almost anything then on the American pop-rock scene that sounded great coming out of the small speaker of a radio. But there was much more top-notch material to satisfy the growing hunger for Beatles music. Just on the B-side of "I Want to Hold Your Hand," there was a hard-driving rocker, "I Saw Her Standing There," which had been selected to lead off the group's first LP nearly a year earlier. Despite the fact that the UK single's flip was the gorgeous three-part harmony showcase "This Boy," Capitol opted for a higher-energy track and the two B-sides followed "I Want to Hold Your Hand" on Capitol's debut Beatles album, *Meet The Beatles!* The rest of that album consisted of Lennon-McCartney originals from the UK *With The Beatles* album, plus Harrison's exotic-sounding debut solo composition, "Don't Bother Me," and their cover of "Till There Was You," with McCartney's endearing vocal and lovely guitar work from Harrison. The LP also included other material nearly as good as the singles that were racing up the charts: instant fan favorites "All My Loving" and "It Won't Be Long," the rocking Ringo showcase "I Wanna Be Your Man," and the Everly Brothers-influenced "Little Child." Nearly overshadowed during those first weeks after the LP's release were two outstanding Lennon tunes, the Smokey Robinson-inspired "All I've Got to Do" and the piano-driven "Not a Second Time," plus an irresistible slice of what would later be dubbed Macca-pop, "Hold Me Tight." The material on *Meet The Beatles!* was so good and so instantly popular that Top 40 radio took the unprecedented step of including tracks from the album in an otherwise singles-only format.

Meanwhile, Swan quickly reissued their lone '63 Beatles release, "She Loves You," and it would become the group's second US No. 1 single late in March. Vee-Jay paired their two unsuccessful '63 Beatles singles, "Please Please Me" and "From Me To You," on one 45 and "Please Please Me" would reach No. 3 in mid-March. As well, the Chicago-based label mined its 16-song inventory of Beatles tracks with singles (released on Vee-Jay and its Tollie subsidiary) for "Twist and Shout," "Do You Want to Know a Secret," and the group's year-and-a-half-old debut single, "Love Me Do"/"P.S. I Love You." "Twist and Shout" would reach No. 2 on the historic April 4 *Billboard* Hot 100, topped by an all-Beatles Top 5, while "Do You Want to Know a Secret" would reach No. 2 about a month later and "Love Me Do" would become the fourth US Beatles No. 1 single in some four months in late May.

Vee-Jay also belatedly released its version of The Beatles' debut British LP as *Introducing The Beatles* on January 10, getting a 10-day jump on Capitol's release date for *Meet The Beatles!* and it would spend nine weeks at No. 2 on *Billboard*'s album chart behind *Meet The Beatles!* with Ringo's debut Beatles vocal, "Boys," getting the most Top 40 exposure of the tracks not released as US singles. All that saturation airplay served The Beatles well because, for those who were willing to listen, it showed just how good this music was and how much high-quality material they had recorded in a very short time. Others would be exposed to the very tuneful melodies in Beatles songs via orchestral interpretations, first by Arthur Fiedler and the Boston Pops Orchestra's version of "I Want to Hold Your Hand" as well as soon-to-be-released LPs of Beatles tunes by a studio assemblage called The Hollyridge Strings and by Beatles producer George Martin and his studio orchestra.

The other crucial element in The Beatles' sudden American success was, well, them. The Beatles were four unique individuals with disparate personalities, even at that early stage in their big-time career, something that can't be said about any of the British Invasion bands of 1964-65 or their American counterparts of the same period. John Lennon was a force to be reckoned with on his own, even though on that first trip to America he was mostly on his best behavior since the group he had founded was finally making it big in America. But he did chafe at the treatment of The Beatles by the upper crust at a reception for the group at the British Embassy after their debut US concert in Washington. Many of the fans, both male and female, liked Lennon's squinty-eyed, aggressively spread-legged onstage stance. And disc jockeys and some newsmen liked his quick wit, frankness and use of wordplay in one-on-one interviews. Lennon's multi-layered personality would emerge in the coming months and years, but this young man was clearly not the typical cookie-cutter teen idol.

Neither was Paul McCartney, despite his genial demeanor and good looks. As one British observer had put it, McCartney had the look of a "mischievous choir boy." He could charm the socks off media types while also slipping one-liners about a song being "originally done by our favorite group, Sophie Tucker" into his onstage intros. And it was McCartney who would shake his hips during the up-tempo songs and most visibly play to the crowd, something he would still be doing onstage a half-century later.

From the start, it was surprising how many Beatles fans immediately gravitated to George Harrison, the skinny, pasty-faced, very young (still shy of 21 during The Beatles' first trip to America) lead guitarist. The girls were turned on by his deep, expressive eyes, the lopsided grin, and his puckish, wry sense of humor. Males admired his crisp, economical guitar work (in that pre-Clapton, pre-Townshend era) and his cool, unassuming public demeanor. Harrison would become at once the most adventurous and most mysterious of The Beatles, but early on he developed a particularly passionate fandom.

However, the early fan favorite was Ringo Starr. He was shorter than the other three Beatles, had the most recognizable name, and had the perpetually vulnerable facial expression that led some observers to claim that he brought out the mothering instincts in the teenage girl fans. But Ringo was also the member of the band who was greeted with the most squeals from the studio audience when he appeared on camera during that first Sullivan show appearance, the one who was filmed grooving on the dance floor at the Peppermint Lounge after the show, and the one who, despite having to manually turn his drum kit, drove the band with his manic, rock-solid drumming during The Beatles' first US concert two nights later at the Washington Coliseum. Of course, Ringo would be later be the pivot point of the first two Beatles movies while also establishing his credentials as a non-flashy but solid role model for more than one generation of drummers.

They were, as Mick Jagger would call The Beatles when he inducted the band into the Rock and Roll Hall of Fame in 1988, "the four-headed monster—JohnPaulGeorgeRingo." Four unique personalities who each brought something special, musically and personally, to the blend that made The Beatles so special, headed by a songwriting team that was maturing with uncommon speed by early 1964.

And it was only the beginning ...

EPILOGUE

The following is a selective list of significant figures born between November 22, 1963 and March 1, 1964:

1963

November 25 – Bernie Kosar, football quarterback

November 27 – Fisher Stevens, film director/producer/actor

December 2 – Ann Patchett, novelist

Dan Gauthier, actor

Brendan Coyle, actor

December 4 – Sergey Bubka, pole vaulter

Kayla Blake, actress

December 5 – Carrie Hamilton, actress/singer/playwright; died January 20, 2002

December 14 – Cynthia Gibb, model/actress/voice coach

December 15 – Helen Slater, actress

December 16 – Benjamin Bratt, actor

James Mangold, screenwriter/director

December 18 – Karl Dorrell, college/pro football coach

Brad Pitt, actor/producer

Allan Kayser, actor

December 19 – Til Schweiger, film director/producer/actor

Jennifer Beals, actress

December 23 – Donna Tartt, novelist

December 26 – Lars Ulrich, drummer

December 29 – Sean Payton, college/pro football coach

December 31 – Scott Ian (Rosenfeld), guitarist

1964

January 1 – Dedee Pfeiffer, actress

January 4 – Dot Jones, actress

January 6 – Charles Haley, All-American/All-Pro football player

January 7 – Nicolas Cage (Coppola), actor/producer/director

January 12 – Jeff Bezos, founder/CEO of Amazon.com Inc.

January 13 – Penelope Ann Miller, actress

January 14 – Shepard Smith, TV news anchor

Mark Addy (Johnson), actor

January 17 – Michelle Obama, first lady

January 18 – Brady Anderson, baseball player

Jane Horrocks, actress

January 20 – Ozzie Guillen, baseball player, manager

 Mark Gottfried, college basketball coach

January 23 – Mariska Hargitay, actress

January 24 – Rob Dibble, baseball player, analyst

January 26 – Paul Johansson, actor/writer/director ("One Tree Hill")

January 27 – Bridget Fonda, actress

January 28 – Justin Fox, financial journalist

Fredi Gonzalez, baseball manager

January 31 – Jeff Hanneman, guitarist, died May 2, 2013

February 1 – Linus Roache, actor
Jani Lane, singer, died Aug. 11, 2011

February 5 – Duff McKagan, bass player/songwriter

Laura Linney, actress

February 10 – Glenn Beck, TV personality

Victor Davis, Canadian Olympic swimmer, died
November 13, 1989

Francesca Neri, actress

February 11 – Sarah Palin, former Alaska governor, conservative
commentator

February 12 – Raphael Sbarge, actor/voice actor

February 15 – Chris Farley, comedian/actor, died December 18, 1997

February 16 – Christopher Eccleston, actor

Fab. 18 – Matt Dillon, actor

February 19 – Jonathan Lethem, novelist

February 20 – Willie Garson, actor

French Stewart, actor

February 22 – James Wicek, actor

February 25 – Lee Evans, stand-up comic/actor

February 26 – Mark Dacascos, martial artist/actor

Mar. 1 – Khalid Shaikh Mohammed, Al Qaeda terrorist

*****

The following is a selective list of notable figures who died between
November 22, 1963 and March 1, 1964:

1963

November 22 – John F. Kennedy, President of the United States, age 46

Aldous Huxley, novelist/pacifist, age 69

C.S. Lewis, novelist/theologian, age 64

November 24 – Symon Gould, founder of American Vegetarian Party, age 70

November 25 – the Rev. John LaFarge Jr., Jesuit anti-racism advocate, age 83

November 26 – Amelita Galli-Curci, operatic soprano, age 81

November 28 – William Embry Wrather, geologist, age 80

November 30 – Phil Baker, comedian/musician/radio game show emcee, age 67

December 1 – Jimmy Hatlo, cartoonist, age 65

December 3 – US Army Capt. Michael Donald Groves, commander of honor guard for JFK funeral ceremonies November 23-25, 1963, age 27

December 6 – Archibald Henderson, historian/biographer/literary critic, age 86

December 12 – Theodor Heuss, first president of West Germany (1949-59), age 79

December 14 – Dinah Washington, jazz/blues/pop vocalist, age 39

December 19 – Irenee du Pont, former president of Du Pont & Company, age 86

December 26 – George Wagner (Gorgeous George), 1940s-'50s professional wrestler, age 48

Jacob. J. Shubert, last surviving founder of the Shubert theatrical empire, approximately age 86

December 28 – A.J. Liebling, journalist/essayist (The New Yorker), age 59

Paul Hindemith, composer/musician/conductor, age 68
<u>1964</u>

January 2 – Helen Lansdowne Resor, pioneering female advertising executive
(J. Walter Thompson), age 77

January 3 – the Rev. Gustave Weigel, theologian/ecumenicist/author, age 57

January 5 – William A. Bartholomae, oil tycoon/Yachtsman, age 70

January 8 – Julius Saab, chancellor of Austria (1953-61), age 72

January 10 – Frank Cleary Hanighen, journalist/author, age 64

January 11 – Sheikh Bechara El Khoury, president of Lebanon (1943-52), age 74

January 15 – Jack Teagarden, jazz trombonist/composer, age 58

January 17 – T.H. White, author, age 57

January 19 – Joe Weatherly, NASCAR champion race driver, age 41 (in a crash during a race in Riverside, CA.)

January 21 – Joseph Schildkraut, actor, age 67

January 22 – Marc Blitzstein, composer, age 58

January 27 – Stuart N. Lake, writer/screenwriter/Old West authority, age 74

Waite Phillips, oilman/philanthropist, age 81

January 29 – Alan Ladd, actor, age 50

February 3 – Sir Albert Edward Richardson, architect/professor, age 83
C.I. Lewis, academic philosopher, age 80

February 9 – Samuel Chotzinoff, NBC-TV classical music producer, age 74

February 15 – Ken Hubbs, baseball player, killed in plane crash, age 22

Robert Lee Thornton, businessman/mayor of Dallas (1953-61), age 83

February 18 – Joseph-Armand Bombardier, inventor of the snowmobile, age 56

Clarence Budington Kelland, novelist/short story writer, age 82

February 25 – Johnny Burke, lyricist, age 55

Grace Metalious, author, age 39

February 27 – Orry-Kelly, Hollywood costume designer, age 66

February 28 – Gus Lesnevich, boxing champion, age 49

About The Author

A former radio analyst for ASCAP, Mr. Sussman is currently the Executive Editor of Beatlefan magazine and has worked in official capacity for the Fest for Beatles Fans since the 1980's. Al Sussman lives in Rochelle Park, New Jersey.

Readers can connect with Al for updates on Facebook (ASuss49) and Twitter (@ASuss49).

Photo by Robert Rodriguez

PHOTO CREDITS

All images courtesy of the Author's Collection, except where noted here:

Cover Photographs
John F. Kennedy motorcade, Dallas, Texas, Nov. 22, 1963 by Victor Hugo King
Library of Congress Prints and Photographs Division Washington, D.C. 20540 USA
LC-USZ62-134844

Kennedy Airport: The Beatles wave to the thousands of screaming teenagers after their arrival
Library of Congress Prints and Photographs Division Washington, D.C. 20540 USA
LC-USZ62-111094

Chapter 3
US Air Force: A1-H aircraft make a low level pass over Vietnamese tanks and ground troops on Nov. 21, 1963 during a training exercise somewhere in South Vietnam.
http://www.arpc.afrc.af.mil/photos/mediagallery.
asp?galleryID=157&page=30

Fidel Castro arrives MATS Terminal, Washington, D.C. April 15, 1959
Library of Congress Prints and Photographs Division Washington, D.C. 20540 USA
LC-U9-2315-6

President Lyndon B. Johnson meets with Sen. Richard Russell, December 7, 1963
LBJ Library photo by Yoichi Okamoto W98-30

Chapter 4
Martin Luther King and Malcolm X waiting for press conference, March 26, 1964
Library of Congress Prints and Photographs Division Washington, D.C. 20540 USA
LC-USZ6-1847

Photo of the Johnson family during the White House years, November 30, 1963.
LBJ Library photo by Yoichi Okamoto B8626-1

Chapter 5
President John F.Kennedy visits Pope Paul VI, July 2, 1963
JFK Presidential Library, White House Photographs JFKWHP-1963-07-02-A

Chapter 8
Seven Days in May poster courtesy of Heritage Auctions

Chapter 9
Ed Sullivan Show ticket courtesy of Heritage Auctions

Index

P

Pope Paul VI 76, 77, 229

R

Robbins, Jerome 133, 140
Rockefeller, Nelson 25, 58, 64
Rometsch, Ellen 61
Rozelle, Pete 20, 102, 112, 122
Ruby, Jack 18, 34
Rusk, Dean 36, 45, 77

S

Sihanouk, Prince Norodom 8, 45
Smith, Merriman 10
Sorensen, Ted 24, 35, 37, 151
Spector, Phil 182, 189
Staubach, Roger 7, 114
Streisand, Barbra 5, 133, 134, 140, 189
Sullivan, Ed ix, 3, 119, 132, 173, 176,
        177, 200, 201, 205, 209, 210, 212,
        214, 229

T

Tittle, Y.A. (Yelberton Abraham) 101

W

White, Theodore 26

X

X, Malcolm 29, 52, 121, 126, 151, 228

29558624R00138

Made in the USA
Lexington, KY
29 January 2014